Frontier Rebels

FRONTIER REBELS

THE FIGHT FOR INDEPENDENCE
in the AMERICAN WEST, 1765–1776

PATRICK SPERO

W. W. NORTON & COMPANY

INDEPENDENT PUBLISHERS SINCE 1923

NEW YORK | LONDON

For information about permission to reproduce selections from this book, write to
Permissions, W. W. Norton & Company, Inc., 500 Fifth Avenue, New York, NY 10110

For information about special discounts for bulk purchases, please contact
W. W. Norton Special Sales at specialsales@wwnorton.com or 800-233-4830

Manufacturing by LSC Communications Harrisonburg
Book design by Daniel Lagin
Production manager: Julia Druskin

ISBN 978-0-393-63470-9

W. W. Norton & Company, Inc., 500 Fifth Avenue, New York, N.Y. 10110
www.wwnorton.com

W. W. Norton & Company Ltd., 15 Carlisle Street, London W1D 3BS

1 2 3 4 5 6 7 8 9 0

To the archivists, librarians,
institutions, and others
who are stewards of the past
and make books like this possible.

Contents

———•———

Maps

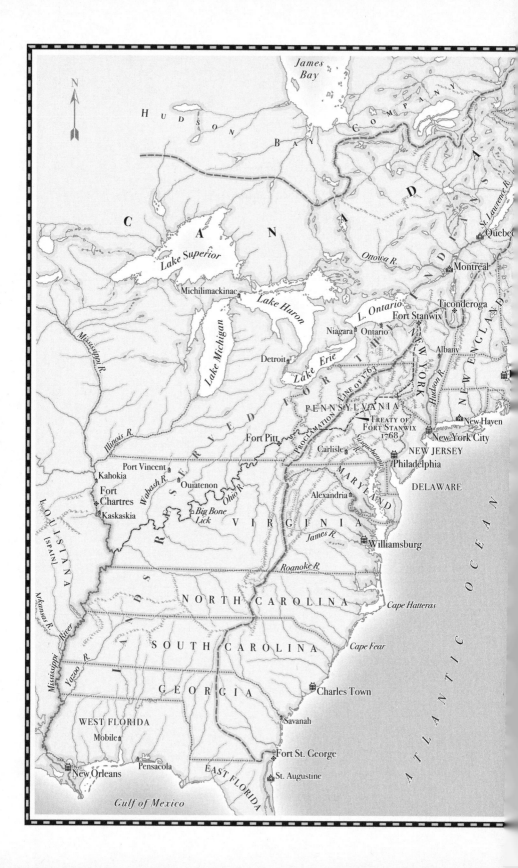

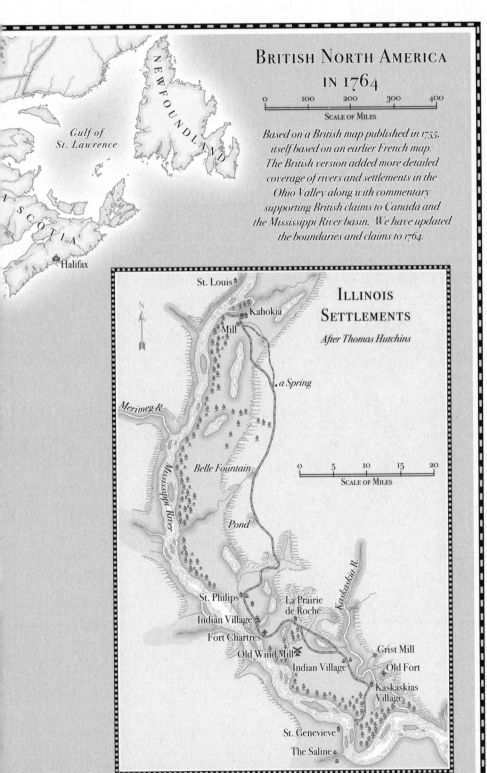

NEWFOUNDLAND

Gulf of
St. Lawrence

A

SCOTIA

⚓ Halifax

BRITISH NORTH AMERICA
IN 1764

0   100   200   300   400
SCALE OF MILES

*Based on a British map published in 1755,
itself based on an earlier French map.
The British version added more detailed
coverage of rivers and settlements in the
Ohio Valley along with commentary
supporting British claims to Canada and
the Mississippi River basin. We have updated
the boundaries and claims to 1764.*

St. Louis

Kahokia

Mill

. a Spring

Merimeg R.

ILLINOIS
SETTLEMENTS

After Thomas Hutchins

0   5   10   15   20
SCALE OF MILES

Mississippi River

Belle Fountain

Pond

Kaskaskia R.

St. Philips

La Prairie
de Roche

Indian Village

Fort Chartres

Grist Mill

Old Wind Mill

Indian Village

Old Fort

Kaskaskias
Village

St. Genevieve

The Saline

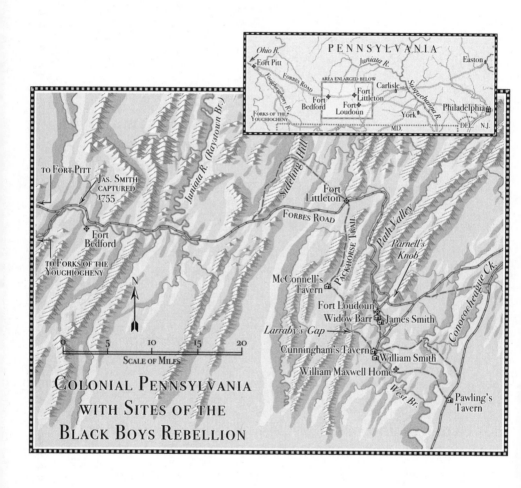

PENNSYLVANIA

Ohio R.
Fort Pitt
Easton
Juniata R.
Forbes Road
AREA ENLARGED BELOW
Carlisle
Youghiogheny R.
Fort
Littleton
Susquehanna R.
Fort
Bedford
Fort
Loudoun
Philadelphia
Forks of the
Youghiogheny
York
MD.
DEL.
N.J.

TO FORT PITT
JAS. SMITH
CAPTURED
1755

Juniata R. (Raystown Br.)

Sideling Hill

Fort
Littleton

Forbes Road

Fort
Bedford

TO FORKS OF THE
YOUGHIOGHENY

Path Valley

Parnell's
Knob

N

McConnell's
Tavern

PACKHORSE TRAIL

Conococheague Ck.

Fort Loudoun

Widow Barr
James Smith

Larraby's Gap

0   5   10   15   20
SCALE OF MILES

Cunningham's Tavern
William Smith

William Maxwell Home

West Br.

Pawling's
Tavern

COLONIAL PENNSYLVANIA
WITH SITES OF THE
BLACK BOYS REBELLION

Cast of Characters
and Important Places

ROBERT CALLENDER Likely born in Ireland around 1726, Callender arrived in America sometime before the Seven Years' War (1754–1763) seeking greater opportunity on the frontiers. By the 1750s, he had found success as a fur trader and by the 1760s had built an extensive trading network and owned at least two significant pieces of property in western Pennsylvania, including a large mill. In the winter of 1765, Callender's job was to cart a massive store of goods from Philadelphia to Fort Pitt to help facilitate a peace treaty between the British Empire and Native American groups.

GEORGE CROGHAN Irish by birth, Croghan arrived in Pennsylvania in 1741 and became a resident of the North American frontier. A successful trader, land speculator, diplomat, and military official, in 1763 Croghan was given responsibility for bringing peace to the frontier by traveling to Fort Detroit to negotiate a treaty with Native American groups who were defending their land against the British Empire. He organized Callender's trip and needed those goods to succeed.

THOMAS GAGE   Gage, an English aristocrat, came to North America during the Seven Years' War (1754–1763) as a military officer. He was promoted to commander-in-chief of North American forces in 1763 at age forty-four, after Jeffery Amherst, his predecessor, mismanaged Indian relations. Gage wanted to restore stability in North America, especially along its frontiers. Croghan's mission was essential to his plans.

ILLINOIS COUNTRY   This territory takes its name from a confederation of related Native peoples who dominated the area of modern-day Illinois and Indiana in the seventeenth century. Prior to the Seven Years' War (1754–1763), New France maintained an official presence in this region through a chain of military bases that followed the Mississippi River and its tributaries, especially the Illinois River. Called the *Pays des Illinois* by the French and governed by an official French commandant, French traders and diplomats living in the area developed strong ties to neighboring Native communities. These Native Americans generally viewed the French as allies whose footprint was contained to the small forts they maintained. After the Seven Years' War, Great Britain claimed this territory as its own, much to the chagrin of Native peoples who lived there. In 1765, these groups included the Illinois and also, according to British references, the Ottawas, Potawatomis, Chippewas (Ojibwes), Kickapoos, and others. Having had good relations with New France and being aware of France's historic hostilities with the British, many of these Native groups were suspicious of the British and fearful that this European power intended to subjugate them and occupy their land. In 1765, British officials wanted to strengthen relations with these groups by trading with them and creating diplomatic alliances.

SIR WILLIAM JOHNSON   Like Croghan, Johnson was born in Ireland but immigrated to North America in 1738 while in his early twenties. He settled outside Albany, where he became the leading frontier diplomat in British North America through his strong ties to the Six Nations Iroquois, a confederation of the Mohawk, Onondaga, Oneida, Cayuga, Seneca, and Tuscarora peoples that exerted influence in New York, Pennsylvania, and the Ohio River valley. Johnson also received a baronetcy for his bravery as a colonel in the Seven Years' War. Johnson respected Croghan and appointed him to be his deputy.

CHARLOT KASKÉ Kaské led a group of Native Americans who refused to accept British peace offers in 1765. Kaské, the son of a German father and a Shawnee mother, believed the British wanted to subjugate Native groups who lived in the Illinois Country. His position gained strength among many of the Native communities in the Illinois region just as Croghan began his peace mission to the Illinois Country.

OHIO RIVER VALLEY The largest tributary of the Mississippi River, the Ohio River begins at the confluence of the Allegheny and Monongahela Rivers near modern-day Pittsburgh and flows west to the Mississippi. In the eighteenth century, Native Americans and colonists alike used its waters to connect eastern North America to interior areas. New France and Great Britain fought the Seven Years' War for control of the Ohio River and the fertile lands that surrounded this strategic waterway. After the conflict, Great Britain began to try to take control of the region, but Native American groups rejected British claims of dominion. Some of these tribes, like the Delawares and Shawnees, had been pushed from Pennsylvania into the Ohio River valley by the pressures of British expansion and colonial advances. Others were members of the Six Nations Iroquois and affiliated Iroquoian cultural groups who also lived in the region. Those who occupied the area therefore had a long and complicated relationship with the British Empire, and often with each other. By 1764, many Ohio groups were willing to negotiate a peace treaty that would establish their sovereignty and re-open trade and diplomatic relations with the British. Their geographic and diplomatic ties often overlapped with those of the Illinois, and the distinctions between the two regions and the peoples who lived there often blurred. For this book, the Illinois Country refers primarily to more-western areas along the Mississippi River in which New France had a military presence, while the Ohio River valley encompasses the more-eastern terrain of modern-day western Pennsylvania and Ohio, although distinctions between the two regions could be amorphous in the eighteenth century.

JOHN PENN   Penn was the lieutenant governor of Pennsylvania and nephew to Thomas Penn, the governor and proprietor of Pennsylvania. Because Pennsylvania was a proprietary colony (meaning that it was controlled by the Penn family in much the same way the British Crown controlled royal colonies), John Penn also stood to inherit the colony. He arrived in Pennsylvania in 1763, during Pontiac's War (1763–1766). As lieutenant governor, he was the British Empire's chief civil officer in the colony and was responsible for enforcing imperial policy as well as governing the colony. He had to juggle these responsibilities in the midst of the Black Boys' Rebellion as he tried to maintain order in the colony and enforce imperial policy.

PONTIAC   Pontiac was an Ottawa warrior, probably a war chief, who launched a siege of Fort Detroit in the summer of 1763 that began the war that now bears his name. Pontiac's early life is clouded in mystery, as there is very little about him in the historical record. By 1765, however, the British had come to see him as the leader of the Illinois Country and the one who could negotiate a peace treaty. He was the person Croghan sought in his mission.

JAMES SMITH   Smith was born in Pennsylvania, probably in 1737, right around the time Croghan was arriving in the colony. As a teenager during the Seven Years' War, Smith helped cut roads for British troops. He was captured and adopted by Mohawks and lived in the Greater Ohio Valley Region for several years. Eventually, he was returned to his Pennsylvania community. During Pontiac's War, he led a local militia that used Native American warfare techniques Smith had learned while in captivity. In 1765, he led a group called the Black Boys, who used the same tactics to challenge the British Empire on the frontiers of Pennsylvania.

WILLIAM SMITH   Smith was a justice of the peace in western Pennsylvania. He was also James Smith's relative, most likely both his brother-in-law and cousin. Older than James, William Smith provided legal cover and advice for the Black Boys.

The Crisis of Empire

The Frontiers of North America

March 1765

The travel was tough, but the mission was important. That was the message Robert Callender and his men had to remember as they marched along the snow-covered roads of western Pennsylvania, at the time the frontier of North America.

Callender was heading up one of the largest diplomatic missions ever assembled in colonial America. Behind him trailed over eighty packhorses carrying several tons of trade goods; the cargo's value is hard to determine because it was so large. It came from Philadelphia, and its destination was Fort Pitt—a three-hundred-mile journey that took Callender and his men from the largest city in British North America to one of its most isolated outposts.

Callender's partner, George Croghan, deputy superintendent of Indian Affairs, was already at Fort Pitt waiting for the supplies before starting his own risky mission. Croghan's task was no small one: he was to bring peace to North America. For the previous two years, Great Britain had waged a deadly and costly war against a powerful Native American military alliance based in the Greater Ohio River valley and the Illinois Country—what the British called Indian Country. The war began in Detroit when an Ottawa military chief named Pontiac made a surprise attack on the British post in the summer of 1763. For the next two years, united Native American forces raided other British forts and colonial settlements, mainly in western Pennsylvania. They fought to reclaim land, to limit the growing power of the British in North America, and to oppose the subjugation British officials tried to impose on them. It was a war to assert their independence.

The conflict tested the British military's capabilities and devastated many colonial communities. By the winter of 1764, several of the warring Native groups, feeling strained themselves and realizing the British would probably agree to their terms, decided to negotiate peace. Croghan was assigned to make this peace a reality, and Callender's cargo was the key to accomplishing it.

Croghan's strategy was bold. First, he would host a major treaty meeting at Fort Pitt to renew old alliances with the Shawnees and Delawares. Then, with their backing, he would travel down the Ohio River with a fleet of flat-bottomed boats loaded with the trade goods Callender was carting across the Appalachians. Croghan planned to dispense the cargo as gifts to the Indian communities he visited while venturing deeper into the American interior. He knew that many of the Native groups were still declared enemies of the British, but he hoped that this show of generosity would reassure them of Great Britain's dedication to cooperation and partnership.

His real goal, however, was to find Pontiac. Croghan expected that his conciliatory message would persuade this leader and his supporters to accept peace, thereby creating the stability the British Empire so desperately wanted on its frontiers. With peace and stability would come the trade and prosperity needed to free Great Britain from the burden of managing its North American colonies. For imperial officials, then, the British Empire's own independence depended on the success of this mission.

However, Callender realized the problem with Croghan's plan as he traveled farther into the frontier and confronted colonists who were opposed to his mission. At every turn, settlers warned him to stop, to return to Philadelphia. They weren't worried about the dangers of his journey. Instead, they were worried that any peace would be false. These colonists had lived through nearly a decade of war—first against the French and their Native allies, and then against Pontiac and his alliance. They had developed a very different understanding of the Empire and its future, an idea of the West that formed during the violence and fear of the preceding years.

At the heart of this disagreement, one that would influence the coming of the American Revolution in this region, was the status of Native Americans within the British Empire. Although imperial officials in London and the eastern seaports wanted to incorporate trade and good relations with Indians into their plans for the empire's future, colonists in war-torn regions felt there could be no peace with Native Americans. These colonists instead saw Native groups as threats that needed to be removed. Their vision was also based on a desire for independence: they wanted to be freed from their fear of Indians. They thus had their own idea of what independence meant on the frontiers of North America.

These conflicting views collided as Callender marched west. And the farther west he went, the stronger the opposition. Insults and empty threats soon turned into physical violence and armed confrontations.

On March 6, as the pack train neared a gap in the Appalachian

Mountains at the base of Sideling Hill, the disagreement between colonists and the British Empire turned explosive.

Shots rang out from the woods, and smoke from long rifles filled
the air. Soon the woods echoed with hollering in the style of Indian
warriors.

As the dust settled, a group of colonists appeared, dressed like
Native Americans and with faces smeared black with charcoal—
therefore earning them the name Black Boys. Leading this group was
James Smith. A former prisoner of war who was captured and then
adopted by Mohawks in 1755, Smith had returned to Pennsylvania in
1760 and taken up arms against his former captors. He, and the men
who followed him that March morning, created a crisis for those trying
to govern the North American frontiers.

The outcome of these interwoven struggles—between the British Empire and colonists like the Black Boys, between Native Americans and the British and colonists, and struggles within each of these
communities—would determine whose idea of independence on the
American frontier would prevail.

———•———

For many years, historians have considered the year 1765 as a pivotal
moment for the coming of the American Revolution, but not because of
the Black Boys' Rebellion or George Croghan's mission down the Ohio
River. Instead, historians point to the Stamp Act and the colonists'
response in eastern seaports. That story also began in March 1765,
when the British Parliament passed a new levy on the colonists that
would raise revenue through a tax on many kinds of printed material.
The colonies, according to those in London who supported the tax,
had avoided paying their fair share for decades, and this law corrected
the situation by treating the colonists more like their peers in England.

Colonists in the eastern cities of North America disagreed with this stamp tax, so-called because all taxable items would now bear a special stamp. Beginning in the summer of 1765 and continuing into early 1766, colonists along the eastern seaboard revolted, denouncing the Stamp Act wherever they could. Politicians gave heated speeches, and preachers delivered grave sermons. Colonists wrote eloquent pamphlets and scathing newspaper editorials. They performed peaceful acts of protest in town squares and formed angry mobs that destroyed buildings and harassed tax collectors. New organizations, in particular the Sons of Liberty, formed to help channel this opposition to imperial policies. Such combined resistance to the Stamp Act aroused animosities that festered until independence. As the renowned historian Edmund Morgan noted, the Patriots in the cities who declared independence from Great Britain "'stood Bluff' in 1776 on the line they had drawn in 1765."[1]

But in 1765, events transpiring on the frontiers of North America also played a central role in the coming of the American Revolution. The upheavals on the eastern and western edges of British North America, however, have rarely been connected. That is a mistake. In order to understand the origins and ultimate success of the American Revolution, we must pay the same attention to the Black Boys' Rebellion that we do the Stamp Act protests; the same attention to colonial diplomats like George Croghan that we do to governors like loyalist Thomas Hutchinson; and the same attention to Native Americans like Pontiac that we do to colonial leaders like Samuel Adams. All these figures played pivotal roles in the beginning of the American Revolution on the frontiers of North America, and it was in 1765 that their interests collided.

The crisis in the West arose for very different reasons than those in the East. For western settlers who supported the Black Boys, the British Empire's willingness to accept former enemies as trading partners and its reduced military presence on the frontiers stirred up heated oppo-

sition that united a spread-out rural population in a common cause—
much as the Stamp Act united city dwellers. The western settlers,
however, focused their anger on eastern elites involved in trade, whom
they accused of controlling government to serve their own interests over
those of rural Americans.[2]

By 1776, the Black Boys' dedication to independence turned out
to be as strong as the urban colonists'. The beliefs that drove the Black
Boys to rebel continued to influence politics in the new nation they
helped to create. Similar beliefs even influenced events well into the
nineteenth century, and they linger today in the resentment of many
rural Americans toward the federal government and coastal elites,
whom they see as wielding power for their own purposes. For these
reasons alone, the rebellion is worthy of our attention.

Aside from a brief moment in the early twentieth century, however,
the Black Boys' Rebellion is largely unknown, overshadowed by stories
of the Sons of Liberty and their leaders such as Paul Revere, Samuel
Adams, and others. There was a fleeting moment of greater renown for
the Black Boys in 1937 when Neil Swanson, a popular author of his day,
wrote a work of historical fiction that chronicled the group's exploits—
especially those of its leader, James Smith. Swanson's book, *The First
Rebel*, was soon optioned by Hollywood. In 1939, RKO produced *Allegheny Uprising*, starring a young John Wayne as James Smith. The film
flopped, but Wayne's role helped establish the on-screen persona that
would later catapult him to stardom. Today the movie, like Swanson's
novel, is long forgotten.[3]

The crisis on the frontiers of North America is relatively unknown
for several reasons. First, the events occurred along the frontiers of
the British Empire, an area that stretched from the western borders of
Maryland, Pennsylvania, and Virginia all the way to Detroit. Historians in the nineteenth century who wrote the first stories of the American Revolution, however, came from eastern cities, the sites of events

like the Boston Massacre and Tea Party. They often based their histo-
ries on local events. The seaboard cities were also home to major printing presses during the revolutionary era, and they churned out fiery
pamphlets that fueled the movement for independence. These easily
accessible materials provided nineteenth-century historians with the
basis for their interpretations. Our nation's first stories of independence,
then, were those of the cities in crisis, and many historians followed this
way of thinking.

Records from the frontiers, meanwhile, are sparse, scattered, and
mostly in manuscript form. The story of the Black Boys, for instance,
rests in collections of letters at the Historical Society of Pennsylvania in
Philadelphia, the Pennsylvania State Archives in Harrisburg, numerous small county archives throughout the state, a large collection of
papers at the Clements Library in Ann Arbor, Michigan, the Sir William Johnson Papers from New York, the Papers of Benjamin Franklin, miscellaneous correspondence at the Virginia Historical Society in
Richmond, and new digital collections.

Perhaps foremost among the reasons the Black Boys have languished in relative obscurity, however, is the way our society wants
to remember the Revolution. Eastern cities, like Philadelphia with
Independence Hall and Boston with the Freedom Trail, are proud of
their revolutionary heritage and make it a part of their identity. Many
twenty-first-century Americans, including historians, consider the
events that occurred in these seaports as constituting the story of revolution. Countless books, numerous television shows, and even major
movies depict events related to the Sons of Liberty, the Tea Party, and
the lives of famous individuals during the 1770s. The traditional story
goes something like this: following the repeal of the Stamp Act, colonists reacted to every new imperial policy that restricted their liberty,
such as the Townshend Duties (a tax on certain items shipped to the
colonies) or the Tea Act, with similar anger, growing unity, and greater

strength. These urban revolutionaries, the story continues, rebelled against taxation, demanded representation in Parliament, and resisted the expanding regulatory state being forced on them by the British Empire. This story is a hopeful one of liberation.

But the story of the Black Boys doesn't fit easily into this idea of the American Revolution as a struggle for liberty. Beneath the Black Boys' desire for liberty and freedom from the British is an unpleasant, perhaps unpopular, truth that may have caused past historians to look the other way: behind the Black Boys' movement was a deep fear of Native Americans that had turned into hatred through war. Its vehemence clouds the heroic narratives of colonial rebels fighting to overthrow a tyrannical imperial regime. Although the Black Boys definitely wanted to throw off the restraints of imperial Britain, much as the eastern colonists did, the frontier settlers were motivated by opposition to the Empire's desire to treat Native groups as allies. The Black Boys wanted to be free of Indians as much as they wanted to be free of their imperial overlords. Their story, driven more by fear and anger than by righteousness, doesn't work well as a morality tale or a founding legend.

These factors make the Black Boys' Rebellion a tough story to tell and a hard one to categorize, but that doesn't mean it should remain unknown. The story isn't the romantic tale that Neil Swanson told and John Wayne performed on the big screen. To be sure, it is dramatic. It is, at times, invigorating and even inspiring, but when we peel away the veneer and see some of the underlying motivations, a darker story with troubling consequences emerges. It is a piece of our past that still reverberates.

Frontier Rebels

Chapter 1

———•———

Setting the Stage

1754–1764

On February 10, 1763, diplomats from Great Britain and France met in Paris to sign a treaty that ended one of the largest wars the world had seen. Known as the Seven Years' War, this conflict had actually begun nine years earlier in western Pennsylvania, near the very region in which the Black Boys would later rebel. In 1754, when the war began, Great Britain and France were competing for control of North America. Both empires knew that whoever controlled the area around modern-day Pittsburgh, and the Ohio River that began there, would control the future of North America. And with North America would come global dominance.[1]

The war's origins date to a century-long rivalry between the British and French over their claims to North America. As soon as Catholic France populated Canada (known then as New France) and Protestant England settled to its south in what is today New England and Virginia in the seventeenth century, the two clashed over boundaries. Indeed, in New England, the seventeenth and early eighteenth centuries saw several clashes between the French and their Indian allies and the English and their own Indian allies. Throughout the eighteenth

century, this competition increased as both empires expanded farther into interior North America. By mid-century, British colonization
stretched along the Atlantic seaboard from Maine to Georgia, and its
settlements sprawled to the Appalachians. Although New France was
more sparsely settled, French influence spread from the mouth of the
Saint Lawrence River across southern Canada to the Great Lakes and
down the Mississippi.

Tensions between the two powers rose in the 1740s when the French
built a string of forts along the Great Lakes and moved military forces
into the Ohio valley in direct conflict with British claims. British colonists refused to sit by idly. Virginia-based land companies sent settlers,
surveyed land, and began constructing their own forts in the region to
assert British rights to the territory. Such provocative moves made a
major confrontation inevitable.

The collision finally happened in the summer of 1754 when Virginia governor Robert Dinwiddie sent a twenty-one-year-old lieutenant
colonel named George Washington to the Ohio River valley to conduct
reconnaissance and confront French officials. Washington asked the
French to abandon their posts, but they soundly rejected his demands.
In May, Washington returned to the area that is now Pittsburgh and
prepared to assert Virginia's claims more strongly. Matters quickly
turned violent. On May 28, Virginian forces aided by Iroquois guides
clashed with French forces over these western lands in the battle of
Jumonville Glen—so named because, near the end of the battle, an
Iroquois warrior killed Joseph Coulon de Jumonville, the officer leading the French forces. Washington's triumph turned out to be fleeting.
On July 4, 1754, twenty-two years to the day before American colonists
declared independence, the French mounted a strong counter-offensive
that forced Washington and his troops to capitulate.

As they beat a hasty retreat into Virginia, reports of the clash began to circulate throughout the colonies. When the reports eventually reached Europe, the British realized that the confrontation gave them just what they wanted. The French, who accused Washington of assassinating Jumonville, felt the same way. In time, this scuffle in the backwoods of America grew into a furious brawl that engulfed the globe. As the war expanded to include Europe, Africa, South Asia, and the Caribbean, the contest evolved from a fight for the control of North America into a battle over the destiny of both empires. The winner, most people believed, would rule supreme.[2]

They were right. As the ink dried on the treaty at Paris, Great Britain became the world's sole superpower. As part of the terms of peace, Britain forced France to relinquish its North American holdings. Spain, which had entered the war late as a French ally, ceded Florida to Britain while keeping control of New Orleans and land west of the Mississippi (something it had received from France in a deal struck in 1762). Britain also secured near-total dominion of India and strengthened its control in West Africa. Ambitious and optimistic Britons soon boasted that "the sun never sets on the British Empire."[3]

But victory came at a cost. Historians have often credited Great Britain's strong financial system as being one of the nation's main advantages over its more autocratic European adversaries. Britain's ability to finance debt, the argument goes, enabled the British to outperform their rivals during the Seven Years' War by expanding the theaters of war and draining the resources of the French and Spanish governments. After the war, however, politicians in London felt besieged by debt payments. The British treasury owed about £130 million to its creditors. The amount was unprecedented, and servicing it placed heavy financial demands on politicians. In 1764, for instance, the entire budget of the British Empire was £10.7 million; £4.9 million went to pay interest on its obligations—a staggering 45 percent of

total government expenditures. Searching for a way to increase reve-
nues, Parliamentarians and imperial administrators turned their eyes
to North America.[4]

———•———

During the eighteenth century, the importance of the North American colonies within the British Empire changed profoundly. Before
the 1740s, the sugar islands in the Caribbean—such as Barbados and
Jamaica—were the source of the Empire's growth. The mainland colonies, meanwhile, seemed like unprofitable backwaters. This contrast
promoted an attitude of salutary neglect in which imperial officials in
London seemed to pay more attention to their holdings in the West
Indies than their North American holdings. The colonists took advantage of this autonomy to develop their economies and pursue their own
interests. For example, iron forges were founded in New Jersey, Pennsylvania, and Virginia. By the time of the Revolution, British North
America had become the third-largest exporter of iron in the world.
Farming in Pennsylvania, Maryland, and Virginia expanded, helping
to feed the entire Empire as well as the European continent. Indeed, the
western areas of Pennsylvania, the region the Black Boys would eventually occupy, became the breadbasket for the British Empire. Wood from
cleared forests fueled the forges and heated the new homes that were
sprouting up rapidly. Abundant supplies of wood also spurred a vibrant
shipbuilding industry, especially in New England. By the time of the
American Revolution, New England–built ships accounted for at least
a third of all British merchant vessels sailing the globe. Rice, tobacco,
and rum rounded out the other major items that colonists exported to
support the Empire's growth.[5]

By the 1760s, this economic expansion and diversification had
changed the colonies' relationship with their mother country. In the
early eighteenth century, Great Britain had a negative balance of trade

with their North American colonies, meaning the colonists exported more to the mother country than they imported. By the end of the Seven Years' War, that balance had been reversed. The thriving colonists became hungry consumers, and the British were aware of it. Now the North American colonies stopped existing on the margins of imperial thinking and instead became a central focus.[6]

Colonists in North America experienced this change as well, though in a slightly different way. They took pride in their display of refined and often-expensive British manufactured items—a sign, they claimed, of the colonies' growing success and importance. There was more to it than conspicuous consumption, though. They imported and wore London's finest to show that they shared the same culture as their distant countrymen. The more they bought from Great Britain, the more British they felt. Consumption allowed the colonists to transcend the physical and metaphorical separation from Britain that was represented by the Atlantic Ocean.[7]

But even amid this buoyant optimism, colonial Americans felt deep insecurities about their future—mostly over what loomed on their western horizon. Many worried that New France, by now extending from southeastern Canada to the mouth of the Mississippi, would hem them in to the coast and restrain their future expansion. Some even feared that New France could assemble the military might to push British settlement back to the east, perhaps even back across the Atlantic. For colonists who lived nearest to New France, like those in western Pennsylvania, the anxiety was even greater because they knew they would be on the front lines in a war between empires.[8]

When war between the empires did arrive in 1754, colonists mobilized to defend their territory. The war was both traumatic and exhilarating. Those living in the Middle Colonies, especially in Pennsylvania, experienced a fury unmatched in the region's history. In the war's early years, colonists endured devastating losses, most notably in 1755 when

Edward Braddock suffered one of Britain's worst defeats at a battle out-side of present-day Pittsburgh. For the two years that followed, Pennsylvania became bloody ground. In fact, one creek near where the Black Boys lived still bears the name Bloody Run, because a successful Indian attack on a colonist settlement supposedly turned the water red with blood. (Some people in the nineteenth century claimed that its name actually came from the Black Boys, whose actions "stain[ed]" the river red with blood from slain horses. But evidence from the eighteenth century, however, points to an earlier date for the name.)[9]

The war transformed the American colonies, especially Pennsylvania. The colony had maintained peace with Native Americans for over seventy years, a record of harmony unrivaled in colonial America. But as Pennsylvania settlements expanded farther west in the 1740s and 1750s, many Native groups grew disillusioned with the colony. The angriest groups used Great Britain's war with France as an opportunity to push Pennsylvania's western boundaries to the east.

Their attacks were devastatingly successful. Pennsylvanians born into its comfortable peace began to live in constant fear of invasion. These frontier residents felt terror and desperation on a scale that is hard for most modern readers to understand. Families spent nights awake, listening to the surrounding woods, aware that every unknown sound could be the signal for an attack. Regular patterns of life were permanently disrupted. Farmers, for instance, hired soldiers to guard them and their families as they tilled their lands. "The most pleasant, peaceable, country in the world," noted a soldier fighting in Pennsylvania, had "become a land of murders and rapine." Colonial fears of retreat were confirmed when French and Indian raids forced Pennsylvania settlements back over a hundred miles, and formerly secure communities within seventy miles of Philadelphia became dangerous frontiers.[10]

For those first years of the war, colonists' fears of a French victory grew as their borders retreated to the east. But in 1758, the British launched a successful offensive that recaptured lost ground and soon seized French territory in Canada. In that year, General John Forbes arrived in Philadelphia ready to march west to reclaim the Ohio valley. He succeeded, recaptured Fort Pitt, helped establish alliances with formerly warring Native groups, and returned peace to the colony.

As British victories began to pile up, the colonists felt a sense of liberation and hope for a return to the growing prosperity they had known before the war. When Quebec fell in 1759—a sign, many believed, of certain conquest in North America—Britain's colonies were aglow with festivities celebrating their new dominance. In Boston, for instance, church bells rang and militiamen fired muskets throughout the day. As dusk fell, taverns swelled and boisterous toasts swirled. Later in the evening, Bostonians gathered around large bonfires and watched fireworks light up the night sky. In 1760, when General Jeffery Amherst captured Montreal, colonists knew that they had achieved a resounding triumph over the French.[11]

The euphoria of Great Britain's victory was short-lived. British administrators' excitement dimmed as they came to terms with the new financial demands of this much-expanded empire. Previously, the Empire had tried to protect its North American settlements against a looming French rival. Now, as administrators balanced their ledger books and surveyed maps of North America with the French gone, new challenges became evident. Britain needed to establish control over this newly acquired area, and it also needed to integrate the region and its people—including Native peoples—into the larger framework of its global empire, all while keeping expenditures to a minimum. These new demands led those in charge of the transition to assert greater authority in the colonies through a stronger administration. They also had to make sure that this larger and more bureaucratic, but also deeply indebted, empire could sustain itself financially, so they sought new efficiencies by improving governance, reducing expenses, and increasing revenue.[12]

As early as 1760, but picking up speed once the Treaty of Paris was signed in 1763, British policymakers began to build a new imperial governing structure in North America. They established more offices and layers of administration, many of which aimed to provide greater oversight of Indian relations and better management of the new western territory. Outside of Albany, Sir William Johnson, a charismatic Irishman turned diplomat, won the new position of Superintendent of Indian Affairs in the Northern District. His task was to maintain peace and negotiate treaties with Indian groups living north of Virginia, and he appointed George Croghan as deputy superintendent for the region around Fort Pitt. The Crown also planned to maintain a series of forts in the west, including a communication line that connected Philadelphia to Fort Pitt. Military officials expected British troops to man these forts and to help Croghan and Johnson do their job by maintaining the infrastructure, overseeing trading posts, and providing protection to officials and colonists. These soldiers symbolized Great Britain's new control over territory and, in this way, served as the primary arm of empire in areas of recent settlement or new acquisition.[13]

Next the Crown announced policies to manage its new acquisitions in North America, especially areas in western Pennsylvania. Imperial strategists knew that the rivers around Fort Pitt provided the best access to the vast American interior and that the roads from Philadelphia to Fort Pitt, built during the war, connected these rivers to the Atlantic world of trade. On the water and earthen arteries of the eighteenth century, raw materials from deep inside the continent could flow to the imperial core, where they could be refined and shipped to eager North American and European markets. In this scenario, Native

American communities in the Ohio River valley and in the Illinois Country would become peaceful trading partners integrated into the new British Empire. This policy, often referred to as creating an "open road" to Indian Country by diplomats like Johnson, was made clear in the King's Proclamation of 1763. The Proclamation declared that "the several Nations or Tribes of Indians with whom We are connected, and who live under our Protection, should not be molested or disturbed in the Possession of such Parts of Our Dominions and Territories."[14]

While the Empire looked to expand its markets into the interior, administrators took a very different approach to the politics of land. Peace again drove their policies. To show the Crown's sincerity to Indians, the Proclamation of 1763 established a boundary line between Indian Country and colonial settlements along the Appalachian Mountains. The Proclamation Line, as it was known, was meant to reassure Native communities in the Ohio valley and Illinois Country that Great Britain respected their territorial claims. While the policy aimed to appease Indian worries, it also reflected the reality of governing an eighteenth-century global empire. Rather than encourage colonial expansion into the newly acquired western territory, imperial officials wanted to restrain settlers, at least for the time being. They worried that a widely spread-out settler population, far from colonial and imperial capitals, would cause disorder and lead to more costly wars. Instead, they wanted to keep colonists confined to the eastern seaboard, where they would be under the oversight of government authorities and connected to the mercantile trade of the Atlantic.[15]

Finally, those in London fretted about finances. They needed to find a way to fund this newly energetic imperial presence in North America. They found their answer in molasses and paper. In 1764, George Greenville, the prime minister, proposed a tax on foreign molasses—a major trade item for the colonists, especially those from New England. Technically, the 1764 molasses tax *reduced by half* an earlier tax on foreign molasses. Colonists weren't happy with this tax cut, however, because the former tax, passed in 1733, had been so high that merchants and most customs officials had ignored it during the period of salutary neglect. The new law included ways to make the tax easier to collect, meaning that it would probably act as a tax increase for those who had ignored the previous law.[16]

Next Greenville eyed the vast amount of paper the colonists consumed. In the eighteenth century, paper was the medium through which life was conducted. Residents of Great Britain had paid a stamp duty—a tax on most printed documents such as marriage licenses, deeds, newspapers, and even playing cards—since 1694. The colonists in North America, however, had avoided such a tax. Greenville reasoned that it was time to establish in North America what was considered a standard form of taxation in Great Britain. Passed in 1765, a year after the Molasses Act, the Stamp Act placed a relatively small surcharge on all legal documents, bills of sale, licenses, newspapers, and even some books in the colonies.[17]

Greenville intended these measures to give the colonies greater financial independence even as he tried to assert greater parliamentary authority over them. The money, as the law stated, would never leave North America. All revenue would go toward the costs of maintaining the British army on the frontiers, thereby contributing to the colonies' safety and security. Moreover, from Parliament's point of view, the taxes were a bargain for the colonists. The revenue raised by the two acts would cover less than half the total operating cost of this force, leaving Britons with the rest of the bill. Greenville simply wanted the colonies to help pay for the troops that protected them. He felt that Parliament had to impose these levies because the colonists would never do it on their own.[18]

Therein lay the seeds for discord. After the Seven Years' War, just as colonists felt burdens lifted and a new sense of freedom and security, imperial administrators felt the weight of new liabilities on their shoulders. They eyed the colonies and their prospering economy as a source for new revenue—revenue, they said, that would help preserve the colonists' well-being. For colonists basking in the glow of victory, news of these new policies dampened their jubilation.

Worse, events in North America quickly intruded on administrators' well-laid plans and made colonists feel even more subjugated. First, the North American economy began to weaken. During the war, as thousands of British troops descended on North America and colonial militias formed to aid in their campaigns, demand for materiel created an economic boom for many colonial merchants. The displacement of the French after the war brought a form of geopolitical security, but at the expense of financial stability. As demand dried up, all of the major colonial seaports suffered a significant recession. In such an economic downturn, the taxation policies that many colonists found odious now seemed noxious. They viewed the taxes as an insult to their wartime sacrifices and sufferings. Moreover, the colonists began to associate the higher taxes with the cause of their deepening economic crisis.[19]

Worse still, an Indian war began on the frontiers in 1763 that threatened the Empire and its new North American holdings. After the Seven Years' War, a Delaware Indian named Neolin began to prophesize near Fort Detroit. He claimed that he had experienced a sacred vision that called for Native groups to give up their European connections and return to their traditional cultural ways. Dependence on Europeans for goods, Neolin warned, had weakened Native Americans and destined them for a hell-like place. He promised his followers that a return to their roots would give them the strength to halt colonial expansion and create a path toward eternal happiness. In the summer of 1763, an Ottawa named Pontiac transformed Neolin's spiritual message into a

political one. He united various groups in the Ohio River valley, Illinois
Country, and the Great Lakes into a coalition that waged a war against
Great Britain to recapture territory the French had ceded.[20]

The united Indians were extraordinarily successful. The war began
with an attack on Fort Detroit. While Pontiac failed to capture this
major military base, he did lay siege to it for over two months. Meanwhile, groups of Native Americans began launching raids on colonial
settlements that dotted the Appalachian Mountains, and many of those
settlements were in Pennsylvania. The warriors succeeded in destroying
at least eight British forts and harassed half a dozen more. For colonists
living on this exposed frontier, the war rekindled the fears of Indian
invasion that they had felt during the Seven Years' War.[21]

In the fall, at about the time the war was reaching the height of
its bloody violence, the Proclamation of 1763 arrived in the colonies.
The Proclamation, issued during a full-scale Indian war, seemed poorly
timed. The war itself made it meaningless. But its issuance alongside
the molasses and stamp taxes seemed to confirm for urban and frontier
inhabitants alike that the Crown was trying to limit their potential for
economic and territorial growth at a time of struggle. The liberation
that colonists thought they had achieved after the Seven Years' War
seemed under assault.[22]

British officials in North America desperately wanted to restore
peace between the warring groups. Pontiac's War tested their military
capabilities and financial reserves at a time when both were thin. In late
1764, a British offensive led by Henry Bouquet put the Shawnees on the
defensive. By winter, they and other Native groups in the Ohio River
valley seemed ready to negotiate, and the British were willing to meet
them on their terms. The Shawnees and other allied Indians accused
the British of treating them like a conquered people after the Seven
Years' War and demanded better treatment and greater recognition.
Weakened by a combination of insufficient funds and military defeats,

imperial officials wanted to correct the situation. Native spokesmen also complained about colonial settlements that threatened to encroach on their spiritual homeland in the Ohio Country. The British promised to restrain such settlement and pointed to the Proclamation.[23]

But words would only go so far. Officials in charge of managing Indian relations knew that specific actions needed to follow. Native Americans believed that one of the most important ways to restore trust was through ceremonial gift-giving at the signing of treaties. The size, value, and types of gifts that allies gave each other were deeply symbolic. Gifts underscored the respect and understanding allies claimed to feel for each other and added weight to words. When the British gave their Native allies guns and powder, they meant to show that they trusted them as friends. Reciprocity was a fundamental part of this exchange. When Native Americans provided valuable trade goods in return for the British goods, they meant to show that an open road of trade existed between the sides. Sir William Johnson, the superintendent of Indian Affairs, explained to his superiors across the Atlantic: "If we conquer their prejudices by our generosity they will lay aside their jealousys and we may rest in security. This is much cheaper than any other plan and more certain of success."[24]

In December 1764, after Bouquet's victory, George Croghan, the deputy superintendent of Indian Affairs, was given the job of cementing this peace in the spring of 1765. He planned to show British sincerity through one of the largest gift-giving ceremonies ever conducted. Croghan's idea was to begin the display of gifts at Fort Pitt, where he would re-open trade and re-establish alliances with Native American communities in the Ohio River valley at a treaty there. Then he would launch a massive goodwill venture down the Ohio River and deep into the American interior in search of Pontiac. All along the way, gifts would stream from his rafts as he floated downriver. Such a show of generosity, he hoped, would reassure distant groups in the

Illinois Country, many of whom were former allies of the French and deeply suspicious of British intentions, that the British Empire could be trusted. If he succeeded, Great Britain's plans for a stable West and a profitable relationship with Native American groups would be guaranteed. Croghan understood the stakes, writing shortly before his departure that "for the Indians in those parts, Detroit and the Illinois . . . the manner the Trade is to be carry'd on and Conducted in a great measure will depend the future Peace of His Majesty's Subjects in this Country."[25]

There was, as was usual with George Croghan, more to his plans than just diplomacy.

Chapter 2

———•———

The Mission

Philadelphia

January 1765

George Croghan was a wily man with often murky motives. His plans usually served his self-interests, but he was also often a well-intentioned man who served the Empire and supported peace. Sometimes the two went hand-in-hand, as was the case in 1765. While his ambiguities have frustrated historians who have tried to make sense of him, Croghan never saw the contradictions that are so evident to later observers, nor did he waste time thinking about them. Put simply, he believed that serving himself and serving the Empire were not mutually exclusive. Such beliefs were not rare at the time, nor are they now. It was this conviction that inspired his secret plans for his trip to Fort Pitt—the trip that sparked the rebellion that began a revolution.[1]

George Croghan's path to Fort Pitt began on a different British frontier: Ireland. While Croghan's birth year remains a mystery, we do know that he spent part of his youth in Dublin. By 1741, he was old enough to cross the Atlantic and put down new roots in western Pennsylvania. He arrived with a heavy brogue and, although literate, had such poor spelling and atrocious penmanship that he was probably self-taught. In short, he was like many aspiring young immigrants—smart enough to learn to write on his own and enterprising enough to cross the Atlantic in search of new opportunity in an unknown land. There also is little evidence to describe Croghan's physical stature. While it's unusual for someone who became so prominent to apparently have no portrait done, it also reflects a key part of Croghan's lifestyle. He was a man always on the move who spent most of his time trading on the frontiers—not the type of person to sit idle for days in Philadelphia for a painter.[2]

We may not know precisely when he was born or what he looked like, but the historic record provides plenty of evidence about Croghan's personality and professional activities. Upon arrival in North America, Croghan quickly entered the Indian trade, a profession that promised profitability but involved enormous risk. He seems to have begun as a carrier of goods from Philadelphia to Peter Tostee, a prominent trader in the western area of the colony. But Croghan was an ambitious man with an independent streak. He soon operated on his own and within a decade became one of the most well-known and respected Indian traders in Pennsylvania. Officially commissioned maps of colonial Pennsylvania almost always marked his house, located near a gap that also carried his name in the Appalachian Mountains just west of the Susquehanna River, because it was a popular waypoint for those involved in the western trade. George Croghan's name may be forgotten today, but almost anybody who was anyone knew it in 1765.[3]

Croghan's success reflected his personal history and abilities. To be sure, he needed incredible cunning to thrive in the treacherous trading world of the American frontier. But there was more to Croghan than his guile. To succeed as a trader, a man needed to bridge the cultures of Indians, colonial frontiers, and the refined society of Philadelphia, one of the largest ports in the British Empire. Croghan's upbringing in Ireland left him well equipped for this American setting.[4]

Although the American frontier was home to a far more diverse populace than the Irish countryside Croghan knew as a child, the frontier's social and economic structures had certain similarities to those of Ireland. Ireland, with its native population of Catholics and its colonial population of British aristocrats who wanted to subjugate the local inhabitants and control the land, looked a lot like British North America. Indeed, many elite Britons considered the Irish as well as American Indians to be savage heathens. Those raised in Ireland needed to be familiar with the ways of often-absentee British landlords, local elites, and the Irish populace, who had their own social structures, beliefs, and dialects, just as colonial traders needed to be deft at navigating imperial policy, colonial politics, and Native American relations. Croghan himself was also competitive, connected, and calculating, which made him all the more ready to dominate the world of Pennsylvania traders.[5]

Croghan was so skillful at navigating these waters that he soon became indispensable to both Native groups and the British Empire. Croghan learned at least two Native languages and built a business empire based on good relations and fair dealing with his Native trading partners. His connections meant that as imperial rivalries heated up in the 1740s, colonial officials called on him for aid. First, they hoped he could help Pennsylvania and the British Empire maintain alliances with Indian groups that were teetering toward a French alliance. Then, once war broke out, they called on him to mobilize Indian allies for war. Croghan held the rank of colonel during the war, seeing action several times, although he primarily served as an intermediary between Great Britain and Native groups. He even practiced subterfuge by spreading false rumors about British victories through his networks in Indian Country, leading to moments of confusion and disorder among the French and their Indian allies.[6]

Croghan's path eventually crossed that of William Johnson, a man whose background nearly mirrored that of his own. Johnson, an Irishman with family ties to merchant networks, arrived in New York at about the same time Croghan did in Pennsylvania. Johnson was even more skilled at navigating intercultural relations than Croghan. A successful trader, diplomat, and politician, Johnson built a grand plantation outside of Albany to reflect his status as the chief cultural broker in British North America. But while the structure of Johnson Hall, as he called it, resembled an English manor, the activities that went on inside it were far from anything that would have occurred in an austere manor. Johnson had several children with Molly Brent, a prominent member of the Mohawks, while also having a relationship with a European woman of German descent. Indian structures and symbols adorned the grounds of his stately mansion. But this combination of European and Indian cultures is exactly what made Johnson influential. On his manor, different cultures mixed rather than collided. As many historians have noted, Johnson almost single-handedly maintained Great Britain's alliance with the powerful Six Nations Iroquois, whose claim to dominion stretched from Canada to Virginia, by his smooth diplomatic maneuverings.[7]

Johnson continued his rise during the Seven Years' War. He served as a colonel during the war, eventually receiving a baronetcy for his bravery at the Battle of Lake George in 1755. In 1765, he held the office of Superintendent of Indian Affairs for the Northern Department, which, after Pontiac's War, now included the Illinois Country. To manage such a large territory, he had a number of sub-lieutenants who represented the Crown in specific regions. When it came to appointing someone for the Ohio valley, probably the most strategically important zone and also the most volatile, Croghan was Johnson's obvious choice.[8]

Ending Pontiac's War through a diplomatic trade mission was one of the first real tests of Croghan's ability to serve in the office. Croghan's plan in 1765 was ambitious—and possibly illegal. Its questionable legal status also means that records of his actions are unclear because many people involved in his scheme had reasons to tamper with and destroy materials. The outlines of Croghan's plan emerges by combining the records that do remain and reading between the lines of what was said. In late 1764, Croghan received £2,000 from Thomas Gage, commander-in-chief of British forces in North America, to purchase goods intended for a peace treaty with Shawnees at Fort Pitt and for his journey down the Ohio into the American interior. He later received official passes from Colonel Henry Bouquet, the most senior military officer in the region, to travel on the roads with these trade items. Ordinarily, during times of peace, the Crown allowed colonial governors to grant trading licenses. During wartime, however, trade with enemies was halted by order of the Crown and by Pennsylvania law, but high ranking military officials could provide a pass for diplomatic or military purposes.[9]

Croghan, while grateful for having received the pass, believed he still faced a problem. Two thousand pounds seemed a tiny sum, given the stakes. As Croghan understood, Indians considered the Empire's cutbacks on gift-giving before Pontiac's War as a sign of hostility. Many Native groups saw the cessation of gift-giving as threatening not only their diplomatic standing but also as a purposeful attempt to weaken their communities by withholding valuable goods. It was, they worried, a sign of Great Britain's desire to subjugate them. Croghan argued that the Empire needed to do more than reverse its policy through written orders. To make peace, he needed to perform the promises made around the fire through an exchange of goods. He worried that Indians would interpret the absence of trade goods following the treaty as a ruse to lull them into a false sense of security before an attack. As Croghan explained to his superiors, "Had the trade been opened for the Indians and they told so, and no goods to be sold to them, that it would be out of my power to persuade them. But that we wanted to put a Trick on them, and deceive them, which might be attended with the worst Consequences."[10]

Croghan, frustrated with stingy military officers untrained in the ways of Indian diplomacy, decided to take matters into his own hands. He worked with the Philadelphia firm of Baynton, Wharton, and Morgan to pull together a much larger shipment. Although the details of their partnership are unknown, it appears that he entered into some sort of loan in which Baynton, Wharton, and Morgan would cover most of the initial costs and then receive a share of the profits. These proceeds were to be funneled to Croghan through a shell company that he had fronted through a relative named Thomas Smallman. A mixture of self-interest and public service guided Croghan's project. While he looked to make a huge profit if his scheme worked, Croghan also felt that this plan of uncertain legality was necessary to secure the interest of the British Empire.[11]

Organizing such an endeavor turned out to be a difficult task. The first problem was the sheer size of his order. Croghan's request for shirts alone exceeded the supply of all the stores in Philadelphia. Baynton, Wharton, and Morgan bought all that they could and then enlisted several women to custom-make thousands of shirts to fill the order. By the end of January, the firm acquired more than 5,700 shirts, which had consumed more than 15,000 yards of cloth—an astounding number. The shipment was enough to clothe more than half of the total male Indian population in the Ohio Country, and Croghan intended to provide every Indian family in the region with at least one shirt through either trade or diplomacy. Baynton, Wharton, and Morgan also acquired a ton of sugar to cart west; over thirty hogsheads of rum (around 1,800 gallons), which weighed more than six tons; and additional bales of cloth. The total weight of the caravan is unknown, but according to receipts that still survive, the horses hauled at least forty-four tons. Its exact value is also tough to determine, but the best estimate is around £20,000, more than ten times the £2,000 Croghan was officially allocated—although some contemporary (and possibly inflated) estimates put it at £30,000. Even at a lower estimate, however, Croghan had organized one of the largest trading missions ever undertaken in North America.[12]

While Philadelphians scrambled to meet Croghan's demand, the weather took a turn for the worse. Heavy snow blanketed the Greater Philadelphia region, blocking many of the roads heading west. Croghan realized that even if he could obtain all of the supplies and leave Philadelphia, the road condition would make travel nearly impossible. In late January, after three frustrating weeks in Philadelphia, Croghan decided to go ahead to Fort Pitt, entrusting one of his partners, Captain Robert Callender, to finish the business and escort the goods west. Croghan, meanwhile, would prepare for the treaty and his own trip farther west.[13]

Croghan left Philadelphia on January 24. The trip was slow and difficult. It took him and his companion, Lieutenant Alexander Fraser, nine days to reach Carlisle, Pennsylvania, 120 miles west of Philadelphia, normally a journey of a few days in fine weather. Snow continued to fall, leaving Croghan stranded for several more days.[14]

Finally, on February 16, after the paths improved slightly, Croghan left on horseback for Fort Pitt with a light load of about £900 of trade goods. The trip was horrendous. Croghan and Fraser were the first travelers on horseback to cross the Allegheny Mountains since the snowfall, meaning they had to clear their own paths. The depth of the snow, Fraser noted, was "extraordinary" and "rendered the roads very bad, if not impassable for wagons." Finally, twelve days later, on February 28, they arrived at Fort Pitt. Once settled, Croghan waited for Callender. He knew his partner faced a difficult journey, but he had no idea of the extent of the difficulties that lay before him.[15]

British Headquarters
New York

January 1765

Meanwhile, Thomas Gage stewed despite the cold in New York City. Gage had become commander-in-chief of North America in late 1763 after Lord Jeffery Amherst bungled the transfer of power from France to Great Britain. Amherst's two tasks had been to establish the British Empire's authority in its new holdings, which stretched from Detroit to Florida, and to keep the peace. Both his temperament and circumstances beyond his control worked against his success in these efforts. A portrait Amherst had commissioned in 1765 captured his overly proud attitude. He is shown dressed in armor, the old metallic uniforms of knights, with his helmet resting on a map of North America—a pose meant to say that this conquered land was his territory to rule.[16]

Amherst's actions confirmed the attitude conveyed by this image. He expected Indians to act like obedient British subjects and follow his commands, and he showed no interest in making the gestures of peace that Native peoples wanted. To the contrary, limited by his own arrogance and by budgetary pressures, Amherst oversaw the reduction of the gift-giving and treaties that had been part of European-Native diplomacy for so long. His rigid policies made it clear to many Indians that the British Empire was no friend and ally but, instead, an imperial power that was determined to subjugate them. In this way, Amherst's actions fueled the pan-Indian resistance to Great Britain that ended in Pontiac's War. As Croghan summarized in a report to the Board of Trade, the imperial body based in England that supervised affairs in North America, "The Indians . . . consider us in a very different and less favorable light as they are now become exceedingly jealous of our growing power in that country." In 1763, London officials recognized their errors and recalled Amherst and replaced him with Thomas Gage.[17]

Born the second son in a noble family, Gage's journey to the position seems unremarkable in an empire in which one's dynasty often determined one's destiny. As was often the case in such circles, his elder brother took over the family's official titles and most of the family wealth. Gage, like many other second sons, became a military officer in order to maintain the status and benefits associated with the aristocracy. The glory, prestige, and patronage of serving in war conferred on him all that his family could not pass on. Gage fought with distinction in the Seven Years' War. After serving alongside Braddock and George Washington in western Pennsylvania in 1755, he was promoted to general three years later. In 1760, after the fall of Montreal, he was appointed military general of Canada. He had seen much of North America. He knew its potential, and he knew its dangers.[18]

Amherst's failures made Gage's current task even more serious and difficult. With Pontiac's War drawing to a close in 1765, Gage knew that the transition from war to peace needed a delicate hand. As Gage noted, "They [Indians] dread our Extension over the Continent by driving out the French and think us too powerfull Neighbours, but with proper care and management it is to be hoped that any Suspicions of bad designs in us will entirely Subside." Gage knew that to show "the proper care and management," he needed people who showed the same moderate and reasoned approach that Gage himself represented. William Johnson seemed like just such a person.[19]

George Croghan did not. When Gage thought about Croghan as

the man who had been given this delicate mission, he worried. Croghan was unlike any of the diplomats Gage knew in England. Croghan didn't come from a well-established English family, nor had he received a respectable British education. He was an uneducated Irishman from a relatively undistinguished family. Worse, and perhaps because of this background, Croghan was hard to pin down, slow to respond to correspondence, and vague when he did so. As Gage confided to his friend, Colonel Henry Bouquet, "There is as much Difficulty to keep these People in Order [meaning diplomats like Croghan], as the Indians they deal with."[20]

What Gage failed to realize was that his model for a diplomat— a deferential person who could perform the protocols of etiquette in the rarefied halls of Europe and serve the Empire's interest without question—would have been unprepared for diplomacy on North America's frontiers. Indeed, as Amherst had showed, displays of European arrogance and condescension were likely to alienate Indians. Diplomacy on remote frontiers called for adaptability and independence. Croghan, who had spent time immersed in Indian cultures, was better prepared to serve the Empire's geopolitical interests, even if—much to Gage's chagrin—he often pursued his own economic self-interest at the same time.[21]

But Gage's concerns about Croghan reflected something deeper about the imperial system in North America. The British Empire suffered from a lack of control. Administrators in London were well aware of this problem. In fact, the stream of regulations and laws they passed after the Seven Years' War were efforts to solve it. The problem of authority was particularly bad in areas where the Empire was asserting new control, like in the recently acquired territory around the Great Lakes, or on the fringes of its established jurisdiction like western Pennsylvania. These areas lacked the personnel and infrastructure to enforce new policies. One of Gage's tasks was to build a new model that also reflected the Empire's desire for efficiency.[22]

The trouble that Gage faced caused him to re-think the future of governing in North America. As he read the reports from his lieutenants exploring the newly acquired territories, he began to envision a new system of colonial settlement that was better suited for America's vast interior. The old models for colonization that stressed local control by colonists, he concluded, had become too problematic in the western areas where violence, shady land deals, and unregulated trade spoiled the Empire's attempt to create stable Indian relations. His plan was simple and designed for the realities of the frontiers. He would create "a military establishment" headquartered around Fort Pitt. It was a strange, idealistic dream that only a general could imagine.[23]

This is how his new colony would function. The commandant of the fort would serve as the governor, and settlers would live on grants of land "in lots of 100 and 150 acres, given on military tenures." It would be a "little community" at first, but eventually the area "should be settled in different townships" along the banks of the various inland rivers. Military culture would be prominent, with regular "mustering and days of exercise" and with every person obliged to possess a "quantity of ammunition . . . to have at all time." Colonists who moved to the new colony would be required to farm and to provide supplies to the fort so it would always be well stocked—a type of tax in exchange for protection. This little inland community would also have a navy, something no eastern colony had. The farmers' supplies would help support a flotilla of boats "always ready for service" because they would be stacked with "months provisions."[24]

Although his colony never took form, Gage's notion of a well-regulated West was shared by many and reflected imperial visions of grandeur. The need for a strong military presence to maintain order

and security also reflected Gage's realization that colonists living far
from eastern governing centers were too free from imperial controls.
Regimenting the people through a military state and its chain of command would allow the Empire to better manage colonists who preferred
to serve their own interests rather than the Empire's. He wanted to create a centralizing force for political power in an empire that appeared
to be rapidly expanding.[25]

Gage's colony never made it further than the pages of a letter, but
he did take steps to increase the Empire's control of these areas. He
maintained communication lines to connect the fringes of the Empire
to its colonial centers. He bolstered forts in recently acquired areas to
establish Great Britain's presence. In the far west, Fort Detroit served as
the largest symbol of the British Empire in the areas of recent conquest.
It was connected to New York and Philadelphia, the two most important seaports, via waterways and trade routes. Fort Pitt, meanwhile,
served as the most strategically important post. Its location provided
officials with easy access to points west via the Ohio River and gave
them a base from which to work as they established British authority in
the Ohio and Illinois Countries.

In January 1765, Gage was still struggling to establish a system of
communication that tied this network together. Fort Pitt in particular
was giving him trouble. He wanted to maintain the outpost, but his officers in the region reported that because of Amherst's cutbacks the forts
that had once dotted the communication line to Fort Pitt were "moul-
dering away." Indeed, Croghan's awareness that information traveled
slowly along an imperial infrastructure tied together by rough roads
and rotting forts gave him the confidence to make such a bold move. He
thought he could pull it off because no one would ever find out. And as
far as he knew, his plan was working. By the end of February, Callender
finished collecting the rest of the goods and prepared to head west into
this region.[26]

Indian Country
Somewhere near Detroit

January 1765

For someone who has received so much attention from historians, we know surprisingly little about Pontiac. His parentage and birth year are unclear. Some say he was fifty when he led the siege of Fort Detroit that began the conflict now known as Pontiac's War; others say he was younger. Most likely, he was born around the same time as George Croghan, in the 1710s, and in the Great Lakes region, perhaps near the Miami River around modern-day Defiance, Ohio. This story, however, may be apocryphal, as Defiance later became the site of a major conflict between Native groups defending their land in the nineteenth century against American forces in much the same way Pontiac did against the British in the eighteenth century. Pontiac's physical appearance is also uncertain. One biographer concludes that he was "not attractive in appearance," while at least one contemporary said he was "a remarkably well-looking man." Even his height is in dispute, with one contemporary describing him as "a tall man" and another claiming he was "a man of medium stature." Aside from confusion about his age and looks, historians have described him as a charismatic leader, a calculating military strategist, and an important but not especially unique Indian.[27]

Even though Pontiac's early life is a mystery, we do know that he was Ottawa. However, his family background is obscured by rumor and speculation. The strongest evidence is that his father was Ottawa and his mother Chippewa, but other sources say it was the other way around. Still others claim he was Catawba by birth and adopted into the Ottawa nation as a child captive. Additional theories are that he came from a further western nation as a captive, that he was Chippewa, or that he was Nipissing. Regardless, having been raised as an Ottawa in the early eighteenth century, Pontiac probably had ties to New France, feared the British, and considered the upper Great Lakes region Indian territory.[28]

As Great Britain and New France collided and war engulfed the region Pontiac considered home, he emerges more clearly in the historic record. Pontiac was an active warrior in the 1740s, fighting alongside the French when they confronted their British rivals. By the Seven Years' War, he seems to have served as a war chief. At a minimum, he was a part, if not the leader, of numerous raids on British settlements in the Ohio River valley and Pennsylvania during the Seven Years' War. One of the first mentions of him in the historical record relates to 1757, when he delivered a fiery speech to French officials in which he berated George Croghan—the very man who was sent to negotiate peace with him in 1765—as a liar. Croghan had apparently spread rumors of a massive French defeat at Quebec among Ohio valley Indians in an attempt to weaken the resolve of Pontiac's warriors. But Pontiac was undaunted by Croghan's subterfuge, rallied his troops, and continued to fight the British. During and immediately after the Seven Years' War, Pontiac comes into even sharper relief. In 1763, he was at the center of a pan-Indian movement to reject the British and assert Native sovereignty over the North American interior—a movement that ended in the war that bears Pontiac's name.[29]

While Pontiac appears in sources more often during the war years, there are few records of what was happening within Indian society. We have only fragments, secondhand accounts, and rumor. We cannot know the exact role Pontiac or other Indian leaders played at war councils. The written record, rather than helping clarify the past, has only made Pontiac more mysterious.

This much, though, is clear: Pontiac was a central figure, perhaps the central figure, of the war.[30] It was Pontiac who launched the initial raid on Fort Detroit, the largest fort in the British Empire's new territory, and this attack triggered all of the subsequent attacks. But his allies were not duped into acting by his charms or coerced by his power. They voluntarily joined the cause out of a shared vision for the future.[31]

By the time Croghan planned his trip to negotiate the end of this war in 1764, Pontiac's stature was under threat, and with it his vision for Indian Country's peaceful future. He had united Native Americans in the Great Lakes region in war, but the prospect of peace fractured the coalition. The division erupted as Native groups considered a world in which they had to accept a British presence in or near their communities, a world that to many looked bleak. Without a French presence in North America, many Native Americans worried that a British monopoly on trade would increase prices in trade goods and leave them wholly dependent on a single foreign empire. They worried further that without their French ally and trading partner, they would be unable to ward off British encroachments. At the heart of this debate, a debate similar to the one colonists were entering into themselves, was the role—if any—of the British Empire in this world remade by the end of the Seven Years' War and a fear that the Empire was now too strong and forceful in North America.[32]

In the winter of 1765, Pontiac the former war leader had become the chief advocate for peace with accommodation. His supporters thought they could benefit from continued trade with Great Britain, but they expected the relationship to be similar to the one that had existed between Native groups and New France. New France had respected Native autonomy and had kept its settlements confined to trading forts. Yet these former allies of New France knew of Great Britain's reputation for territorial growth through colonization. All Native peoples strongly opposed Great Britain's unfettered landed expansion. Those who were open to peace, however, were willing to switch one European trade partner for another without giving up their sovereignty or rights to land.

Pontiac's change from warrior to peacemaker may seem odd, but it makes sense in light of the historic record's scattered information about his life. Taken together, these bits of information reveal a fundamental part of what drove this Native leader as both a warrior and a diplomat. Pontiac had no ideology other than advancing the interest—and preserving the independence—of Ottawas. His actions as first documented in the historic record from the 1750s to the 1760s were always intended to weaken the expanding British Empire and assert Native strength and sovereignty in the West. Although his dramatic transformation in 1765 from a fierce warrior to peacemaker may have confounded historians, his actions show that he was as well-versed in the art of realpolitik as any European diplomat. For Pontiac, the war against the British was a means to an end, not an end unto itself. The early success of Pontiac's War brought the British to the negotiating table, and Pontiac saw in Croghan's diplomatic excursion the opportunity to accomplish the aims of his war through peaceful means.

There may also have been a bit of self-interest at play in Pontiac's decision to negotiate. Great Britain needed Pontiac for two reasons, and he leveraged their desires to his advantage. First, those from Great Britain were preconditioned to see history made by singular leaders, like kings and great generals. Thus, when they sought out a cause for the war, they concluded that Pontiac was a singular chief who was solely responsible for it. They therefore thought he was the only person who could bring it to an official close. Pontiac could confirm their desire and advance his cause. In contrast, those better versed in Native ways, such as William Johnson and George Croghan, realized that the war's causes were more complex and that Native groups had worked together and had shared models of leadership. They, however, saw another reason to boost Pontiac's position. By treating Pontiac as the most important Indian in the Illinois Country, they would strengthen their own hand through a coalition built on valuable trade items with a leader whose power would partly come from this alliance. As William Johnson reminded Croghan before he left, a happy Pontiac "may prove of great service" to the British interest.[33]

By the time Callender was heading west to Fort Pitt, Pontiac was in desperate need of such bolstering. There was a growing movement led by a Shawnee named Charlot Kaské to reject any peace overtures. Kaské and his followers believed that any accommodation with the British would eventually lead to the expropriation of Native lands. Those in this camp pointed to history as evidence, arguing that giving the British an initial toehold would only lead to Indian removal and eradication. Kaské is reputed to have said to a delegation of British soldiers, "You English, when you first came amongst us, only settl'd upon the Sea Coasts and ask'd for a small quanitity of land . . . but as more and more of you came over and as you increased, you ask'd again again for a span lengthen and then for a step, which we poor Indians always gave you. Now you envy us every good spot of Land we have, even for our hunting." Kaské and his supporters wanted to continue to fight, seeing this moment as the best time to strike back and restrict a weakened British Empire to the eastern seaboard.[34]

Pontiac knew that support for Charlot Kaské was growing stronger by the day. He knew that he needed to stop Kaské's movement if he was to maintain his own power and that an alliance with Great Britain would strengthen his own hand within many Native communities. Since he would be acknowledged as the chief spokesman for Native groups in the Illinois Country, he would have an influential role in the diplomacy and trade that would follow peace. As word of a diplomatic mission began to circulate through Indian Country in early 1765, Pontiac no doubt realized that the sooner Croghan arrived with goods, the better for his own position—and for the British Empire.[35]

Chapter 3

The Convoy Departs

Carlisle, Pennsylvania

Somewhere near Croghan's Home

February 1765

As Robert Callender, one of Croghan's business partners, sat in a cold and snowy frontier town in late February 1765, dreams of quick riches warmed his thoughts. Callender was a prominent figure on the frontiers of Pennsylvania in his own right. He had served in militias during the wars, eventually reaching the rank of captain. He was a justice of the peace, a powerful position that made him essentially a judge and a police officer. He also operated a trading firm based out of Carlisle, a growing market town on the frontiers of Pennsylvania. Respected by colonial authorities and military officers alike, Callender was a man on the make. In December 1764, he had invested in Croghan's trading mission, and by the end of February 1765 he was sitting at the head of one of the most valuable trading caravans ever assembled in the colonies. Callender's aim was to transport these goods

over snowbound roads and rough terrain to George Croghan at Fort
Pitt. For his efforts, Callender looked to reap a profit of about £2,470—
at a time when the average property owner in Pennsylvania had only
£186 to his name. Croghan, waiting 300 miles away at Fort Pitt, and
the principals of the prominent Philadelphia trading concern Baynton,
Wharton, and Morgan, expected to earn double that.[1]

Carlisle, the staging area for the caravan, was a booming frontier
town that only existed because of George Croghan and his allies. When
Croghan first arrived in Pennsylvania, he had headed west in search of
opportunity. At the time, the Susquehanna River marked the extent of
British control in Pennsylvania. The river was an artery that allowed
goods to flow to and from the Atlantic Ocean. Lancaster, situated near
its eastern banks and closer to the Chesapeake, was the region's chief
town. Founded in 1729, by 1765 Lancaster was a thriving inland trading
hub on its way to becoming the largest interior city in North America.
When the British scientist Charles Mason took a break from surveying
the Mason–Dixon line (which later marked the border between Maryland and Pennsylvania) to visit Lancaster in 1765, he noted in his diary
that it was "as large as most market towns in England." Most recent
arrivals to the region, especially those emigrating from Ireland, found
their way to Lancaster.[2]

Croghan, as usual, cut his own path. He explored areas west of the
river and discovered a convenient gap in the Appalachian Mountains
that connected to rich valleys and gave traders easier access to points
west. The path was so convenient that he settled near it. Croghan
launched long-range trading missions from this base, some reaching
as far as the Great Lakes. His risks paid off, and by 1745 he owned a
large plot of land on the western banks of the Susquehanna River and
numerous storehouses throughout the region. His property became a
manufacturing hub that included a tanyard, large warehouses, and

stables. As Governor James Hamilton noted in 1752, Croghan's post and his sophisticated operations "drew a great trade to that part of the country."[3]

In 1750, as more colonists crossed the Susquehanna, Pennsylvania's government created a new county that encompassed Croghan's home. The government's aim was clear. The rush of new settlers—many of whom were squatters living illegally on Native lands—challenged Pennsylvania's policy of ordered expansion and raised tensions with Native neighbors. Having a county on the western side of the river allowed the government to exert greater control over the region and its people.[4]

As the government considered a location for a new county seat, a group of wealthy and well-connected men began lobbying for a place near Croghan's home. Many in this group owned property near their proposed site, and—no surprise—Croghan was among those who supported the location. Their proposal was to build a planned community named Carlisle that would serve as the headquarters for government in the region. Among counter-petitions that argued for a different spot, the loudest voices came from colonists who lacked the powerful connections that the Carlisle camp had. Indeed, some came from the very area in which the Black Boys' Rebellion would occur. They argued that it made no sense to designate Carlisle as a county seat. It was too close to Lancaster, they complained, and too distant from where most of the new settlers lived. Instead, they wanted a county seat located further west. Some even threatened to leave the colony if Carlisle became the county seat. Actually, there is much to be said for their argument. In time, the government created new counties in the very areas where these most-western petitioners lived because of their distance from Carlisle.[5]

But there was something about the Carlisle location in 1750 that those farther west didn't take into account: the importance of Croghan's trading post to the government. For a colony whose economy was deeply connected to the Indian trade, it made sense for the government to locate a town near the heart of the action. As a result, the better-connected camp won and Carlisle was established with Cumberland County in 1750. And the government rewarded the already well-heeled Carlisle camp for its advocacy by giving the town's choicest lots to many of those who had lobbied for its location there. This decision reaffirmed the impression of many westerners that the government served the elite, not the common settlers.[6]

Robert Callender saw opportunity in the new county seat and seized it. He was one of the first to settle in the town, earning the label "town pioneer," and quickly entered the Indian trade. By 1765, his stature rivaled Croghan's. Callender, also an Irishman, was aided by a background and personality that mirrored Croghan's. He too earned a reputation for fair dealing and good relations with his trading partners. During the war years, he served the colony with distinction. After it, he returned to trading but maintained ties with the military and government, often winning lucrative contracts to supply the British Army. By the 1760s, he operated skillfully in the world of traders, government officials, and Indians. Callender may have rivaled Croghan, but they were not competitors. Croghan welcomed Callender into his trading networks and became a business partner with him.[7]

By 1765, war had transformed Carlisle from a fledging backcountry town into a major trading hub. During the Seven Years' War, colonists carved a new road, called Forbes Road, out of the woods that connected Philadelphia to Fort Pitt. Although the road was cut for the British Army (and therefore was also called the King's Road), it became the chief artery for trade—and it ran through Carlisle. Callender himself was one of the most frequent travelers on this highway. As a result, when he was given the job of organizing the pack train in 1765, he went to Carlisle, now a major center for travel and trade.

Throughout the cold January and February of 1765, twenty wagon loads of goods from Baynton, Wharton, and Morgan arrived at Callender's home about ten miles outside of Carlisle. While the goods streamed in, Callender worked out the logistics of moving such a massive cargo across such a long distance. First, he had to procure reliable men and sturdy horses. By February, he seems to have contracted for upward of 100 horses and employed at least a dozen men. Callender also had to figure out how to store such a huge amount of material through bad weather. As early as December 24, he had sent inquiries to traders in the West asking if they could help. In January, after deciding that Fort Loudon, the last fort in the settled part of Pennsylvania, was too small to hold a shipment of this size, he sent one of his clerks to scout the area for a private warehouse that was large enough. He finally found one in Antrim Township in southern Cumberland County. It was on a large plantation associated with Henry Pawling, a large landowner in the region, who had either rented it or recently sold it to a man named John Howe. The compound would serve as Callender's second staging area before making a final push to Fort Pitt.[8]

But the site in Antrim provided something more than just space. By choosing Pawling's farm, Callender could also leave Forbes Road before encountering the line of forts that dotted its route to Fort Pitt. Thus, Callender and his teamsters could avoid British troops who regularly patrolled the road and searched goods traveling on it. Callender surely worried that the troops might question the size of his shipment. Indeed, while his conclusion that Fort Loudon was too small for his purposes seems plausible (it was a small garrison), the scrutiny the goods were sure to receive there may have made his decision easier. But if evasion was part of Callender's plans, as it probably was, it was wishful thinking. Secrecy, it turned out, only made matters worse for him.

The Pennsylvania Frontier
Conococheague

February 1765

As Croghan settled into Fort Pitt at the end of February, the caravan began its trek west from Callender's home to the warehouse. As it trudged along, rumors raced ahead of the cargo. Colonists in the area had never seen a peace treaty require so many goods. Some said that part of the shipment was to serve private interests rather than the public good. Others claimed that the entire shipment was illegal. The most troubling rumor of all was that the drivers were avoiding the King's Road because their barrels were stuffed with ammunition—contraband that many western colonists feared would be used by Indians to launch more attacks on settlers' homes.[9]

Callender and his men encountered tough conditions that made their trip slow going. The sheer size of the endeavor made travel unwieldy under the best circumstances, but the weather and roads made it only worse. Even Forbes Road, a new and well-traveled thoroughfare, was a good road only relative to those around it. The smaller roads that Callender chose were even worse, and the horses lumbered because of the weight of the cargo.

But the gossip that followed the caravan was the real problem. By the time the traders left the warehouse in Antrim on about March 1, residents of the countryside were mobilizing against them. As the pack train, which now numbered eighty-one horses, took Callender's more southern route through frontier settlements, the traders encountered "repeated interruptions . . . from companys of people armed."[10]

The circuitous route that Callender followed brought him into a region of Pennsylvania known by the locals as Conococheague. It sat on the border of Maryland and Pennsylvania along the Appalachian

Mountains. The name came from a creek that fed into the Potomac River; but as colonists built homes alongside it, the name began to refer to a series of interconnected settlements and small towns that lined the base of the mountains and filled the fertile valleys surrounding the tributary. Many of the settlers were from Scotland and Ireland, although there was a smattering of German and English stock as well. Some were new settlers recently arrived from Great Britain in search of what they couldn't achieve in the Old World: their own independence through landownership. Others were children of families from Lancaster and other, older communities who had been crowded out of these eastern regions when available land became scarce.

As colonial farms displaced Native American communities in the Conococheague, many Native groups, some of whom were allies with Pennsylvania's government, saw these homes as intrusions on their sovereignty. During the Seven Years' War, many of these groups turned against Pennsylvania and the British in hopes of reclaiming this ground. As a result, the colony became the site of some of the deadliest attacks on colonial communities, precisely because Indians wanted to re-establish their claims to this land. The scale of the devastation in Pennsylvania is long forgotten in Americans' collective memory today, but it produced a death toll comparable to that of the Civil War. Most of the combatants, too, were civilians who had turned their farmsteads and mills into makeshift forts during the recent wars. These militarized colonists, many of whom lived in and around Conococheague, became something new in Pennsylvania: "frontier inhabitants" or "frontier people" who lived "upon the frontiers" of the British Empire in North America.[11]

The significance of such language is essential to understanding the governing crisis that was unfolding on the frontiers of North America at the time. In eighteenth-century America, to be a "frontier inhabitant" carried a specific meaning that is very different from our modern conceptions. Today we often associate frontiers with areas of exploration, opportunity, and expansion. In colonial and revolutionary America, however, the term carried almost the exact opposite definition. Frontiers in the eighteenth century were specific sites within a governed area that emerged when invasion threatened. As such, they were prone to contraction rather than expansion, and most people fled from frontiers rather than flocked to them. For people living in them, fear and uncertainty rather than hope and opportunity filled their lives, and they looked to their government for military aid and security. As Benjamin Franklin summarized in an influential pamphlet published in 1760:

> The Frontier of any dominion being attack'd, it becomes not merely "the cause" of the people immediately affected, (the inhabitants of that Frontier) but properly "the cause" of the whole body. Where Frontier People owe and pay obedience, there they have a right to look for protection. No political proposition is better established than this.[12]

With that idea as their guiding principle, self-described frontier people believed that they should be the government's central concern during wartime. During the Seven Years' War, however, those living on the frontiers of Pennsylvania felt that the government failed to keep up its side of this bargain. Instead of feeling supported, they felt ignored and neglected. A popular refrain from the war was that the government did not care if they died, since those in the East felt they had people to spare on the frontiers.[13]

The terror and sense of marginalization that frontier people felt during the war only made them more politically engaged. As they sought answers for their lack of security, they blamed their legislature and the large and wealthy Quaker population in the east that seemed to dominate it. Representation in the Assembly, the name for the colo-

nial legislature, was heavily weighted toward Philadelphia and its surrounding area. The colony's Frame of Government, which established
the institutions of government and their form, stated that each county
should have four representatives and the city of Philadelphia should
have two. Throughout the eighteenth century, however, the practice
had changed. The three Original Counties (those founded by William
Penn in 1682) sent eight representatives each, while the newest counties
sent anywhere from one to four. In total, the eastern counties and Philadelphia sent twenty-six representatives, while the five frontier counties
sent only ten.

Although the Assembly may have originally allotted these frontier
counties fewer representatives because of their smaller populations, by
1765 the colony's population had shifted west. If one were to base representation on taxables in the 1760s, then the frontier counties should
have sent at least twenty-two representatives, and the eastern counties,
including Philadelphia, should have sent no more than twenty-three.
The population in the West steadily grew larger in the 1760s and 1770s
as migration increased after peace with France, and along with it the
sense of disproportional representation grew stronger.[14]

The eastern control of the legislature created another problem
for frontier people. Gerrymandering meant that Quakers, who were
pacifists, and Philadelphians aligned with the Quakers' political party
(known, aptly, as the Quaker Party) dominated the Assembly. For two
years—from 1754, when George Washington was defeated at the Battle of Fort Necessity (in what is today southwestern Pennsylvania), until
May 1756, when Great Britain officially declared war against France—
the colony had no formal defensive measures. The frontier people
asked for forts, a militia law, and supplies. Instead, they were forced
to form their own volunteer militias and build their own forts. People
whose towns had become frontiers during the intervening years blamed
Quakers for both the current legislative lethargy and the preceding

decades of leadership that left Pennsylvania unprepared to defend its own colonists.[15]

While most Quakers left politics in 1756 because their pacifist principles conflicted with Great Britain's formal declaration of war, frontier anger toward the group continued unchanged. When a group of Quakers created the "Friendly Association for Regaining and Preserving Peace with the Indians by Pacific Measures," a charitable organization that sought to restore peace with Native Americans through nonviolence, frontier people worried that this new entity was simply a front for wealthy Quaker merchants intent on continuing to trade with enemy Indians in the midst of war. Quakers, in the minds of frontier people, had become treasonous, self-serving profit-seekers. As one person writing from the frontiers reported in 1757, the frontier people "exclaim against the Quakers and some are scarce restrained from burning the houses of those few who are in town."[16]

After the war, many frontier people harbored an almost pathological fear of Quakers, as well as a belief that this group intended to harm the colony and its western people, a perception that Quakers and many of their friends and political allies found wholly illogical and unwarranted. Nonetheless, frontier people thought that the Quakers still exerted undue influence on the government through the Quaker Party and continued deceptive trading activities at the expense of those who lived on the frontiers. Traumatized by war, these settlers also had developed a constant fear of Indians that had turned into a deep hatred. As peace between the British and French began to return, these issues lingered in the minds of frontier people and became interwoven. As John Armstrong, a military hero from Carlisle, said after he put his rifle down and tried to return to civilian life, he could "forgive everybody except the Assembly and the enemy Indians." A justice of the peace in Cumberland County in 1760 noted that "so many cruelties have been practiced upon the whites by the Indians, that the innocent (Indians) are not secure from their revenge." Such feelings were common among the frontier inhabitants. The idea that there should be free and open trade and a return to a *status quo antebellum*, a view held by the governing elite, was completely unacceptable to frontier people, who assumed that there would be more wars with Indians. In fact, the re-opening of trade and diplomatic relations with former enemies seemed to confirm the frontier people's suspicions that the eastern-dominated legislature ignored those suffering on the frontiers in order to enrich themselves through trade.[17]

These beliefs crystallized a year before Croghan's mission in what was probably the largest political movement in early American history up to that point. The mobilization had brutal beginnings. In December 1763, in the midst of Pontiac's War, a group of militiamen called the Paxton Boys raided the manor of the Conestoga Indians near Lancaster and killed all those present. A couple of weeks later, they killed the remaining Conestogas, who had been relocated by government officials to Lancaster's jail for their protection. Although the Conestogas had been longtime friends of the colony and had maintained neutrality throughout the wars, the Paxton Boys justified their action by accusing a Conestoga man of breaking the neutrality and secretly helping enemies allied with Pontiac's movement launch raids on frontier towns. The government was skeptical of such a claim and, more important, viewed the attack as illegal and unauthorized. Following the massacre, the government provided other friendly Native groups living in the colony with additional security by bringing them to Philadelphia for protection. At this, the frontier people were furious. They saw the government's aid to Indians as an affront. Hundreds of men from Lancaster and Cumberland Counties banded together in the middle of the winter and marched the nearly ninety miles to Philadelphia to protest the government's policies. In the months that followed, Pennsylvania became awash in paper as writers debated the merits of the Paxton Boys in pamphlets, broadsides, and political cartoons.[18]

Not having a printing press, the residents of Cumberland County— the same angry people Callender encountered as his caravan of goods headed west—joined this debate by writing a petition that stated their position. "The source of all their grievances," they proclaimed, "is their not being fairly represented in Assembly"—a complaint that sounds eerily similar to protests against an unrepresentative British Parliament that colonial seaports would soon be making after passage of the Stamp Act. The structure of colonial government, the frontier petitioners noted, ran "contrary to the design and letter of our excellent Charter, contrary to the rights of British Subjects, contrary to reason and common sense." Revealing how they imagined their place in the colony's political landscape, they said the "interior counties" (meaning those sitting safely in the East) would never "have sympathy with the frontier counties." Therefore, because of this breakdown between East and West, they needed equal representation in the legislature to make sure they received the security they were owed.[19]

They then listed the specific ways their lack of representation hurt them. They complained that civilian volunteers had saved the colony from destruction through their military service during the past two wars, but that these "brave adventurers" had never received any public recognition or compensation for their sacrifices. Instead, the wounded languished without any financial support, while Indian allies like the Conestogas—"pretended friends," they claimed—"are taken care of" with "public money." They then demanded that all Indians be "sent away" so that the "bereaved" frontier inhabitants would never "have the additional trouble of seeing their enemies, murderers of their friends, caressed and cherished by the public." Finally, they demanded that "no commerce be allowed" with Indians until the war was con-

cluded and, more important, that any and all captives be returned to
their homes before trade resumed. They asked that this demand be
conveyed to the generals and diplomats, meaning Croghan, to make
sure "the restoration of the captives be . . . accomplished previous to a
conclusion of a peace."[20]

Greater representation, resentment of and hostility toward Native
American groups, a desire to physically remove all Indians from the
colony, a sense of being taken for granted by easterners, and a desire
for a highly regulated Indian trade—those were the driving beliefs of
the frontier people that Robert Callender and his men met as they and
their eighty-one packhorses marched west in March 1765. Frontier people saw in Callender and his huge cargo all that was wrong with the
colony and the Empire. They were sure that Callender's goods were
meant to serve the private interest of eastern merchants at the expense
of the frontier people. They were determined to stop it.

British Headquarters
New York City

February 1765

As the pack train wound its way west, Thomas Gage began receiving
more information about the caravan. He, too, began to question its
purpose. First, he learned that Croghan had spent far more than Gage
had allotted. Worse, he had billed it to the Crown. Gage, still operating
under significant financial constraints, knew what this meant. Since
the Board of Trade hadn't approved this expenditure, Gage could be
held personally liable for it. He was, to put it mildly, displeased with
Croghan. That isn't to say he failed to recognize the need for goods.
As he confided to Henry Bouquet, without a plentiful supply of trade
goods, "We must have war again."[21]

And in other matters, Gage had reason for optimism. At the moment, the Ohio River valley seemed to be settling into a comfortable truce. "The present disposition of the Shawnees," he noted, "seems as favorable as we could wish." At a conference with Henry Bouquet in late 1764, the Delawares also agreed to stop fighting and promised to return captives. Regarding Pontiac, Gage also held out hope, writing to William Johnson in late February that "I think He will come in to Us and He certainly may do us great Service." Even if Croghan was up to something with his purchases, Gage hoped it would at least cement this peace and smooth things over with the Native groups living farther west in the Illinois Country, who harbored deeper suspicions toward the British.[22]

Gage's relationship with William Johnson also grew stronger as the likelihood of peace increased. Johnson's home, located near Albany 150 miles up the Hudson River from Gage's headquarters in New York City, meant that the two were in constant and, more important, easy communication with each other. Johnson shared Gage's agenda for reform. Both wanted stronger imperial institutions in North America that could control the development of the British Empire and maintain strong Indian relations. Trust between the two began to form around a shared vision for the future.[23]

Both Gage and Johnson were a new breed of political officer in North America: imperial official. To be sure, there had been appointees of the Crown in North America before the 1760s whose job was to represent the interests of the British Empire over that of the colonies, such as customs officials and royal governors. But the men in such positions were often either pliable (as was the case with customs officers, who lacked any real powers of coercion and often preferred to receive a bribe from a smuggler rather than dole out a hefty fine) or too dependent on colonists (as was the case with governors, whose job was often to oversee a strong legislature that had the power of the purse, including the governor's salary). Johnson and Gage represented something different. They were part of the British Empire's attempt to strengthen its hand in North America by taking power away from colonies and colonists and placing it in individuals who were wholly dependent on the Crown.[24]

Gage and Johnson, as two of these new position-holders, operated free from colonial restraint and could implement policy without fear of reprisal from colonial constituents. They needed such a position in order to enact the two things they knew were important for maintaining peace in North America. Both the opening of the Indian trade and the creation of a clear boundary between colonial settlements and Indian Country were unpopular issues in colonial capitals and among colonists who hungered for land and feared Indians. But colonial opinion didn't concern these men. As Johnson fully acknowledged in a letter to Gage, writing of colonists, "Their hatred must be expected against One whose duty is to hear and represent the Indians Grievances, which if I neglect to do, I must be deficient in the discharge of my Trust, and this I flatter myself none of my Enemys could ever make appear."[25]

With peace in the offing, Johnson in control of Indian Affairs, and trade about to re-open, Gage felt that things were coming together for him in the West. He even began to consider grander schemes, such as opening a factory in the South that would use American clay to produce Chinese-style porcelain for European markets. Gage decided that such a venture made little sense because the population was still "too thin," but the idea reflects a more general excitement about the untapped potential of a British-dominated North America. Arthur Dobbs, the royal governor of North Carolina, captured the enthusiasm of the moment when he wrote (a bit prematurely) to Gage in early March that "the confirmation of the Peace with all the Indians has given me great Pleasure as we can now improve all our Colonies and have the Benefit of all the inland Trade of the vast Continent and be in Danger of no future Indian War as they can have no supplies but from Britain and her Colonies." Whatever Croghan was up to, his scheme seemed a minor irritant that Gage could ignore—at least for the time being.[26]

Fort Pitt

February 1765

George Croghan, still waiting for his supplies to arrive at Fort Pitt, began acquiring intelligence that seemed to confirm Gage's optimism. Croghan knew that the Native communities in the Illinois Country were likely more hostile to the British than those in the Ohio River valley whose homes were closer to British colonies, like the Shawnees and Delawares. Native Americans who lived along the Mississippi and in modern-day Illinois and Michigan had long been allied with the French and saw the British as their enemies who, they feared, aimed to subjugate them. Rumors that were likely based in fact circulated that these Indians continued to receive encouragement and supplies from French traders who were equally unhappy with the British takeover. But events began to change in late February and early March. The Senecas, Delawares, and Wyandots—groups whose homes were in the eastern part of the Ohio River valley and who had a longer history of working with Great Britain than those in the Illinois Country—held a council near Fort Pitt, where the leaders decided to renounce their French partnerships and create closer ties with the British. First, a council vote in Indian Country by leaders of each of these Ohio Indian groups agreed to uphold the unofficial terms of peace they had entered into with Bouquet as long as "the English would open a free trade and intercourse with them, and supply them with ammunition, goods and rum, as usual, and not prohibit the sale of powder and liquors, as they had done before the difference happened." Further, "in Order to convince the English of their own sincerity," the council sent "a message . . . to the French Traders which was following them to return home, as they had no further Ocassion for them having made Peace with their Brethren the English." Since in Indian diplomatic protocols trade symbolized a group's relationship with a foreign entity, their decision to stop trade with the French was a clear sign that these peoples were willing to accept, although tentatively, the British as their new and sole trading partner as long as they supplied the Indians with the goods they expected from allies.[27]

Croghan was happy with this decision, but he still worried about negotiating with the groups who inhabited what the British termed the Illinois Country, groups like the Ottawas, Chippewas (Ojibwes), and Potawatomis, whose ties with the British were weaker and whose hatred was stronger. He had a plan, though: it involved the Shawnees. The Shawnees were an extraordinary group whose presence stretched across North America, with some settled in areas from Georgia to Canada and others traveling between various trading posts. Their expansive networks allowed them to be crucial and trusted diplomatic connectors within Native America. Before the fighting upset trading networks, Croghan knew the Shawnees well through previous trading relationships and diplomacy. Before the war, they seemed to trust him. Croghan hoped that he could repair relations at Fort Pitt through a display of British generosity. Then he planned to enlist them as emissaries who would travel with him down the Ohio River and help open diplomatic relations with those in the Illinois Country. The Shawnees—and therefore his treaty at Fort Pitt—became the key to his entire mission. And the trade goods that he expected any day were the key to securing their trust. Without trade goods to display the "sincerity" the Native groups wished to see, Croghan would be unable to show the reciprocity of trust that the Indian council expected from the British and that they themselves were showing by snubbing French traders.[28]

Indian Country
Illinois

February 1765

As part of Great Britain's attempt to transfer power, small groups of British agents streamed into the Illinois Country. Although none had the same heady task as Croghan, the broker of peace, they were part of an effort to reconnoiter the area in preparation for the control of it. The French installation of Fort Chartres was one of the strategic sites the British wanted to claim quickly. Sitting near the eastern banks of the Mississippi in what is today Illinois, the fort served as a key waypoint for goods traveling along the river toward New Orleans. The fertile river valley surrounding it meant that the soil was rich for farming, something men like Croghan noted on their travels as they imagined a future in which Great Britain controlled the territory. Fort Chartres was, in short, a prize possession.[29]

In mid-February, two emissaries—Hugh Crawford, a Pennsylvania trader who knew Pontiac and was a former prisoner of war, and Lieutenant John Ross of the 34th Regiment—were the first to reach the Illinois Country. They had left from Mobile weeks earlier and traveled up the Mississippi with an eye on Fort Chartres. Crawford, perhaps not coincidentally, was also a close associate of George Croghan. Their goal was to meet the French commander of Fort Chartres, Captain Louis St. Ange, who was still supervising operations until the formal transfer of power happened, in order to lay the foundation for the transfer and begin to build ties to Native groups in the region.[30]

Shortly after arriving, Crawford, the trader and former captive, got to work by organizing a ceremonial meeting between Ross and the Native leaders. The meeting did not go as planned. During the proceedings, Crawford presented a pipe that was to be shared as a symbol of a new era of friendship and cooperation. As one of the Chippewa chiefs prepared to pass the pipe to Ross, the official representative of the British Empire, he handed it instead to another chief, who "behaved very insolently" toward Ross. The disrespect was meant to send a signal to the British that not all Native groups shared an optimistic view of them.[31]

From there, things only got worse for Crawford and Ross. More Native groups arrived, and at several subsequent gatherings they made clear that they "were of the same opinion" as the Chippewas. None seemed open to treating the British with respect. Finally, a large formal gathering of Native leaders met to discuss their position toward the British. Much to Crawford's chagrin, the assembled Indians performed a war song and "resolved not to suffer the English to come into their country"—all signs meant to tell Crawford that he and the Empire he represented were unwanted.[32]

Crawford realized that the war faction was gaining strength in the Illinois Country, so instead of trying to learn about trading opportunities, he turned to gathering military intelligence. He accumulated information on the Indians' strength by using his networks in the region. His best estimate was that there were about 6,000 Indian warriors ready to fight, a powerful force. With the enmity palpable, the clearly overpowered Crawford and Ross quickly fled the region, returning south to New Orleans before eventually returning to New York to report on matters to Thomas Gage. Croghan, stationed at Fort Pitt, far removed from the usual communication lines, remained unaware of the growing hostility to the British and, therefore, his mission in Indian Country.[33]

Chapter 4

————•————

The Attack

The Great Cove
Western Pennsylvania

March 5, 1765

As Robert Callender and his men continued on, fending off threats and insults, they felt the anger among colonists in the region grow stronger and more unified the farther west they traveled. Advertisements lined the road calling for colonists to join together "to prevent the carrying ammunition and the like to the Indians." Finally, the pack train met well-organized resistance as it neared a largely Scots-Irish settlement tucked into a fertile valley near modern-day Mercersburg. A group of men from Maryland and Pennsylvania approached Callender's pack train and pleaded with them to stop. The drivers paid the men no heed. When they arrived at the center of town, they found a tavern named Cunningham's opposite the house of the local justice of the peace, William Smith. The traders let their horses mill about Smith's house, leaving the animals and goods unguarded while they headed to the comfort of Cunningham's Tavern. The traders figured that everything would be secure because Smith, being justice of the peace, was essentially the government in this area of the frontier.[1]

Meanwhile, the frontiersmen then sitting in Cunningham's Tavern were talking about the new arrivals in town. The word swirling around the bar was "that the goods then going to Fort Pitt were private property belonging to some merchants in Philadelphia, who were sending them contrary to all law and justice into the Indian Country." Worse still, rumors circulated that a barrel had burst during their travels, exposing scalping knives among the cargo. Defenders of the traders claimed that they were pruning knives, but for the residents of the Conococheague there was little doubt that the traders intended to give weapons to the Indians.

When the traders entered Cunningham's seeking refreshment, things got heated. The frontiersmen accused the traders of sending ammunition to the Indians "to enable them to continue the war and again kill and murder his Majesty's Subjects on the frontiers who had already suffered the most extream misery and distress." As the confrontation spilled out into the streets, the crowd grew larger, with fifty angry colonists shouting threats at the horsemen. When one of the drivers made a move to leave, a local walked up to him, rifle in hand, and "told him if he did not stop they would blow his brains out."[2]

Uncertainty reigned. Soon William Smith was called to mediate. Elias Davison, a driver who oversaw the horses, tried to quiet the frontiersmen's concerns by producing documents that showed George Croghan's signature and insisting that they traveled under the orders of Henry Bouquet. The frontier people were incredulous. They refused to accept the passport's validity because it lacked an official seal from Pennsylvania's government—further evidence, they felt, that trade was still stopped because of the war. The group demanded to know why the traders had avoided Fort Loudon, implying that they had bypassed the post because they were transporting illegal goods. William Smith only added to the traders' woes. He inspected the passport and suspected that the signature wasn't really Croghan's, having himself seen Croghan write before, although it's unclear if he told anyone of his misgivings. In any event, rather than provide assurances, the passes only deepened the frontier people's fears that this caravan was illegal and was carrying arms and ammunition destined for the Indians.[3]

Finally, Davison, frustrated and intimidated, agreed to go to Fort Loudon with some frontier people to speak to Lieutenant Charles Grant, the commandant. Davison's colleague Robert Allison, meanwhile, took a set of packhorses over the mountains to McConnell's Tavern, about ten miles west. McConnell's sat in the tip of the Great Cove, a well-known valley that served as an inland harbor for travelers seeking safety and comfort during rough mountain crossings. It was called a cove because it was surrounded by hills, with Sideling Hill bounding it in to the west and small ridges separating it from Mercersburg to the east. Approximately thirty-six horses and their drivers, including Callender, stayed behind near Fort Loudon and stored their material at two local farms for the night.[4]

Back at the fort, Davison had Lieutenant Grant confirm that he had received orders from Bouquet to expect this trade mission and to let it pass through. Grant also assured the frontier people that there was no contraband in the cargo. But when Davison asked Grant to sign the pass, Grant, being a by-the-books officer, refused because he hadn't personally seen the items. He scolded Davison for not bringing them to him in the first place. The frontiersmen remained unconvinced.[5]

With neither side entirely satisfied but with little else to do, the groups dispersed. The frontiersmen promised Davison that they would leave him "unmolested" but sent him off with a word of caution: they thought some Virginians might still try to stop the traders. Davison caught up with Allison that night outside McConnell's, where he related the events

and warned off a group of colonists who had pestered Allison and his
men. The frontier delegates, meanwhile, returned to Cunningham's
Tavern, where some still lingered waiting for news from Fort Loudon.
The representatives relayed what had happened and told their friends
they were satisfied that "the said goods were going out by authority." But
they also mentioned that Grant refused to sign the passes because he was
unable to inspect the barrels. It was late on a long and eventful day, so
the men at the tavern accepted what they heard and went home, even as
some still had doubts about the contents of the cargo.[6]

The town that night was, as William Smith later testified, calm.
But there were stirrings across the mountains at McConnell's. Later
that evening, as the traders unloaded their horses near McConnell's
house, the drivers saw a group of thirty men leave McConnell's and
follow them. Once they caught up to the caravan, they rifled through
the goods and continued to accuse the traders of carrying ammunition.
The anxious residents eventually left and let the men sleep. At dawn,
the locals reappeared and leveled the same accusations that had trailed
the caravan since its departure. The drivers again denied carrying contraband and offered their invoices as proof. The frontiersmen let it go
at that and promised to let the men proceed. But as they "went off into
the woods," they warned the drivers that they thought "the Virginians
would Stop them." As the men disappeared into the forest, the drivers
began to "suspect that they had some Ill Design."[7]

James Smith's House
Conococheague

March 5, 1765

James Smith had led a remarkable life. Born on the Pennsylvania frontiers around 1737, Smith, like most of his neighbors, came from Scots-

Irish stock who took pride in their reputation as warriors. Members of the colonial government embraced this culture and used it to their advantage. In the 1720s, as the first wave of immigrants from Scotland and Ireland arrived, officials purposely placed the Scots-Irish on the western edges of settlement "as a frontier in case of any disturbance." In doing this, the officials noted that the Scots "had so bravely defended Londonderry and Inniskillen," a reference to a 105-day-long siege of Ulster in 1689 in which Scotsmen repulsed a Catholic assault during the ascension of William and Mary. The circularity of this logic meant that the Scots' reputation as a people who were ready to fight became a self-fulfilling prophecy in the Seven Years' War as a result of government policy.[8]

Smith, though, was a different story. He was quite literally born to fight. According to his autobiography, because he was "born between Venus and Mars," the stars dictated that he was destined to find glory on the battlefield. When war between France and Great Britain broke out in 1755, he left behind a young fiancée and joined the cause. The teenager relied on William Smith, the same justice of the peace the pack train met in 1765 (and who also happened to be James Smith's relative), to find him a job helping the war effort. During the war, William oversaw the construction of new roads that were to help the British Army march into the Ohio Country to defeat the French and their Indian allies, so he set James up as a young laborer felling trees and the like.[9]

Clearing the roads one afternoon, Smith's team was attacked by a group of Indians. James, the youngest of the crew, watched as his friends were killed. Smith was carted to Fort Duquesne, which would later be the site of Fort Pitt. Once there, he witnessed several executions, always expecting he would be next. He was not. The Indians decided to spare his life. He was instead adopted into a Mohawk family. Such adoptions were a common Native American practice, in which groups depleted by warfare replenished their ranks through the ritual adoption of captives. Smith's youth and fitness made him a likely target for acculturation. For the next four years, Smith lived in Indian Country, where he became immersed in Native cultures, learning languages, practices, and, most important for our story, their mode of fighting.[10]

In 1760, Smith was released and returned to his settlement in the Conococheague. His arrival shocked his friends and family. They had all assumed he was dead; they had grieved and moved on. His fiancée had already married another man. Smith, upset by the loss of his love, nonetheless readjusted to frontier life. But he never forgot his experience on the other side of that cultural line.[11]

When war returned with Pontiac in 1763, the stars again proved prescient. Smith's neighbors asked him to form a local militia to protect their community, and he applied the skills he had learned as a captive to fight his former adoptive kin. Smith rejected the stiff uniforms and regimented style of the British Army and thought the open-field style of European warfare was inappropriate for the American frontier. Instead, he thought that the best way to beat one's enemy was to know him and be like him. Smith taught his men the Indian styles of camouflage and their quick-hitting guerilla tactics.[12]

Smith's regiment served with distinction, and Smith soon was promoted to the position of officer in the Pennsylvania Line, the official colonial militia. When Henry Bouquet and the British Army prepared to launch a fall offensive into Indian Country, they asked Smith and his "Indian" regiment to join them. And so, when Bouquet and the British Army marched out to Indian Country in 1764, the British troops in their red coats and the Highlander regiments in their plaids had attached to them an American group dressed in "breechclouts, leggings, mockesons, and green shrouds" and with "red handkerchiefs [in place of hats] . . . and painted faces red and black." After success in the battlefield, Smith and his men witnessed the Delawares and Shawnees accept peace and deliver 200 captives to the British with the promise that the remaining British prisoners would follow shortly. The men then returned to their homes and waited for peace to be formalized and for the promised return of their kin. Croghan, of course, planned to accomplish those two objectives at Fort Pitt, so long as he had the trade goods to exchange as a peace offering.[13]

Now, on March 5, 1765, as George Croghan's pack train under the command of Robert Callender reached the Great Cove, Smith's remarkable life was about to become a revolutionary one. He knew that the peace had yet to be formalized and that some colonists still remained in captivity. He also knew that the Great Cove was the last major colonial settlement before Fort Pitt. If the traders made it over Sideling Hill, the western extent of colonial settlement, there would be little left to stop their cargo from reaching Indian hands. Smith, like most of the other frontier people, believed that the traders carried supplies that would embolden the Native groups to launch new raids on the frontiers, not bring the peace Croghan expected. The ammunition that the traders supposedly carried would, in the words of one frontiersman, "bring fresh distruction on the frontier inhabitants when put into the hands of a people with whom no peace it yet fully made." He and those who followed him wanted to starve Indians of necessities and force them to ask for peace and return Smith's kin. They, rather than imperial officials, saw subjugation as the Empire's best policy.[14]

When Smith learned that the frontier people's previous efforts failed to stop the convoy, he decided to act. Just as Davison rejoined Allison outside of McConnellsburg on the night of March 5, Smith "collected ten of his old warriors," veterans of Pontiac's War, and headed to Sideling Hill. He knew that the traders would follow the road that ran along its base to a gap leading to the open road to Fort Pitt. As dawn broke, they prepared for combat. They darkened their faces with charcoal, put on their Indian outfits, and prepared their rifles. By noon, they lined the road with five pairs of men crouching behind trees sixteen feet apart. Then they waited.[15]

The Pack Train
Sideling Hill

March 6, 1765

Robert Allison, Elias Davison, and the rest of their crew spent the morning of March 6 loading their cargo back onto the horses. Their goal for the day was to make it past Sideling Hill and closer to Fort Ligonier, the last fort before Fort Pitt.

Their brigade, as they sometimes called it, started its march to Sideling Hill with Allison in the rear and another driver, John Sampson, in the lead.[16]

At one o'clock, as they traveled along the hillside, the sound of gunshots filled the afternoon air. As the smoke cleared, Allison heard war cries and whoops in the Indian style and saw men with blackened faces and outfitted in Native dress prowling about the front of the train. Soon Sampson came sprinting from the front, yelling that they were under attack by the locals.[17]

Allison raced to the scene. He found horses lying dead and cargo spilled. There was so much blood from the horses that it ran into a nearby stream, turning its water red. Residents of McConnellsburg, it was later said, learned of the Black Boys' success when "the rivulet . . . dyed with blood . . . ran into the settlement below, carrying with it the stain of crime upon its surface." At the time, there was a creek in the region that bore the name Bloody Run. There is disagreement about the origins of the creek's name. Some say it was named after an incident in 1755 when Indians killed a group of colonists trying to build a road. Others claim it dates to an Indian massacre of colonists and their cattle. And then there are claims it was blood from the horses the Black Boys killed in 1765. All are legitimate reasons for the creek's name. The many different origins of the name illustrate the violence that many colonists on the frontiers of North America experienced during the previous decade of warfare, especially in the region where the Black Boys lived. When Allison arrived at the head of the cargo train, he confronted a people whose rivers had been stained with blood for a decade.[18]

Allison surveyed the destruction and demanded explanation.

"Pray, gentlemen, what would you have us do?" a report written by James Smith claims the drivers asked of the Black Boys.[19]

"Collect all your loads to the front, and unload them in one place; take your private property, and immediately retire," was their supposed reply.[20]

Such polite talk certainly did not happen at the base of Sideling Hill on that March afternoon. Allison, for instance, testified that the Black Boys warned him that "if they did not leave the Goods and go off the Ground with the Horses in 15 Minutes they would Shoot the Horses and them Afterwards." But there's a truth to Smith's recollection. Testimony from the drivers confirms that the Black Boys allowed Allison and the other drivers to collect their private belongings, telling them in words very similar to Smith's account that "if they pleased they might bring off . . . anything that belonged to them."[21]

When the Black Boys opened the traders' casks, their suspicions were partially confirmed. They discovered "blankets, shirts, vermillion, lead, beads, wampum, tomahawks, scalping knives, &c"—some of the items the frontier people feared would strengthen Native Americans for war. But they found no ammunition. As Allison and his crew retreated to Fort Loudon, he turned to see the cargo go up in flames—except for several large barrels of rum, which sat untouched. The Black Boys saved the rum and let the traders collect their belongings because they wanted to send a larger message to the authorities: they weren't a lawless mob that simply destroyed private property, but instead a lawful group that targeted specific items they considered illegal.[22]

The drivers arrived at Fort Loudon that night. Callender, who traveled behind the lead caravan, was furious when he heard the news. This was no lawful action, he declared. It was an insult to the Crown of unimaginable proportions: an estimated sixty-three wagonloads destroyed, worth £30,000, some said, more than most men will earn in their lifetime, destroyed. The commander of the fort, Lieutenant Charles Grant, was shocked.[23]

What happened next set the course for the rest of the Black Boys' Rebellion and helped transform a single action by a vigilante group into a movement that would shake the foundations of the British Empire. Callender asked Grant for an armed guard to retrieve whatever remained of the cargo and arrest any bandits still milling about. Callender also offered compensation to the soldiers. While Grant worried about how such a scheme might look, he did little to stop him. Grant's instincts were right. The Black Boys would later use the payment to attack the integrity of the British Army, claiming that the money amounted to a bribe that turned soldiers protecting civilians into mercenaries who served traders and violated the rights of frontier people. Otherwise, Grant agreed with Callender's plan and quickly gave orders to Sergeant Leonard McGlashan to round up twelve soldiers to scour the countryside for salvageable cargo and the guilty parties. At 9:00 p.m, McGlashan had his men ready to leave.[24]

The troops who accompanied Callender into the March night were one of the most respected—that is, feared—regiments in the British Army. They were the 42nd Regiment of Foot, also known as the Black Watch for the dark-colored tartans they wore. During the Seven Years' War, they became an indispensable unit to military strategists who sent them to the most important military theaters. They first served in the Army campaigns in North America and were among those who seized Montreal. After that, they shipped off to the Caribbean to wage amphibious assaults on French and Spanish islands. After the peace with France in 1763, they were sent to the American frontier to fight against Pontiac and his allied Indians. Now, with that war dying down, their task was to help the Empire transition to a new, stable, and peaceful order. They were a good choice for the job, at least in theory. As Scotsmen, they felt a bond of kinship with many of their civilian neighbors—a connection that might ease tensions between civilians and the military. Britons had a fear of standing armies embedded deep in their cultural DNA. They believed that an army stationed among a civilian population symbolized a tyrannical government that used the military to oppress its own subjects. In theory, the Highlanders, the frontier people's kinsmen, might feel like less of a foreign occupation force than the traditional redcoats.[25]

However, a gulf as wide as the Atlantic had developed between the two groups. While the Highlanders became more loyal to the Empire over time and served its interests without question, frontier people became less British and more, well, independent. As civilians, frontier people had a very different sense of the Empire. Unlike the Highlanders, who felt their duty was to serve the Empire, frontier people felt that the Empire existed to serve them. As self-described inhabitants of a frontier, they expected a particular type of support: protection against their Indian enemy. As long as the military seemed to be doing that, the frontier people were happy with the Highlanders' presence. When the situation changed, anger arose that could turn violent—as the Black Watch soon learned.

McGlashan discovered this division as he headed out into the American frontier. His task was to police the civilian population, a new role for him and the troops stationed in Fort Loudon. In this new role, his first chance to exercise the power of arrest came at about midnight. As the Highlanders made their way up the mountain that

formed the eastern wall of the Great Cove, they heard men scrambling
through the forest. McGlashan, benefiting from a nearly full moon,
saw the flash of bright, new linen through the trees. He was sure the
men were wearing clothes stolen from the caravan for extra warmth
in the cold night. McGlashan chased them through the woods, eventually capturing two. While the men denied any involvement in the
Black Boys attack, they were wearing new blankets used in the Indian
trade and carrying weapons—all clear evidence of guilt, McGlashan
believed. Following Grant's orders, he seized their guns and had the
men bound and held.[26]

The soldiers continued with their prisoners to the Great Cove, the
site of the attack. Their first stop was McConnell's Tavern, the suspected
meeting point of the Black Boys. McGlashan stormed into the tavern
and interrogated everyone present. Although the tavern was probably
filled with talk of the attack, no one admitted to knowing anything
about it. Incredulous, McGlashan left the two prisoners under guard at
the inn and continued on to Sideling Hill. They arrived at about 6:00
a.m., the sun just peeking above the horizon, and found dead horses,
the barrels of untouched rum, and "the dry goods in ashes." Aside from
the rum, there was little else he could save. Having completed his mission, McGlashan began his return to Fort Loudon.[27]

Meanwhile, word of the arrests spread throughout the frontier communities. It seemed to the Black Boys that the British Army had now
turned on them. As the Highlanders crossed the ridge where they captured the two men, McGlashan noticed some scalping knives strewn
on the road. When he began to investigate further, fifty men appeared
from the forest with their rifles cocked. One of the Black Boys boldly
declared "that he would shoot [McGlashan] through the heart" if he
didn't release their friends and their guns. But McGlashan was undeterred. Force, he felt, was necessary to win submission. He challenged
the man to shoot, and when the man hesitated, McGlashan stole the

gun out of his hand. Soon the Highlanders fell on the frontier people, scattering the fifty men. When the dust cleared, the Highlanders held four more men and their weapons.[28]

The seizure of more men and their arms made the Black Boys increasingly determined to confront McGlashan. When he neared Fort Loudon on Forbes Road, the same men reappeared and blocked the soldiers' path. This time the Black Boys seemed ready to fight.

"Where are you going?" McGlashan asked them.

"Hunting," they answered, staring at McGlashan and his men as if they were targets of the hunt.

"If you are hunting us, you should find us better game," McGlashan replied before ordering them to clear the road. The Black Boys stood their ground. The Highlanders refused to be intimidated by civilians. McGlashan ordered his men to form a line and fix their bayonets for close combat. With bayonets that these men regularly used to kill now aimed at them, the party disbanded, and McGlashan returned to Fort Loudon. Once again, a show of strength ended the standoff.[29]

Fort Loudon

March 9, 1765

Lieutenant Grant's decision to send McGlashan out to the scene and McGlashan's actions that night all make sense. They were doing their duty to protect the Crown's property and to aid a diplomatic trading mission. The power to arrest civilians without going through the usual civil legal channels, however, was a new assertion of imperial might, one taken in the moment without much thought. Traditionally, arrests were performed by local authorities, while the Army, as a representative of the Empire, was to steer clear of civilian affairs. The Empire delegated criminal matters to colonial authorities specifically as a way to maintain British liberty—which was based on a legal system managed by civilians, not the military—and as a pragmatic matter, since colonial governments had the courts to try subjects.[30]

The arrest of six men and the seizure of their guns, done without going through these usual legal routes, gave the Black Boys a reason to persist and grow bolder. They worried that if the captured men were convicted, imperial officials would make examples of them and impose harsh penalties, maybe even death. The Black Boys also needed to secure their guns—private property that the Empire had illegally seized and that they felt provided them with security. Many of them thought that the Empire had completely abandoned its purpose. Rather than supporting the frontier people, that "fundamental political proposition" that Benjamin Franklin wrote about, their government was providing goods to Indians, protecting traders and eastern interests, arresting civilians without the usual legal protections, and seizing civilians' only means of defense. Rescue seemed to be the only remaining option.[31]

Smith, again, felt compelled to act. On March 9, with James Smith at their head, the Black Boys took their boldest action yet—more brazen than anything authorities in British North America had ever seen. Smith organized between two hundred and three hundred men, a staggering number for a frontier community, and surrounded Fort Loudon.[32]

Lieutenant Charles Grant understood siege warfare firsthand. He had been involved in the successful assaults on Montreal and Quebec that won Great Britain's dominion over New France. But he never thought he would find himself besieged by his fellow British subjects. Grant responded to the assault by keeping armed and on watch at all hours. The Black Boys also understood sieges. They stopped any person who tried to go into or out of the garrison, cutting the fort off from its supply chain.[33]

Grant soon realized that the Black Boys, now supported by the surrounding community, had the means to persist. He decided that the only thing possible to end the confrontation, short of open warfare, was to negotiate. In a move that was the exact opposite of McGlashan's show of military might and confidence in the field, Grant sent flags of truce to James Smith. Smith accepted and entered the fort with a bravado intended to show Grant and the Highlanders who had the upper hand. The negotiation between Smith and Grant was terse but, from the frontier people's point of view, productive.[34]

"What do you mean appearing with such a mob before the King's fort?" Grant asked Smith.

"I came to demand the prisoners," Smith replied, and threatened to rescue them if Grant tried to move them to the Carlisle jail for trial.

"Suppose they were sent to Carlisle and escorted by the King's troops. What would you do then?" Grant asked.

Smith's answer showed the growing resolve of the frontier people.

"We would first fire over the soldiers, and if they would not give up the prisoners, then we are determined to fight the troops. We would die to a man sooner than let them prisoners go to jail," he warned.[35]

Grant, an officer with his honor at stake, knew that a deadly engagement with civilians would leave an embarrassing legacy that would be hard for him to escape. Maybe even worse, being surrounded by two hundred to three hundred men, Grant was also outnumbered and probably outgunned, so he risked losing to a group of ragtag frontier people—a shameful outcome for a unit that took pride in its valor. But there was more to the situation. Grant was encountering colonial resistance—armed resistance—to imperial policies. He was unprepared for this type of situation and worried that a wrong move could be disastrous for the entire British Empire. As one of Grant's colleagues explained later, Grant, stationed on the frontiers far from the security of Great Britain or even the urban seaports of North America, feared that

he was on the precipice of a "civil war," a term many British commanders would use to describe the skirmishes at Lexington and Concord a
decade later. Grant wanted to avoid such a conflict, so he was willing
to cede authority to colonists in order to preserve the greater good. He
released the prisoners.[36]

The Black Boys disbanded for the night, but rumors of a secret
stash of ammunition that the Black Boys had missed persisted. Eventually, the gossip began to focus on the home of William Maxwell.
Maxwell's farm had served as a rest area for some of the traders, and
many suspected that it had stored some of the traders' goods that had
not traveled with the lead caravan. Maxwell's son James was also a justice of the peace, and, unlike William Smith, he tried to help Callender
recover his destroyed property. These two facts led the Black Boys to
view the Maxwells as allies of the traders and as enemies of the local
residents.

On the night of March 13, talk turned into action when Richard
Brownson, a physician living in Maxwell's house, answered a knock at
the door. A group of about twenty men with faces blackened confronted
him and demanded to speak to the master of the house. When Brownson let them know that the Maxwells were away, they broke down the
door to make sure.

"We want Croghan's store of powder and lead," they told Brownson, but, once again, promised to leave any private property of the
Maxwells untouched.[37]

The Black Boys then began searching storehouses in the yard.
Eventually, Brownson heard a pistol fire from one of the outhouses.
About twenty more men, some of whom appeared to speak German
and may have come from Maryland to support the original Black Boys,
emerged from the woods at the sound of the shot and helped lug eight
barrels into the woods. Soon a massive explosion rocked the neighborhood, a sign that the Black Boys had found their target. All the rumors

that had trailed the caravan were true. There was ammunition heading to Fort Pitt.[38]

The explosion on March 13 revealed something that would, in time, have even more powerful consequences than the black powder that shook the night. While the frontier people thought the goods were contraband, Croghan and his supervisors took a very different view, one that showed the growing divide between imperial interests and those of the frontier people. While the Black Boys saw the ammunition destined for Indian Country as weaponry, Croghan saw the munitions trade as a way to establish peace. Indians needed powder to hunt, an essential practice for sustenance, for economic endeavors, and for their cultural practices. For Croghan, gunpowder was both a trade good and a tool of diplomacy. Supplying gunpowder would win the good graces of former enemies because exchanging ammunition signaled a critical level of trust between the British Empire and Native groups. Gage and Johnson never disagreed with Croghan's opinions on ammunition because they felt the same way. These imperial officials all wished for former enemies to become trading partners and diplomatic allies who could be trusted with weaponry, while the Black Boys felt the Indians would simply use the items to carry out future attacks on their communities. The contrasting outlooks on gunpowder reflected a larger difference between imperial concerns and the frontier colonists' views. In time, these differing views would become explosive for the Empire as a whole.[39]

The raid on the Maxwell house by a handful of German-speaking colonists who may have come from Maryland illustrated something else: the Black Boys' evolution into a political movement that transcended colonial borders and united colonists of various backgrounds. The Black Boys began as a small group acting on Sideling Hill, but by March 13 it encompassed an entire region and its peoples. After the initial attack, one frontier person reported that "the current prevailing opinion of the frontier people on both sides of Susquehanna runs in favor of stopping the goods" and that the support came from all quarters: the "Irish, English, Dutch and Welch." The fact that this region of Pennsylvania bordered Maryland and Virginia allowed the Black Boys to shield their members by pointing fingers every which way, claiming the attackers were from Maryland or Virginia—which was surely true, though most came from Pennsylvania. Actually, we can never be sure if the attackers at Maxwell's were from Maryland or if they spoke with a true German accent. James Smith, for instance, was fluent in German as well as English and Mohawk, because colonists needed such a diverse set of skills to thrive on the frontiers. In this way, the Black Boys used the fluid nature of frontier life to hide their identity and confuse officials back east.[40]

British Headquarters
New York City

March 1765

News of the happenings outside of Fort Loudon soon found their way to Thomas Gage's desk. The more Gage learned, the more he regretted having Croghan in the service. He was sure that the goods were illegal and that Croghan had used his position to take liberties in purchasing items. He even began to question the treaty at Fort Pitt, which he thought was nothing more than a sham for Croghan to reap a profit.[41]

The destruction of so much property meant that many empty hands began appearing at Gage's doorstep seeking restitution. Baynton, Wharton, and Morgan asked the Crown to cover the costs of the goods, since they were intended for a treaty. Callender, too, expected to be compensated. Gage was sick of it all. He knew the truth, which he shared with his confidant, Henry Bouquet: "Many pretences will be made and Story's told to conceal the truth, but it appears pretty plain, that tricks of this kind were intended amongst them all for Croghan had else no Business that I can see to assemble any great number of Indians at Fort Pitt, for his journey to the Illinois."[42]

William Johnson, however, held a different view, one based on his own experience with Indian diplomacy. He defended Croghan's choice and helped calm Gage down by producing letters that he and Croghan had exchanged that showed Croghan's reasoning. Johnson assured Gage that Croghan was serving the British interest and that such a large shipment was necessary for a diplomatic mission as ambitious as Croghan's. For Johnson, the real problem the Empire faced was with "the frontier people" who had shown "a great inveteracy to all Indians" and had "laid Aside all obedience to the Laws or public authority." Johnson urged Gage to focus his energy on establishing order and deference to authority within these "frontier people."[43]

Johnson's opinion helped ease Gage's anger at Croghan. But the news that really gave Gage peace of mind was that the value of the goods destroyed was far smaller than originally reported. While the total value of Croghan's cargo was large, the most recent estimates put the value of the destroyed goods at a few thousand pounds—still a large sum, but one that seemed more manageable. In the weeks that followed, Gage began to shift his focus from Croghan to the frontier people, who seemed to pose the greatest problem to the Empire's interest. But not before he scolded Croghan in a sharply worded letter:

> If you had only minded the Business you was employed in, fol-
> lowed your instructions, and made use of the permit given you by
> Colonel Bouquet for carrying up the goods to Fort Pitt, without
> taking upon you to encourage traders to act contrary to the law
> of the province, you would not have been involved in any diffi-
> cultys on this account. The Government of Pennsylvania know

when it is proper, will issue Proclamations to that effect and
when that happens there will be no danger of any want of goods
at Fort Pitt.[44]

Fort Pitt

March 1765

Croghan, however, remained undeterred. The Shawnees were the key
to his plan, and diplomacy was the way to win their support. Benefiting
from the slow and unreliable system of communication in North America, Croghan brushed off Gage's reprimand and continued to delay,
waiting for the Shawnees to arrive. But as Croghan waited for his goods
to arrive at Fort Pitt, things grew tense in his own convoy. Lieutenant
Alexander Fraser, a French-speaking officer who had been appointed
to travel with Croghan as his military escort, became more anxious by
the day. His orders from Gage were clear. He was to travel down the
Ohio River into the Illinois Country with all possible speed and deliver
certain documents to French officials who still occupied forts. Croghan,
however, insisted on waiting so he could conduct a treaty. Croghan
tried to dispel Fraser's concerns. He promised that the Shawnees were
expected any day and that the treaty and exchange of goods were essential to their success.[45]

Fraser gave Croghan an ultimatum. If the Shawnees didn't arrive
by March 15, then he would round up his men and head down the
Ohio without Croghan. When neither the goods nor the Shawnees
showed up, Fraser stayed true to his word. He left Croghan at Fort Pitt
and entered the most volatile region of North America. It seemed that
the diplomatic convoy that was intended to save the British Empire in
North America was crumbling from within.[46]

Indian Country
Somewhere in Illinois

February 1765

Just as Fraser headed down the Ohio River, Charlot Kaské, Pontiac's chief rival, was returning to the Illinois Country from his own diplomatic journey down the Mississippi River. Kaské is one of the most enigmatic figures of Pontiac's War, even more so than Pontiac. Unlike Pontiac, who was a full-blooded Indian, Kaské had strong connections to Europe. His father was a German who had escaped colonial society for Indian life, and his mother was a Shawnee. He was likely raised in Native communities in the Illinois Country and inherited his father's apparent animus toward English society. Later in life, Kaské married an English woman who had been captured as a child in a war and adopted into the Shawnee nation. But his blood had little to do with his current allegiances. Although he was of mixed blood and his children were three-quarters European, he was one of the most vocal opponents of British colonization.[47]

Kaské's name rarely appears in the historic record. When it does, it's mostly in letters written by Europeans describing encounters with him. In fact, many of these accounts are rumors filtered through various sources. However, the common theme of all these stories suggests that Kaské was a fierce fighter who had served as an aide and ally to Pontiac for much of the war. His strong opposition to the British won him many followers, and he began to challenge Pontiac as the leader of a pan-Indian resistance movement.[48]

In the fall of 1764, as Bouquet was launching an offensive into the Ohio Country, Kaské developed a plan that he hoped would further his cause and keep the war alive. On November 9, he and his wife left the Illinois Country and headed down the Mississippi River for New Orleans. The city was technically in Spanish hands, but the Spanish government hadn't yet sent any officials. In the meantime, the French kept a governor there in order to maintain law, and the city became a refuge for French merchants hoping to keep their former trading connections alive and dreaming of recapturing their lost territory. Kaské lobbied the French for money and supplies in an effort to re-ignite a war between Great Britain and the Indians in the Illinois Country. He promised that he could rally more warriors if he secured aid. In return, he vowed to keep the British confined to the eastern seaboard and thereby re-open the Illinois Country to the French.[49]

Kaské eventually secured a meeting with Charles Aubry, the French governor in New Orleans. On February 24, Kaské made his case to Aubry. British observers also sat in the audience to make sure the French kept the terms of peace. Kaské began by scolding the French for ceding the Illinois Country, land that he said they never truly owned.

"I am surprised that the great emperor of the French has given away our land," because, he continued, "there belongs to the emperor only what lies across the lake"—meaning France.

More important, he vowed to fight the British until the very end, noting that even though the British had halted the ammunition trade, he would fight them with "bows and arrows, and if there were no wood we should find rushes."[50]

Then he turned to the British spectators, representatives of his enemy, to convey his hatred and distrust.

"You English only ask to kill; you have caused the red men to die; do not be surprised if I speak to you likewise; if I scold you, my heart is still sore because I have seen so many French and Indians die together," he said.[51]

Aubry's response, however, rebuffed Kaské's impassioned plea.

"All men are united and peaceful," he chastised Kaské; "you are the only ones who in this corner of the world, wish to make war, and it is for your misfortune."[52]

But more important, he told Kaské that he must trust the British as new partners and tried to reassure him that Native Americans in the Illinois Country would continue to enjoy their freedom even with the French departed.

"They do not wish to make you slaves as you think; you are free men and will be always," Aubry reassured Kaské.[53]

"Make peace with the English and you will have abundance," Aubry continued, in words that must have felt like a betrayal to Kaské.[54]

He ended with a firm refusal to aid Kaské in his attempt to re-arm Indian warriors.

"It is impossible for me to send you powder and ammunition to destroy them. I cannot and ought not."[55]

But Aubry's answer didn't matter much to Kaské, because he had a plan even if the French government refused to help. His plan was one that would further threaten Pontiac's position—and Fraser's life.

Chapter 5

Transformation

Pennsylvania Statehouse
Philadelphia, Pennsylvania

April 1765

The Black Boys put John Penn, the thirty-six-year-old governor of Pennsylvania and heir to the colony, in a predicament. Penn arrived in Philadelphia in November 1763 and immediately entered into a difficult political environment. Pennsylvania's government, called a proprietary one, was an unusual entity in the liberalizing world of eighteenth-century Great Britain. It meant that a family controlled a governorship and staked a claim to most of the colony's land. In Pennsylvania, even those who owned their property owed the Penn family an annual tax called a quitrent. Critics complained that this form of government was feudalistic and anachronistic and demanded radical change.

On top of that, Pennsylvania was facing immediate problems that tested the new governor's acumen. Since Penn's arrival, he had moved from one crisis to another, all of which involved frontier issues. First, he took office at the height of Pontiac's War, a war the British didn't want but had inadvertently begun. Then, in December, just a month after he arrived, the Paxton Boys massacred a peaceful Indian group and marched on Philadelphia to challenge the foundations of government there. The Paxton Boys' political movement continued until October, at which point the most divisive election in Pennsylvania's colonial history gave Penn and his allies greater clout in the Assembly. But their victory didn't bring stability. Disgruntled members of the Quaker Party saw the failure to prosecute the Paxton Boys as even more evidence for a need to change the government. Leaders of the legislature organized a petition to the Crown asking that it seize control of the colony from the Penn family, arguing that the family was unfit to govern. And now Penn had to deal with the Black Boys' Rebellion.[1]

People in elite governing circles, officials like Thomas Gage and William Johnson, expected swift and full justice. The government needed to exert more authority over frontier people, in Johnson's view, not less. Penn's problem, however, was that the politics of Pennsylvania made his influence on the frontiers weaker. At the very moment imperial officials were hoping for a show of strength from the governor, powerful forces in Philadelphia were trying to take the colony away from Penn. He knew that Benjamin Franklin, perhaps the most respected colonist, was then in London lobbying with officials to turn the colony run by the Penn family into a royal one administered directly by the Crown—perhaps even with Franklin as its new governor. Penn therefore needed to maintain some semblance of order, lest imperial officials agree with Franklin that a proprietary colony was incapable of governing in this new North American empire. But Penn also needed allies to support his government—and therein lay his problem. As Penn discovered, frontier people—the ones creating disorder on the frontiers—blamed the Assembly and the Quakers for their situation. Fearing that a royal colony would mean greater rule by the coastal elite, the frontier people were among the strongest opponents of the proposal and, therefore, the most likely to side with the proprietor, who they saw as more willing to provide them with the defensive support they sought. In 1764, as support for a royal colony gained steam in the East, a countermovement sprung up on the frontiers, culminating with a petition containing around 14,000 signatures opposed to a royal takeover.[2]

The alliance between the proprietor and frontier people was odd, although much about Pennsylvania was unusual. Proprietary colonies were a rare thing in 1765, a holdover from an earlier English Empire in which King Charles II doled out lands in North America to his closest friends as patronage. At various points, New Jersey, New York, the Carolinas, New Hampshire, Pennsylvania, Delaware, Maryland, and Georgia were propiertary colonies. Proprietors were like feudal lords. They owned all land, could create governments as they saw fit, and collected annual land taxes from their colonists in exchange for protection. By the eighteenth century, colonists generally despised proprietors and felt they had no place in a liberal British Empire. In fact, except for the Penns' continued management of Pennsylvania and Delaware and the Calvert family's control of Maryland, the Crown had transformed its other North American proprietary governments into royal colonies throughout the eighteenth century.[3]

One of the chief complaints against proprietors was that they claimed ownership of all undeveloped land and placed a tax on all landowners. Therefore, the political coalition between frontier people, who occupied the most land and wanted to acquire more, and their proprietor was an awkward one. But their ties were forged through war. The proprietary family served as both governor and commander-in-chief, and since the 1750s, when war came to the colony, the proprietors' representatives regularly toured frontier areas promising support and blaming the Assembly for any deficiencies. Both the Penns, who had left the Quaker fold in the mid-eighteenth century, and the frontier people loathed the Quaker elite, whom they saw as their chief adversaries. As a result, in 1765, as the Black Boys gained steam, John Penn worried that swift—indeed, any—justice against them could threaten this most unusual political alliance.[4]

Penn's predicament was doubly difficult because the Black Boys' actions forced him to reconcile conflicting responsibilities. He was both the chief magistrate who enforced colonial law and the captain-general who oversaw the colony's defense. He was also the chief representative of the Crown in the colony and the head of diplomacy with Native American groups. The issues raised by the Black Boys' Rebellion made juggling these various roles impossible. Frontier people wanted a stronger defense against Indians, and Penn was expected to provide it. Indeed, this relationship was the foundation of their alliance. To the Black Boys, Croghan's trading mission seemed to weaken these defenses and break the law. The Empire and the traders that served it, meanwhile, wanted the Black Boys prosecuted for unlawful actions, and they looked to Penn to maintain the open road to Indian Country that the Crown desired. The destruction of trade goods forced Penn to try to balance the demands of these competing constituencies, all while worrying that whatever he did on the frontiers of Pennsylvania might affect decisions being made about the colony's future back in London.[5]

Carlisle, Pennsylvania

March 1765

Penn confronted his political dilemma as soon as he arrived in snow-covered Carlisle in late March with his attorney general and two close advisors in tow. Word of the Black Boys' attack had reached Philadelphia soon after it took place. As soon as Penn heard of it, he knew he would have to venture to the frontiers to sort things out. A scene of confusion greeted the governor. Traders sought retribution, colonists demanded protection, and local government officials were unsure of who was on the right side of the law. William Smith, of course, took the side of the Black Boys, but James Maxwell supported the Black Boys' arrest. John Armstrong, a war hero who was the most powerful justice in the region and who was known as caring mostly for his own reputation, tried to avoid the mess and seemed to think the government should ignore the incident.[6]

The sentiments of the local residents, however, made Penn's job especially tough. Once he was in Carlisle, a group of colonists who supported the Black Boys presented him with a long petition summarizing the frontier people's beliefs and reminding Penn of his alliance with them. The petition is one of the most remarkable documents produced from the entire affair. In it, the frontier inhabitants expressed their views on Indians, politics, trade, and the Empire. The petitioners laid bare their fears and justified the Black Boys' actions in terms that reinforced Penn's obligations as captain-general. Above all else, the frontier inhabitants feared "being again involved in another war." The "supplies of cloathing and warlike stores"—especially "ammunition; powder, lead and scalping knives"—that the attacked traders carried triggered their memories of war and its "images of murdered families, captivated brethren and friends, men, women and children, exposed to all the cruelties and miseries."[7]

The petitioners pleaded with Penn for sympathy, begging him to restrain the grasping hand of the eastern elite. "Permit us honorable sir," they wrote, "to implore your protection against the attempts of our fellow subjects who being remote from danger, sit at ease and know not what we feel." This single sentence expresses the foundation of something powerful that coalesced in the aftermath of the Seven Years' War, something we might think of as frontier society—a political identity that

shaped the way certain colonists viewed government and elite society
and that drove their actions. Frontier people, those who had suffered
through war, believed that their government, especially the Assembly,
was no longer working for them: because the government didn't "feel"
what they felt, they claimed that it ignored them.[8]

The petitioners focused their anger on the Quakers in particular,
who continued to loom large in the psyche of frontier people. This lingering fear bred a conspiratorial notion of this religious community
that formed the heart of the petition submitted to Penn. They complained that Quaker merchants were unfazed by the implications of
continued commerce with Native peoples. The Quakers' pursuit of
profit over the public good, according to the petitioners, made Indians feel more secure through a brisk trade in military goods—the very
items that would, according to the petitioners, incite a "third Indian
war." Indeed, the frontier people went so far as to accuse the Quakers of
being enemies to the colony, the Empire, and its frontier people, similar
to—perhaps even worse than—Great Britain's long-time rival, France.
"What does it avail us," they continued, "that the French are removed
out of country, that they can no longer excite and assist the Indians, to
ravage our settlements and murder our friends, if our own fellow subjects regardless of his Majesties, of his officers proclamations, nay all
the laws of God and man are still continuing to supply them with the
means of our Destruction?" They even claimed that the Quakers had
a financial stake in prolonging the conflict. "A certain faction," they
wrote, meaning Quakers, "tho void of compassion for the distressed
people of the frontiers long drenched in blood, were profuse and liberal in their presents to the Indians." Quakers, they wrote, were a self-
serving group "so bent upon enriching themselves by an Indian trade
that they will do it at the expence of so much blood and treasure as it
must cost the Crown and Colonies."[9]

The situation exposed a society and its government that was in a dire state. The problem the petitioners identified was one of shared feeling. A healthy political body was supposed to be connected and functioning in union, but the wars had exposed Pennsylvania as a fractured colony in need of repair. In the traditions of eighteenth-century British political culture, this disconnect between the people and their government justified rebellions like the one the Black Boys were leading. As one pamphleteer wrote during the Paxton Boys crisis, "the people . . . seldom or never assemble in any riotous or tumultuous manner, unless when they are oppressed, or at least imagine they are oppressed." In this atmosphere, the Black Boys wanted their actions to have an immediate effect—the stopping of a specific convoy—that would also send a message to the government that those in power back east, especially the Quakers, who seemed to control the legislature and trade, needed to heed the demands of frontier people whom they had ignored. The petitioners therefore looked to Penn, as captain-general and protector of the colony, as the only person in government who understood their plight and could convey their interests back east.[10]

Penn did sympathize. When he first heard of the attack, he disapproved of the violence but also expressed concern about the legality of the trade goods. In language reminiscent of the petitions he received from frontier people, he confided to William Johnson that "General Gage having sometime since desired to know my sentiments upon the subject of opening an Indian trade in this province, I wrote to him that I very much disapproved of such a measure as yet, as it might attend with dangerous consequences till the Delawares and Shawnees had actually satisfied and concluded a peace with you agreeable to their engagements; especially as the hostages of the latter had made their escape from Fort Pitt." As far as he was concerned, the traders had operated without his approval and were therefore illegal. It's unclear if Penn knew of Gage's support for the mission or Bouquet's pass when he fired off this missive to Johnson. But if he did, his opposition to the pack train hints at tensions developing at the time between imperial institutions as new officers like Gage took power from governors. The traders did carry legal passes. Those passes just came from military authorities rather than the traditional civil one.[11]

But Penn also worried about Gage's order that the perpetrators meet strict justice. Since the Paxton Boys still remained untried, his failure to prosecute the Black Boys might confirm that the Penn family was incapable of managing such a large colony. He therefore decided to conduct a thorough investigation and prosecute those he could catch. As he was well aware, the trial would take place in Carlisle, meaning that the local residents in the jury box would offer a sympathetic ear to the Black Boys. This approach would satisfy both his constituencies. Penn could then claim to Gage that he was doing all he could but was stymied by Great Britain's legal system, while the Black Boys could return to their homes, acquitted but chastened by the experience. Although Penn never expressed this as his strategy, one of his advisors on the frontier, John Armstrong, did. Armstrong confided to George Croghan that while "neither office nor inclination admits me to advise winking at the offences of these people, I'm fully of opinion that a rigourous prosecution is not likely to answer any good purpose, but has a fearful affect on the publick tranquility."[12]

For over a week, Penn and his advisors remained in Carlisle. They took sworn depositions and met with officials and traders. Penn also sent out the sheriff with a posse to find those accused of being a part of the Black Boys, but after five days in the Great Cove they came back empty-handed, claiming that the suspects had "absconded."[13]

Finally, at the beginning of April, a grand jury convened to indict those believed to be guilty. The trial records have never been found, but we can get a hint at the proceedings by piecing together the evidence that makes reference to it. Traders and British soldiers all testified and identified specific people as Black Boys. William Smith, the justice of the peace, came under heavy scrutiny. Many accused him of aiding and abetting the Black Boys. Smith testified in his own defense. He claimed to have no involvement in the attacks and denied, rather unbelievably, any knowledge of its perpetrators. Before he was done, he offered a stirring defense of the frontier people, echoing the same sentiments as the petitioners, saying that the countryside feared a re-opened gun trade with Indians.[14]

The jury weighed the evidence. They found, as Penn noted in a letter to Gage, the sworn depositions "not sufficient testimony to convict a single person." The bills of indictment were returned "ignoramus." When Penn relayed the news of the acquittals to Gage, he washed his hands of responsibility. "I have the satisfaction to acquaint you," he wrote, "that in a regular course of justice I have done everything on this occasion, that could be done consistent with the law." The acquittal had given Penn the cover he needed. Thomas Gage knew what the verdict meant. Not only did the Black Boys go unpunished, it also provided the Black Boys with legal cover to continue. The Black Boys would become, he predicted, "more bold and audacious" because their actions now appeared "legal and warrantable."[15]

Penn left Carlisle shortly afterward, but before he did, the frontier people gave him one final reminder of their beliefs and expectations. They sent him "sundry petitions from both sides of the Susquehanna against any goods going out at present but what is for his majesties presents only." The frontier people were taking a stand on the issue of re-opening the Indian trade. They wanted it stopped except for the purpose of diplomatic treaty-making. And even in that context, ammunition and powder were to be excluded because of the frontier view that Indians posed a perpetual threat to their communities.[16]

Conococheague

March 1765

Gage was right about the jury's power. A colonel traveling through Conococheague soon after the judicial inquiry reported to Gage that the Black Boys "have become more daring and insolent." New groups formed throughout the region, all inspired by the Black Boys. Near Lancaster, for instance, a group referred to as the Paxtonians—and if not involving the same people as the Paxton Boys' movement, this party at least included imitators—"stop'd three or four waggon loads of goods at Harris's, which was intended for Shamokin [a trading post on the Susquehanna River]." They all had the same purpose. Any trader heading west was likely to be searched by a Black Boy under an improvised inspection system that supervised the road. If a trader's carriage contained no "warlike stores," then he would receive a passport that he could show if approached by other Black Boys. At least two British soldiers were stopped and searched, too, showing that these local groups wanted to assert their authority over imperial officials as well. At one point, a Black Boy with the last name Wilson captured an official express runner and told him that one of the Black Boys' goals in regulating the roads was to weaken the British troops in the region by "stop[ing] the cloathing of the regiment."[17]

As the Black Boys groups expanded, it was evident that a small band of vigilantes without any goal other than the destruction of a specific pack train had sparked a larger political movement. This expanded and more organized group also began to assert new claims to authority. Their actions took on a function of government—regulating trade—and made use of new arguments to give legal legitimacy to what they were doing. They were aided by a particular interpretation of the law and the Empire offered by Smith's relative, William Smith. William Smith argued that in the British Empire, the Crown conveyed the power to regulate the internal trade of a colony to the governor. Because the governor's chief representative on the frontier was the local justice of the peace, the power to inspect goods rested in local justices like him.[18]

Smith's argument gave the Black Boys an official capacity, rather than an extralegal one, that rested in his authority as a local government official. The Black Boys, in this rationale, became an arm of the Empire, rather than an enemy to it. Smith was able to make his argument because of the Empire's history, before the Seven Years' War, of delegating authority to colonies to manage the process of empire-building in North America—salutary neglect, then, applied to the frontiers as much as it did to the seaports and to trade. Smith could confidently make this legal interpretation because it had some validity and because there was no clear way to tell him he was wrong other than a conviction by a jury, something he no longer needed to worry about. The Black Boys' acquittal, then, only strengthened Smith's position as an officer of the law. He could now claim that what they did was "legal" because a jury had said so. This argument placed enormous political power into the hands of common settlers at the very time imperial officials were trying to centralize such powers in the hands of designated officials like Gage and Johnson.

These two competing ideas of power soon collided when some traders refused to comply with the Black Boys' inspections. The results were not pretty. In early May, about a month after the trial, Joseph Spears, a trader passing through the region, refused inspection. Knowing that he was a potential target, Spears chose to park his cargo outside of Fort Loudon. A British fort manned by the 42nd Regiment would surely provide him with cover, or so he hoped.

Spears represented a serious challenge to the Black Boys. Allowing him to ignore their inspection process would show them to be nothing more than weak-kneed bluffers and would encourage other traders to ignore their claims to authority. It would undermine their whole enterprise. The Black Boys refused to let that happen. One day, as some of Spears's drivers went out to check on the horses, the Black Boys struck. Perhaps encouraged by the jury's decision or emboldened by the growing support for their movement, these Black Boys took even more liberties than those who made the original attack at Sideling Hill. They beat and whipped the men, killed five horses, and stole their goods, essentially making these men victims of the struggle for political power on the frontiers of British America.[19]

Grant reacted to the destruction of goods as he had before. He sent Sergeant McGlashan into the countryside with twelve armed soldiers. McGlashan showed the same determination to use force to subdue the Black Boys—the "mob," as the British officers now called them, a derogatory term in the eighteenth century that distinguished unruly but legal protests in the streets from the illegal and destructive acts of rioters. But the Black Boys refused to be so easily cowed this time. Contrary to what traders and officials said about them, they now enjoyed the veneer of legality.[20]

McGlashan and his men scoured the villages outside Fort Loudon seeking information on the whereabouts of the Black Boys. He finally got a bead on Roland Harris's house. When he arrived at the house, the Black Boys were gone, but McGlashan was sure that he was on the right path. He "pressed" Roland to tell him where they had gone. Eventually, Harris sent McGlashan to Widow Barr's house, a community meeting place that may also have functioned as a tavern.[21]

As McGlashan approached the home, he heard a warning shot from the woods. He ordered the Black Boys to cease their fire and surrender. Words were exchanged, and in that tense moment one of McGlashan's troops fired a return shot, apparently without orders. All hell broke loose. The Black Boys, numbering between seventy and eighty, unleashed a stream of fire at the British troops, who stood exposed in a cleared field next to Widow Barr's house. McGlashan ordered his men to return fire, intending to intimidate the Black Boys into submission and to provide cover for their retreat. The troops raced into Widow Barr's house. In the midst of the melee, McGlashan was able to grab a stray man trying to escape the house. His face was blackened, and McGlashan was sure he was a Black Boy.[22]

Once inside, McGlashan surveyed the scene. He realized that for the moment they were safe, being protected by a sturdy house and with a clear line of sight into the woods. Outside, the Black Boys were in no position to launch an assault. Huddled behind trees, staring at the field before them, the Black Boys came to the same conclusion. Rather than try to take the house, the colonists kept up a constant fire on it. The standoff lasted for about an hour, when finally a messenger emerged from the woods and headed to the house. The Black Boys were willing to offer a truce: they would allow McGlashan to return to the fort in exchange for their prisoner. McGlashan, pinned down and with limited ammunition, agreed.[23]

The battle outside Widow Barr's only made the Black Boys more determined to assert their newfound power. As they regrouped, they turned their sights on a new target: Lieutenant Charles Grant and Fort Loudon. They knew that Grant and his fort were the symbols of imperial authority on the frontiers. They needed to let Grant know that they wouldn't accept his position. Instead, they wanted to bring him to heel as they had McGlashan.

On May 10, four days after the engagement outside Widow Barr's, two hundred men appeared outside of Fort Loudon, their faces painted black and their posture defiant. James Smith stood at their head. He brought three justices of the peace willing to back the Black Boys' right to search traders, a further show of legal support for the Black Boys' actions. Smith demanded that Grant allow the Black Boys to enter the fort and search what remained of Spears's goods. Grant refused, but he did offer a compromise that he hoped would de-escalate the situation. He promised to let the justices inspect the goods in a few days, as long as the armed bandits disbanded. He also produced passes from high-ranking British officers that permitted Spears to trade at Fort Pitt.[24]

William Smith refused the offer. Instead, he used the confrontation to assert the Black Boys' new understanding of the British Empire on its frontiers, one in which he as justice of the peace held the most power in the region. He rejected the authority of military commanders to offer passes, telling Grant that "the Commanding officer's pass was no pass, and that no Military officer's pass would do without a Magistrate's pass." Smith then went a step further. He rejected the Empire's control over the forts and roads in the region and insisted that they were under civilian authority—meaning his authority. "This was not a King's fort, nor was this the King's road," Smith declared. Smith's reinterpretation of these spaces meant that colonists controlled spaces previously over-seen by imperial authorities. To have command over the forts and the roads meant that colonists could then shape larger imperial policies. They could regulate who traveled where and what those travelers could carry. Indeed, they could close the road that imperial officials were then trying to open to Indian Country.[25]

Smith's argument was a refinement of what the Black Boys had offered earlier to justify their acts, and in its logic something truly rev-olutionary began to take shape. Before this time, frontier people had accepted the presence of British military outposts. They had seen the British Army and its forts as defenders of frontiers and protectors of colonists. Now, however, Smith insisted that the British military posts were under local civilian oversight. By doing this, he was inverting the traditional power dynamics of the Empire. Where Gage and others believed the Empire should be hierarchical, with colonists being duti-ful subjects obeying Crown decrees and deferring to their superiors,

Smith was arguing that the British Army was in fact subject to local civilian officials and that these civilians could determine the policies of the Empire. Smith was taking great power from the governing elite in the East and placing it in the hands of common people on the frontiers. His goal, like that of the Black Boys he supported, was very much a revolution—a complete overturning of political power—on the frontiers of the British Empire. He did so because frontier people had lost faith in these political institutions and, instead, trusted only their neighbors. Smith's view on the power of the people to make decisions for themselves would come to define the era.

Fort Pitt

May 1765

As the Black Boys coalesced into a region-wide political movement, George Croghan's own plans started to come together outside Fort Pitt. More representatives from various groups in the Ohio River valley like the Seneca and Delaware descended on Fort Pitt ready to talk peace, and they brought prisoners to exchange as a show of sincerity. Some of the captives were so young that even though they looked European, they had known only Indian culture. Croghan hosted several private meetings with these Indians to talk about the future. All signs pointed to an agreement to end the war. Four Shawnee emissaries confirmed Croghan's optimism when they arrived carrying a "calimet of peace" (a peace pipe) and word that a large delegation that included more prisoners was on the way. Finally, on May 2, the rest of the Shawnees appeared outside of Fort Pitt, guns blasting in a sign of peace. Croghan responded with his own salute of cannon fire.[26]

On May 7, Croghan's long-awaited treaty began. His patience was worth it. More than five hundred Indian leaders sat around the council fire, and hundreds more—probably over a thousand total—waited outside. Croghan disproved Gage's skepticism about the treaty's importance. The turnout showed that Indian groups in the Ohio River valley desired such a meeting, and by holding it Croghan solidified these alliances before venturing into the interior, where groups in Illinois remained more hostile to Great Britain's rule.[27]

The speeches at the treaty revolved around the causes of Pontiac's War. The Indian groups insisted that their ill treatment by Great Britain after the Seven Years' War had led them to fight. All they wanted was to "enjoy a free trade and intercourse," something that Great Britain had denied them after the Seven Years' War. They worried that Great Britain had misread the geopolitics of the postwar world. After receiving fair treatment from the British before the war, "as soon as you conquere'd the French, you did not care how you treated us, as you then did not think us worth your notice," they complained. They had waged Pontiac's War to remind the British that Indians could upset imperial plans and that their cooperation held the key to the Empire's stability.[28]

These Native spokesmen well understood their economic importance to the British Empire and used their role as key suppliers of raw materials for British manufacturers to force Croghan's hand. "Do not act as you have done for a year or two before those late troubles, when you prohibited the sale of powder, lead, and rum," they warned. "Open the trade, and let us sell our skins which we have brought here." They refused to accept any excuse for delay. Failure now, they cautioned Croghan, would mean that they "[could] not put dependence on what you tell us for the future."[29]

Croghan accepted their demands. He was, however, hamstrung in his generosity by the Black Boys' destruction of his goods. But he knew how important it was to supply his guests with something, so he petitioned the commandant of Fort Pitt, William Murray, to release some of the rum and ammunition meant for the troops. Murray agreed, believing "it was for the Good of the Service." Through this symbolic exchange of pelts for rum and gunpowder, Croghan was cementing the newly reciprocal bonds of an alliance in which Indian allies provided furs to British merchants in exchange for the manufactured necessities they demanded of Great Britain. In opening such trade, Croghan transformed this frontier from a war zone that divided people into an open road that connected far-flung parts of the Empire.[30]

After this success, Croghan shifted his gaze further west, where he hoped to carry out similar rituals and secure even more territory for the Empire. On the morning of May 15, he left Fort Pitt and headed down the Ohio on boats filled with traders, soldiers, and his new Indian allies. The future, he thought, looked bright.

Thomas Gage agreed. After hearing of the treaty, he wrote optimistically to Johnson that "our Indian affairs seem to take a favorable turn, and we might expect a long series of peace with them." But he added a note of caution. Peace was only in the offing "if not interrupted by the licentious lawless proceedings of the frontier inhabitants of Pennsylvania, Maryland and Virginia."[31]

Illinois Country
Fort Chartres

May 1765

At that moment, however, Indian affairs appeared far darker from the perspective of Alexander Fraser. After leaving Fort Pitt in March, Fraser had made a successful trip down the Ohio River and up to Fort Chartres. Fraser had, as ordered, traveled there to meet the French commander who still occupied it as part of the transfer of power from the French to the British. His time there was brief and chaotic.[32]

Fraser met a cool reception upon his arrival. The French were reluctant to cede power and appeared dismissive of the British emissary. Native Americans in the area were far more resolute. Fraser and his small party encountered constant harassment wherever they went. The French commander of the fort, meanwhile, did little to aid Fraser, although he occasionally expressed his sympathy. Eventually, a group of Chippewas attacked the British camp and seized the troops. Fraser narrowly escaped, but with his men held hostage and threatened with execution, he surrendered to his captors.[33]

Fraser refused to cower in captivity. He defused the situation—and saved the lives of his troops—by slowly convincing the Chippewas of Great Britain's peaceful intentions. When he won his release, the Chippewas appeared, he noted proudly, "disposed . . . entirely for peace." Even better, several other Indian groups seemed agreeable as well and lingered in the area waiting for Croghan to discuss terms of peace. At the head of those expecting Croghan was Pontiac himself, who arrived in the midst of Fraser's visit and seemed, according to Fraser, to be "ador'd by all the nations hereabouts."[34]

But Fraser's luck soon fell victim to rumors and the lingering distrust that swirled around the British in the Illinois Country. Soon after his release, an Indian rushed into town carrying distressing news: a war party of British and Cherokee warriors had killed and scalped fourteen Illinois Indians, a clear sign that the British calls for peace were nothing more than a ruse. A group of Native warriors seized several of Fraser's men in retaliation and raced into his quarters, armed and ready to kill him.[35]

But before they could commit the deed, Pontiac appeared.[36]

He stopped the attack on Fraser and took the British official into his protection. He then demanded the release of the other prisoners and promised that he and his supporters "would die in [their] defence." After that strong display of support, Pontiac and Fraser became allies.

Fraser, admiring of his protector, later said of Pontiac: "He is more remarkable for his integrity and humanity than either French Man or Indian in the colony."[37]

Once they trusted each other, Fraser began to relate all he knew to his new friend. He told Pontiac about the Ohio Indians' desire for peace, as well as Croghan's planned treaty at Fort Pitt and mission down the Ohio River with the goal of re-opening trade. It was all news that seemed to reinforce Pontiac's decision to negotiate an end to the fighting. Perhaps the most important piece of news for Pontiac was that the Ohio Indians seemed ready for peace, since war without these powerful allies would probably be futile for the Native groups in the Illinois and Great Lakes regions. As Fraser noted to Thomas Gage, "The Indians seem at present very well inclined to peace if Mr. Croghan has put matters on a good footing with the nations on the Ohio." He even began to suspect that the Indians would make "peace on our own terms."[38]

"Everything was on the best footing imaginable," Fraser later reported. It was a remarkable and quick turn of events.[39]

Just as Fraser was beginning to think the future looked bright, however, Charlot Kaské arrived from New Orleans carrying a war belt and carting a barrel of rum—a sign, he said, of French promises "to supply them with ammunition and arms to carry on the war." Soon more goods arrived, and "the shops and most of the stores in town" began to overflow with provisions sent up the Mississippi. Kaské's news changed the dynamic yet again. Emboldened by the promises of the French and, it was rumored, the Spanish as well, Indians who were still uncertain about Fraser became openly hostile once again. Rumors that were likely true circulated that Kaské plotted to kill Fraser in an attempt to end the movement for peace and continue the war.[40]

No one, it appears, knew that Kaské had made up the story about receiving support in New Orleans—or perhaps he hadn't. While the official record of his visit to the governor in New Orleans shows that the French rebuffed his entreaties, it's possible that he received secret support from French merchants because he did arrive with substantial supplies, and more goods followed. We'll likely never know, but we do know that Kaské's arrival caused, as Fraser noted to a superior, "a very great alteration in the disposition of all the Nations hereabouts."[41]

Pontiac considered the situation grave. With Kaské's promises and supplies streaming into the region, Pontiac realized his own influence was declining. Fraser's death at the hands of Kaské would only further weaken Pontiac's authority and destroy his vision of peace through diplomacy. Pontiac had to act quickly in order to preserve his power and the future he envisioned. He took Fraser to the side and gave him three options: stay and die, follow Pontiac to his home, or escape down the Mississippi.[42]

Fraser opted for the safety of New Orleans and dashed out of town. Pontiac headed to his base to wait for Croghan and plot his next move. Kaské also waited for Croghan. But he knew what his next move would be: he wanted to burn Croghan alive.[43]

Chapter 6

———◆●◆———

Crisis

Fort Loudon

Summer 1765

While Fraser's experience in the Illinois Country dampened Gage's rosy take on the state of Indian affairs, Lieutenant Charles Grant soon proved that Gage's worries about "the licentious lawless proceedings of the frontier inhabitants" were well founded. As the Black Boys' activity was reaching its height, Grant, who had been confined to Fort Loudon, a prisoner in his own castle, decided to take "some air on horseback" on May 28. Little did he know that his innocent ride would deepen the growing imperial crisis on the frontiers.[1]

The Black Boys held the entire region under surveillance, and word of Grant's venture into the forest soon worked its way back to James Smith. Smith saw in Grant's outing an opportunity for the Black Boys to assert their dominance in the region. He called together a crew and hid along the road about a mile outside of Fort Loudon waiting for the officer to appear. As Grant approached, five men sprung from the woods, armed and ready to fight. They told Grant to halt, but instead he snapped his horse to attention and raced toward them. One of the Black Boys reached out to grab the horse, but Grant pushed him off. For the moment, he appeared home free.

"Shoot the bougar!" James Smith shouted to his men.

A shot rang out. Frightened, Grant's horse ran into some bushes, bucked, and threw him.

"Take the durk of the rascall," were the next orders. Grant, the most senior British military officer in the region and the Empire's representative on this frontier, soon found himself, in the ironic words of his captors, "the King's prisoner."

"For what?" Grant asked.

"We will let you know," they replied.[2]

Grant's captivity was not only unexpected but also surely a deep insult to a man whose service had to this point been so remarkable. Indeed, he had led a life at least as remarkable as James Smith's. Grant was a Scotsman descended from a long line of prominent warriors. His father had fought in the Jacobite uprising, an attempt in 1745 by some Scotsmen to overthrow the British monarchy and replace it with a new one. Perhaps in an attempt to salvage the family name and reputation, or simply following in the footsteps of his family, Grant volunteered to fight in the Seven Years' War under the command of the 77th Regiment of the Highlanders. He found himself at the front lines of the war immediately upon arriving in America. He fought in western Pennsylvania and was captured by the Wyandots in 1758. Grant then spent the next two years, like James Smith, a captive in Indian Country.

After securing his release in 1760, something Croghan helped arrange (though neither Grant nor Croghan seem to have noted it later), Grant went back to the field. He saw action in the Canadian campaign and then in the Caribbean. Grant continued his service when Pontiac's

War broke out, fighting under Bouquet and, yes, alongside James Smith and his Indian Regiment during Bouquet's successful fall offensive into the Ohio Country. Soon afterward, Grant was appointed commandant of Fort Loudon. His career had been, so far, one of exemplary service. Indeed, Grant's life and career were a near mirror of Smith's, except for one thing: Grant's first loyalties were to the Empire and his military superiors. Smith's were to his local community.[3]

Standing in the woods, these two Scots warriors and former captives were now at odds with each other because of their different allegiances, and Smith had to decide what to do with his prisoner. He decided not to use more violence against Grant and instead carted him seven miles farther into the forest to try to intimidate him. As Grant plodded along with his new captors, the Black Boys heckled their prisoner, mocking his behavior and letting him know their objective: they wanted the handful of guns the British Army had seized after the initial raid and still held at the fort. If Grant refused to return them, the Black Boys vowed to "carry [him] away into the mountains and keep [him] there."[4]

Grant responded by pleading powerlessness. He told Smith that he was unable to act until he received orders from his superiors to release the weapons, and he warned Smith that if the Black Boys persisted, the British military would make an example out of them. The Black Boys were unconvinced. Indeed, they met Grant's tough talk with their own.[5]

"We are as ready for a rebellion as you are to oppose it," Smith threatened. And he had his own warning for Grant. Fort Loudon now was leaderless, and the Black Boys were prepared to "take the fort by force of arms and by that means . . . have all the goods in the fort as well as their own arms."[6]

Grant stood firm. Smith, sensing that Grant's determination was growing stronger, stopped their march to confer with his men. It's unclear what happened during their meeting, but it's clear that the

Black Boys wanted to get two things out of the episode. They wanted their guns back, and they wanted to assert their superiority over Grant. His continued possession of their guns represented his supremacy over them and implied that members of the British military had the power to seize property whenever they wished. The Black Boys realized that if they got Grant to submit now, they would deny Grant a precedent and instead show their control over the region. When they broke from their huddle in the woods, Smith told Grant that they had decided to take him to North Carolina, and they began the hike.[7]

As they trekked eight miles deeper into the wildness, Grant became convinced of Smith's determination to take him to North Carolina and decided to negotiate. He now promised to do everything in his power to give the guns back. But Grant also had a hidden objective: he wanted to win his freedom without the immediate return of the guns. Smith made him an offer that played right into Grant's plan. Grant would sign a £40 bond for the guns. If the British Army still held the firearms in five weeks, then Grant was liable for the money. Before Smith released him, he brought Grant to William Smith's house to sign a legal document committing to this agreement. Grant thought the entire contract was invalid because he was being coerced, something he planned to let Smith know after he won his release.[8]

Grant's signature at William Smith's home secured his release, but his frustrations only grew in the weeks that followed. First, Grant's troops suffered the same type of treatment he had received—maybe worse. A few days before his own troubles, nine Black Boys seized one of his sergeants (possibly McGlashan), stripped him, and threatened to tie him to a tree and flog him. This was one of the most humiliating things colonists could do to a man who often used the lash against his own unruly subordinates. A separate group seized a second sergeant a few days later. When a colonel arrived to suppress the Black Boys, James Smith refused to bow to the pressures of rank and instead publicly defended his treatment of Grant and his sergeants. Grant "had used the country ill," he told the colonel, by sending troops into civilian communities. He especially targeted McGlashan, though, stating that "I don't accuse Mr. Grant with all the Hostilities committed by McGlashan, for I have reason to believe McGlashan acted contrary to his orders and concealed many of the actions from his commanding officer." In saying this, Smith was hinting at rumors that McGlashan and his men had taken illegal bribes from the traders. Colonists were, according to Smith's logic, within their rights because the British military had violated long-held and much-beloved British liberties involving the protection of private property, illegal searches and seizures, and the proper role of the military in civilian communities.[9]

In the midst of this tumult, a strange advertisement was found tacked to a post on the road that only confused matters further. A day after Grant's seizure, Thomas Romberg, the commissary at Fort Loudon, went out searching for the missing lieutenant. Although he didn't locate his commanding officer, he did return with a battered parchment that called for the Black Boys to meet at William Smith's house. The text played on the hard-drinking and lawless stereotypes associated with Scots-Irish frontier settlers. It enticed recruits with a promise of free-flowing booze: "Come to our tavern and fill your belly's with liquor and your mouth with swearing," it declared. And it flaunted the frontiersmen's disregard for established authority: "We will have Grant, the officer of Loudon, whip'd or hang'd." It also cast Penn as weak, possibly on the side of the Black Boys: "The governor will pardon our crimes," it told prospective recruits. And it touted the Black Boys' popularity, bragging that "the country will stand with us." It ended by naming William Smith, the justice of the peace who permitted "free toleration for drinking, swearing, Sabbath breaking, and any outrage we have a mind to do," as the group's leader.[10]

Everyone involved in the Black Boys' Rebellion viewed the advertisement through their own conspiratorial notions. The Black Boys and their supporters were convinced that their opponents had fabricated it, with many thinking it was Romberg's work, as a way to weaken the group. Such a notice would surely put pressure on officials like John Penn to come down hard on William Smith, a strategy that would deprive the movement of a leader. The Black Boys' main evidence in support of their suspicions about Romberg's authorship was that the only remaining copy was in Romberg's own handwriting. He had destroyed the original, he claimed, because it was "so much blotted with durt." Left only with a duplicate in Romberg's penmanship, the Black Boys argued that the ad was a fake and pointed the finger at Romberg as its forger. However, it could also have been propaganda written by one of the Black Boys to terrorize their enemies with its threats. Whether or not it was propaganda written by the Black Boys or, more likely, a fraud by their opponents, its contents reveal a truth about the political situation as those on the ground perceived it. People in the area thought that Penn and the rioters worked together, and the Black Boys' strength came from the broad support they received from their neighbors and a justice of the peace.[11]

While the outlandish language seems to support the document's inauthenticity, those at a distance from the action took the ad very seriously. Its contents floored Thomas Gage. He immediately forwarded a copy to Governor Penn, demanding "that these insurrections [be] immediately quelled, and the authors and abettors of them brought to punishment." The broadside also infuriated Penn. He called on William Smith to appear in Philadelphia on July 30 to answer for the advertisement and explain Grant's capture. He also required Grant to produce depositions supporting his position and asked the Black Boys' opponent, Justice James Maxwell, to testify against Smith.[12]

As soon as Penn's correspondence arrived, William Smith knew he had to marshal a defense to protect himself and the Black Boys. On July

18, William Smith and other magistrates crowded into Fort Loudon to conduct an inquest into the events, the outcome of which would likely be shared with Penn. The tensions must have been high as the former besiegers of the fort now occupied it to clear their names of any crime. Although the records of the proceedings appear to be lost, we can get a sense of what happened by reading between the lines of the few references to it. According to Romberg, who was brought in as a witness, and Henry Prather, who also testified, the proceedings focused on identifying the author of the advertisement and examining the actions of Justices James Maxwell and William Smith, leader of the Black Boys. Smith called many supporters to testify, including the person who led the attack on Joseph Spears, and one of his tenants whose deposition he supposedly coached. Privately, some confessed that the proceedings seemed a sham, with the judges requiring witnesses to tell only "the truth," purposely omitting the word *whole* from their oath.[3]

Once in Philadelphia, Smith had an easy time convincing Penn that he wasn't the author of the advertisement. In fact, Penn, who was used to viewing every insult through the paranoia of partisanship, had already decided that the advertisement was the work of "a party in this province, who have been indefatigable in their endeavors to malign and traduce me"—meaning the Quaker political party. Gage, of course, disagreed with Penn, believing it the work "of some leader of the rioters." Indeed, the suspected identity of the poster's author depended on one's own view of the frontier and its politics. At every hurdle Penn faced during this affair, he suspected the hidden hand of the Quaker Party trying to weaken his control on the colony. Gage, meanwhile, viewed the frontier settlers with the jaundiced eye of an elite British aristocrat inclined to see those lower on the social scale as rash and uncontrollable. Gage therefore suspected a frontiersman as the author, while Penn blamed his political adversaries. In any case, Smith, armed with depositions attesting to his lawful behavior and a defense against the advertisement, was once again cleared of any wrongdoing and returned to his home with as much power as when he had left.[14]

Conococheague

Summer 1765

Official word of Croghan's treaty, which soon followed the discovery of the advertisement, did little to change the unfolding of events. In June, John Penn issued a proclamation re-opening trade. News of it arrived at Fort Loudon on June 14. The British Army, meanwhile, began escorting traders on the roads, creating even more tensions between the civilian population and the military. Providing protection to the people whom the Black Boys considered to be treasonous easterners only reinforced the rebels' belief that the British army was opposed to their interests.[15]

While the inspection activity seems to have stopped in the wake of Penn's proclamation—though traders still might encounter unofficial harassment—the Black Boys continued to confront the British military, the key imperial institution in the region, in order to recover their property. Throughout the summer, colonists found new, less violent ways to oppose the troops' presence. One jury issued a warrant for Sergeant McGlashan's arrest. Another jury rendered a verdict declaring Grant's seizure of guns an illegal act and demanded their return.[16]

As the Black Boys achieved a new level of dominance, they also developed a stronger sense of cohesion and purpose. The two Smiths served as the heads of this movement. James oversaw the inspection activity, while William used his position to provide legal cover for their actions. Meanwhile, local supporters pooled their money to fund the Black Boys' operations. William Smith's house became the central meeting ground for the organization, earning it the name Fort Smiths, a plural use in recognition of the two Smiths as the movement's leaders. Fort Smiths also provided the Black Boys an air of authority that challenged, if not replaced, their rival, Fort Loudon.[17]

The Black Boys even adopted an anthem. It was written by George Campbell, a recent Irish immigrant from Dublin who now found himself, like Croghan, on the American frontier. Unlike his fellow Irishman, however, Campbell sided with the Black Boys. They sang his song as they traveled along the roads inspecting traders and in taverns as they recounted their exploits and plotted their next ones. Its stanzas echoed the petition that frontier inhabitants had given to Penn at the start of the rebellion, and its words reminded the Black Boys and their hearers of their common purpose. It began by complaining of an eastern elite dominated by profit-seeking merchants who cared little for the plight of frontier people. It then bemoaned the partisanship back east as empowering a self-serving faction that obstructed the public good— the public good being the defense of frontiers against a hostile Indian threat, what the song called "the enemies of mankind."[18]

After the opening lament, the song continues with a stirring defense of the Black Boys' righteousness. They were "patriots" and "brave souls" who knew what the proper government policies should have been, while traders were "treacherous." As the song ends, the Black Boys defend their actions against accusations that their destruction of property was the unlawful act of a radical mob. They instead insist that "frontier inhabitants" are loyal subjects acting as their king would want them to if he truly understood their situation. According to the song, the truly treasonous people were the traders and those who served their interest, like the soldiers at Fort Loudon. Their actions only helped the "enemies of mankind"—meaning Indians.

The ditty, sung to the tune of the British tavern ballad "The Black Joke," is reproduced here:

1. Ye patriot souls who love to sing,
What serves your country and your king,
In wealth, peace and royal estate;
Attention give whilst I rehearse,
A modern fact, in jingling verse,
How party interest strove what it cou'd,
To profit itself by public blood,
But justly met its merited fate.

2. Let all those Indian traders claim,
Their just reward, inglorious fame,
For vile base and treacherous ends.
To Pollins, in the spring they sent,
Much warlike stores, with an intent,
To carry them to our barbarous foes,
Expecting that no-body dare oppose,
A present to their Indian friends.

3. Astonish'd at the wild design,
Frontier inhabitants combin'd,
With brave souls, to stop their career,
Although some men apostatiz'd,
Who first the grand attempt advis'd,
The bold frontiers they bravely stood,
To act for their king and their country's good,
In joint league, and strangers to fear.

4. On March the fifth, in sixty-five,
Their Indian presents did arrive,
In long pomp and cavalcade,
Near Sidelong Hill, where in disguise,

Some patriots did their train surprize,
And quick as lightning tumbled their loads,
And kindled them bonfires in the woods,
And mostly burnt their whole brigade.

5. At Loudon, when they heard the news,
They scarcely knew which way to choose,
For blind rage and discontent;
At length some soldiers they sent out,
With guides for to conduct the route,
And seized some men that were trav'ling there,
And hurried them into Loudon where
They laid them fast with one consent.

6. But men of resolution thought,
Too much to see their neighbors caught,
For no crime but false surmise;
Forthwith they join'd a warlike band,
And march'd to Loudon out of hand,
And kept the jailors pris'ners there,
Until our friends enlarged were,
Without fraud or any disguise.

7. Let mankind censure or commend,
This rash performance in the end,
Then both sides will find their account.
'Tis true no law can justify,
To burn our neighbors property,
But when this property is design'd,
To serve the enemies of mankind,
It's high treason in the amount.[19]

What is especially significant about this song is how it mirrors complaints about government that were coming from the seaports at the same time as news of the Stamp Act was spreading through those eastern communities. The two movements, one based on the frontiers and the other on the coasts, were traveling parallel paths, disconnected and yet headed in the same direction. The key difference was the target of colonial anger. Like the Black Boys, colonists in the seaports claimed an unyielding loyalty to the Crown, so they blamed the passage of the Stamp Act on a dangerous combination of corrupt British ministers and unfeeling Parliamentarians. They also claimed that the source of their dissatisfaction was a lack of representation in Parliament. If they had representatives in Parliament, they argued, then those who legislated for the Empire would have better knowledge of what the colonists felt. Without such representation, they took to the streets to protest, including the targeting of stamp collectors and the symbolic destruction of the stamps, as a way to awaken their well-meaning king to his misinformed and unscrupulous advisors. Their acts, much like the Black Boys', were supposed to reveal to their king the bad policy that Parliament had adopted.[20]

Frontier people leveled similar attacks, although their anger mainly focused on eastern elites and institutions rather than imperial ones. They complained of corrupt traders encouraged by what they saw as a Quaker-dominated government that protected its own economic interests instead of providing security for the frontiers. In their governor, who represented the King, the Black Boys saw an ally who was frustrated by the elite merchant groups. These western colonists saw in Philadelphia the same things eastern colonists saw happening in London. In 1765, colonists in the East and West were developing similar anxieties about governing, although the causes of these feelings were different. In the East, they focused on taxation, a freer trade, and representation in Parliament; in the West, they focused on greater military support, a restricted Indian trade, and greater representation in the colonial government. In the West, also, there was a pronounced fear and hatred aimed at both an eastern elite and Native Americans writ large, something that would continue to linger in their psyche and that distinguished them from the movements in the East. At this moment, however, the two movements remained separated. But in time their shared desire for a more representative government would fuse to create something revolutionary.

British Headquarters
New York City

Summer 1765

The Black Boys' actions flummoxed imperial officials. Those stationed around Fort Loudon thought the situation resembled a civil war. The commanding officer of Fort Pitt, for instance, mustered his troops after Grant was captured. When reports reached his office that the Black Boys had executed Grant, he and his troops began marching to Fort Loudon to retake the post and secure the region. He turned back only when he learned of Grant's release. But his actions and assumptions about the Black Boys showed that the chief representatives of the British Empire on its frontiers viewed these colonists as rebels to be suppressed rather than as aggrieved subjects whose complaints needed to be addressed. As Croghan noted in a letter to Henry Bouquet, if the Black Boys went unpunished, then it would "be an end to sivel and military power" on the frontiers. The situation for these managers of empire was a profound crisis of governing.[21]

The abusive words that Gage, Johnson, Bouquet, Grant, and other officials hurled at the Black Boys reflect these sentiments. Gage saw the attacks as the acts of a "lawless banditti," a group of "miscreants," "traitors" who were in "an actual state of rebellion" and deserved "exemplary punishment." One of his most senior subordinates in the region, Colonel John Reid, agreed and demanded a strong show of military force to compel obedience. These "villains," he wrote, should "have a body of troops quartered upon them till they are brought under proper subjection to the laws." Bouquet called them "seditious." Grant considered them "my enemies." Penn referred to them as "an ungovernable people."[22]

While imperial officials agreed that the Black Boys were acting outside the bounds of legitimate political protest and needed to be punished for their illegal behavior, the problem, as Thomas Gage realized during the crisis, was that the British Empire lacked the strength it claimed to possess. All the imperial officials agreed that more force was needed to bring these colonists in line with the Empire's new policies toward the West. But when they tried to use this power, they found it absent. Gage and his peers may have thought like powerful magistrates but in actuality, they lacked the means to enforce their will.[23]

Recognizing his own weaknesses, Gage instead looked to Pennsylvania's government to fill this void. The imperial structure was such that colonies had the authority to do much of the internal policing that Gage thought was necessary. Colonies controlled the civil and criminal law, employed sheriffs to arrest the accused, and assembled county courts to hand out punishments. But fierce partisanship in the East between the Pennsylvania Assembly and the governor hampered Pennsylvania's adoption of new laws that would have strengthened its powers of coercion. In fact, Gage and others in his group suspected that Pennsylvania's partisanship had made the chief law enforcement officer sympathetic to the rebels. Charles Grant reported that "the Governor may be too apt to listen to their false assertions," and Colonel John Reid, Grant's superior, agreed, writing to Gage that "Governor Penn has issued no Proclamation, nor taken any other steps as yet, agreeable to his promise to me, to quell these insurrections, and as the rioters openly avow his countenancing them, I fear little is to be expected." There were even rumors that William Allen, chief justice of the Pennsylvania Supreme Court, threatened to arrest Grant for his actions if the officer entered Philadelphia. These reports, combined with his own observations, made Gage reach a pessimistic conclusion about the colony's government: "the factions in the government of Pennsylvania, if it can be called a government, seemed to have favored the infamous riots of the banditti upon the borders of the province." Such paralysis occurs, he noted, "when party unhappily overcomes all other considerations."[24]

Penn denied the accusations that he supported the Black Boys, but he would have agreed with Gage's analysis of the situation. In a letter to Gage explaining his inability to punish the rioters, he blamed the colony's politics, especially the Assembly's lack of cooperation, for his apparent impotence. If he had a militia law (something Penn pointed out to Gage he had asked for but the legislature had refused to provide), then he would have the necessary powers of enforcement. A colonial militia would, he explained, "aid the civil powers" by giving officials new policing power.[25]

Penn's proposal was meant to correct the problem imperial administrators were confronting. Put simply, Penn wanted to transform Pennsylvania's colonial government into a more modern state. He believed a permanent militia, something the colony had avoided throughout its history, was now necessary to meet the new demands of a growing colony. The chief issue driving Penn's reform wasn't Indians or the fear of warfare. It was the need to control the colony's own people. As one of Penn's allies realized after the Paxton Boys massacre, "There is no standing army to inforce its laws and support the government." Penn wanted a militia so he could do on the frontiers of his colony what imperial administrators wanted: use force to make the people comply with policies with which they disagreed. As he explained to Gage in

June of 1765, if the Assembly had "paid any regard to my recommenda-
tion . . . and framed a militia law, all the late mischief and disturbance
might have been prevented, such a law being absolutely necessary to
aid the civil powers, and indeed the only natural defence and support
of government."[26]

Even Penn's strongest political adversaries agreed with his vision.
As John Ross, a prominent Philadelphian, confided to his friend Benjamin Franklin after the Black Boys' first attack, "What is lamentably
too true, [is] that we have only the form without the powers of government." Ross also recognized the divisions that were developing in the
colony along regional lines, complaining to Franklin that the colony
now had "two kinds of governments on the East and West side of the
province." Worse still, he reported to Franklin, was that those in the
Conococheague showed a growing sense of independence and autonomy. "The Conegochieg Settlement on the Frontiers are all Governors," he wrote, "and Claim a Superintendancy over the Whole." The
frontier people, according to Ross, with their inspection activities and
control of the courts, showed a level of self-government that undermined traditional forms of colonial and imperial authority.[27]

Franklin, an ocean away, agreed with his friend's assessment, writing, "The Outrages committed by the Frontier People are really amaz-
ing!" For him, the Black Boys provided evidence that the colony and
the Empire needed serious reform to strengthen the powers of government on the frontiers. As he noted in his reply to Ross, "Such Practices
throw a Disgrace over our whole Country, that can only be wip'd off
by exemplary Punishment of the Actors, which our weak Government
cannot or will not inflict."[28]

Franklin, however, influenced by his hatred of the Penns and the
proprietorship, wanted to strengthen imperial powers at the expense of
colonial ones. Instead of creating a colonial militia, Franklin wanted
the British Army to expand its jurisdiction to include policing frontier

populations. As he wrote after the Paxton Boys incident, colonists were shortsighted to fear a standing army and wrong to oppose the taxes necessary to support it. Instead, he said that a more strenuous use of the British military in the colonies would encourage the "security of internal peace among ourselves without the expence or trouble of a militia." But Franklin was out of touch with colonial sentiments in 1765. For instance, he used his influence in London to have his friend John Hughes appointed a stamp collector in Philadelphia, believing the post would provide his friend with a financial windfall. It instead caused his friend to become, like Lieutenant Charles Grant, the target of irate pro-testors who rejected new imperial policies that were intended to address the demands of an enlarged and indebted empire.[29]

Here, then, rests one of the causes of the imperial crisis on the fron-tiers. Most governing officials agreed that there was a problem of order on the frontiers and that a stronger, more centralized government in these regions was necessary. Gage and others in his group all agreed that they were in a moment that demanded state-building. But the poi-soned politics in the colonies between easterners and westerners, and the growing feud between the colonists in the seaports and Parliament, undermined the resolve of officials at all levels to strengthen govern-ment at this crucial moment.[30]

There was another element to this governing crisis. There was a cultural disconnect between colonists on frontiers and those managing the Empire that deepened the rift between the governing and the gov-erned. First, there was disagreement over who, exactly, these colonists were. Time and again, military officers living in the West referred to the Black Boys and their supporters as "country people." The Black Boys, in contrast, never used such a phrase to describe themselves. They instead used the phrase found in their anthem: "frontier inhabitants." In the eighteenth century, this difference in language was significant. When British soldiers called colonists country people, they were using English imagery to describe a North American context. Their words evoked images of peaceful farmlands in the English countryside. They saw stability as they marched through the Conococheague and other small frontier communities. Colonists in the region, however, considered their homes under threat of invasion from surrounding Indians, regardless of what their governors said about alliances with Native groups. They lived in fear, not tranquility. They were not country people. They were the people of the frontiers, a distinctive identity forged in war.[31]

As the Black Boys gained more support, this disagreement over the region's geopolitics bred a lasting distrust between the governed and governing that weakened the bonds that had held the British Empire together for most of the eighteenth century. Frontier inhabitants felt that their imperial government failed to protect them from an enemy threat, and imperial officials considered the Black Boys lawless ruffians who were upsetting the attempt to maintain peace with Native American trading partners. This divide was the root cause of the entire rebellion, and it grew worse as the Black Boys became more assertive.

But it didn't have to be so. Consider the dilemma William Johnson found himself in during the Black Boys' Rebellion. As the Black Boys developed their own inspection program, even receiving donations from their neighbors to offset its costs, Johnson was calling on Parliament for more funds to support his own inspectors. Johnson, however, never considered giving the self-sufficient Black Boys any authority because his prejudice toward colonists on the frontiers prevented such innovative thinking. But if he had thought more creatively about policies that could have served his interest and those of the Empire, he might have found a way to resolve the predicament by giving people like the Black Boys a role to play in the Empire. For example, if he had commissioned frontier people as inspectors under his office and established a clear chain of command, then Johnson might have been able to integrate these communities into the imperial structure and defuse the bitterness between the frontier people and Empire. There was precedent for such actions. During wartime, the British military had depended on the support of local militias and community leaders for supplies, troops, and leadership. In peacetime, however, imperial policymakers seemed unable—or unwilling—to involve ordinary colonists in support of their new plans. Instead, the biases of Gage and Johnson blinded them from seeing frontier colonists in any light other than a lawless rabble to be punished rather than incorporated.[32]

The Ohio River
About twenty-five miles south of modern-day Cincinnati

June 1765

Cruising down the Ohio River, George Croghan was unaware of all that was happening further east. He was instead enjoying the peace of the calm Ohio waters and the beauty of the surrounding landscape. Croghan's journal is filled with the notes of an optimist buoyed by his success at Fort Pitt. As he scanned the shorelines and took excursions inland, his imagination ran wild with the future prospects of such territory in British hands. He awoke to a "fine fertile country" on May 16, the second day of his trip. The next day, they "embarked and were delighted with the prospect of a fine open country." "A good hunter without much fatigue to himself could here supply daily one hundred men with meat," he observed on May 19.[33]

There was even time for unexpected digressions. Colonists had long heard stories of mammoth bones buried at a salt lick a few miles from the river. Croghan was determined to find the site. On May 31, he led an outing through "fine timbered clear wood[s]" in search of it. He was thrilled by what he discovered. Fossils protruded from riverbanks, and his expedition found larger ones buried in the ground. Croghan took a six-foot tusk and other bones back to the boat—remains, he believed, of elephants that once roamed in North America. Natural wonders and beauty, an inspiring mix of tranquility and fertility: these were the things that defined this new territory. It was, he concluded on June 6, "one of the finest countries in the world."[34]

But there were signs of trouble that interrupted his otherwise clear vistas. He saw remnants of war dotting the lush landscape. Formerly thriving Native American towns and French trading villages sat abandoned, leaving hollowed-out homes and crumbling chimneys as reminders of the massive shift in global power that had occurred at the Treaty of Paris in 1763. During their travels, they heard rumors of French traders aiding Indians who were still opposed to British rule, and they ran into Cherokee war parties scouting for captives. But Croghan seems to have brushed away these concerns. When one of his men went into the woods on the night of June 7 and never returned, Croghan figured the man had simply gotten lost.[35]

Croghan's pleasant fiction exploded at daybreak on June 8. A party of Indians formerly allied with the French and distrustful of the English blasted their way into Croghan's camp. When the smoke cleared, two of Croghan's men and two of his Native escorts lay dead. The rest were injured. Croghan himself received a tomahawk blow to his scalp—the only thing that prevented his death, he later joked, was his "thick scull."[36]

A bloody and bruised Croghan was then bound and taken prisoner, sure that his fate would be death. But then one of his Indian escorts from Fort Pitt, a Shawnee elder, came to his defense. The Shawnee had been wounded in the assault but managed to escape and hide in the woods nearby. He confronted Croghan's captors and explained who Croghan was and what he intended. They seemed surprised, explaining that they heard that Croghan was part of a war party meant to "inslave" western Indians—a view likely based on the rumored British-

Cherokee assault that had interfered with Fraser's work. The Shawnee's pleas somewhat satisfied Croghan's captors, although they continued to hold their prisoner under close guard as they marched him 250 miles to Ouiatenon, a major Indian town on the Wabash River in what is today northern Indiana. His captors wanted to present Croghan to their superiors, who would determine his future.[37]

During their travels, Croghan learned of Alexander Fraser's fate. He soon realized that he and Fraser, the two symbols of Great Britain's new diplomatic outreach to western Indians, had become proxies in a power struggle between competing Native American groups. Croghan realized that here, too, in the distant west, Great Britain's most recent acquisition, Native Americans were facing their own crisis as they came to terms with a new imperial regime. And once again, he was at the center of this predicament.

For Croghan, there was more at stake than just peace. His life now symbolized the future of Indian Country. Charlot Kaské had missed his opportunity to kill Fraser earlier, but he refused to let this powerful envoy escape so easily this time. He vowed to find Croghan and burn him alive, hoping that the death of such a high-ranking diplomat would destroy any hopes for peace. When Kaské learned of Croghan's capture, he demanded that Croghan be released to him. Croghan's captors refused.[38]

On July 18, as Croghan came to better understand the politics of Indian Country, he met Pontiac on the road outside Ouiatenon. Croghan knew that with this encounter he would soon learn his fate, and with it, the future of the Empire and Indian Country.[39]

Chapter 7

———— •◆• ————

Independence

As Pontiac's and Croghan's lives converged near the banks of the Wabash River, the twists of history had turned these former adversaries into confederates. Pontiac saw in the diplomat—the man he once called a liar—a person who was now indispensable to Pontiac's own future, and Croghan saw an opportunity to save his thick skull—and with it, the Empire's vision for the American West. As a result, when the two former enemies met in the woods that July day, each man needed the other to resolve the crises that were disturbing their worlds. More immediately, they needed each other for sheer survival. Pontiac quickly took Croghan in and reassured him that he was in safe hands now. They then headed to Ouiatenon for preliminary talks that would solidify the foundation for this new era of peace.[1]

Pontiac's words at this early meeting conveyed the same thing his actions had shown. He began by explaining the reasons for the war, telling Croghan that Great Britain's behavior toward Native groups in the Ohio and Illinois Countries after the Seven Years' War had been unacceptable. Instead of welcoming them as partners, the British had reduced the gifts they provided, confirming earlier French warnings that the British intended to "make slaves of them." Pontiac went on to say that he and his followers felt reassured that these concerns were ill-founded, taking comfort in knowing that the Shawnees and Delawares, his former allies and fierce warriors in their own right, had traveled with Croghan as friends.[2]

But Pontiac refused to show deference to the British Crown or offer any sense of Indian dependency to the diplomat representing the world's largest empire. Instead, he remained firm in his assertions of Indian independence. He made clear at this first meeting—as he would in subsequent ones—that the French never owned any of the western lands and were instead tenants of the Indians. Pontiac expected the British to tread just as lightly on Native ground as the French had, warning that "the King of England might not look upon his taking possession of the forts which the French formerly possest as a title for his subjects to possess their country, as they never had sold any part of it to the French." Pontiac was willing to accept a British presence in the West, but he wanted to set the terms of their settlement and the relationship between the Empire and the Indians. His vision matched what the British had in mind: a trading alliance in which the British occupied specific confined spaces, mostly forts.[3]

Croghan and Pontiac both left their initial talk satisfied and decided to host a larger, more formal treaty in Detroit, the site of the war's beginning. As Croghan traveled along Indian pathways, he passed Indian villages abuzz about the impending treaty. In some communities, the leaders he met expressed hope for peace. In others, he found the men already gone to Detroit for the meeting. But as he traveled from village to village, one thing became perfectly clear: the Indians he met were far more open to an alliance with the British than they had been at his first arrival. At one meeting, Croghan produced a belt that was "to open a road from the rising to the setting of the sun," which symbolized the free flow of goods from the eastern seaports to trading posts in Indian Country. At the end of the council at which this belt was presented, all sides promised to ignore rumors of ill intention and "promote the good works of peace."[4]

Croghan's plan to win the Delawares and Shawnees to his side first at Fort Pitt proved to be the linchpin he had hoped it would be. In his journal, he noted that the delegation of Shawnees that traveled down the Ohio with him now raced ahead, alerting Indians hostile to the British of their recent treaty at Fort Pitt and Pontiac's position on the matter. These other communities began to see the benefit of joining in a trading partnership with the British, but like Pontiac, expected to maintain their sovereignty.[5]

Finally, on August 27, more than a month after Croghan's first meeting with Pontiac, the formal treaty meeting began in Detroit. It was a grand affair, with over five hundred Indian men present. Representatives from the Ottawas, Chippewas (Ojibwes), Hurons, and Potawatomis participated, groups that considered the Illinois Country their own.

Croghan opened the council with warm words and pleasantries. He hoped that this treaty would establish a lasting and "happy union" so that "those unborn may enjoy the blessings of this general peace." He closed with words that echoed those he spoke to other groups he met on the road to Detroit, vowing that the British Empire would "promote the good work of peace."[6]

Then it was Pontiac's turn to speak.

"The war is all over," Pontiac declared, while presenting a peace pipe that he wanted sent to Sir William Johnson so "he may know I have made my peace."[7]

Pontiac ended his speech by making concrete demands that he said would cement this alliance. While Croghan had spoken in metaphoric pleasantries on the previous day, describing a "road from the sun rising to the sun setting" that would be "good and pleasant to travel on," Pontiac made specific demands for goods that he expected would travel on this road—especially "powder and lead" for their hunting. These were the very items the Black Boys wanted to prohibit, but Pontiac pointed out that "our fathers the French" had provided such items and Indians expected their new partners to do the same. Croghan agreed, and at the end of the conference Croghan and Pontiac passed the peace pipe. Pontiac promised that in the spring he would go to William Johnson's home in New York to further strengthen the bonds of peace.[8]

Over the next month, Croghan held at least half a dozen separate meetings with leaders of various tribes, including another one with Pontiac, to confirm the terms of the peace that had been solidified at the earlier Detroit treaty. Throughout these councils, two themes emerge. First, Indians expected a steady flow of trade goods to come from the British, especially ammunition, an item that was mentioned specifically several times. Croghan answered their call with a supply of goods, including powder and lead, that he had likely procured from Fort Pitt before departing. When he made these gifts, he noted that he did so "to convince you further of my sincerity." Second, Indians refused to acknowledge British sovereignty over the territory. Instead, they asserted their own independence and demanded that the British recognize it. As a group of Indians from the Wabash area of Illinois warned:

We have been informed that the English where ever they settle
make the country their own and you tell us that when you conquered the French, they gave you this country. That no difference
may happen thereafter, we tell you now the French never conquered neither did they purchase a foot of our country, nor have
to give it to you. We gave them liberty to settle for which they
always rewarded us and treated us with great civility while they
had it in their power, but as they are become now your people,
if you expect to keep those posts, we will expect to have proper
returns from you.[9]

Pontiac again met with Croghan in September to repeat his position on land rights, echoing the same sentiments the Wabash Indians
had expressed. As Croghan recorded in his journal, "Pondiac with
several chiefs . . . complained that the French had settled part of their
country, which they never had sold to them, and hoped their fathers the
English would take it into consideration and see that a proper satisfaction was made to them." Pontiac expressed his willingness to part with
some land, but only "as was necessary for their fathers the English, to
carry on a trade at, provided they were paid for it and a sufficient part
of the country left to them to hunt on."[10]

Croghan agreed with all that the Indians said during his foray. He
did try to subtly assert greater British control over the Indians, at least
in theory. He repeatedly called these western Indians *children* and the
British their new *fathers*, a language of diplomacy that to British people
implied Indian subservience. To Indians, the metaphor was more complex. Because Indian cultures had different understandings of the role
of women and men and fathers and mothers, they didn't have the same
ideas about patriarchal dominance that influenced British culture. In
their treaties, Native leaders made it clear to Croghan that they had
accepted the French as their fathers because of how well the French

had treated them. *Father* to the Indians was a term of mutual respect and reciprocity that indicated an alliance, not necessarily a subjugated dependent.[11]

Through these meetings, Indian groups in the West were trying to set the terms by which the British Empire could function in this region. And there was remarkable unanimity in their positions. They rejected any hint of British authority over them, expressed their continued opposition to previous British practices toward Indian groups in the territory, and made it clear that they used war to show their displeasure and would do so again if the British didn't keep their promises. Many of the Native groups in the Illinois Country decided that they would, for the moment, accept British forces at forts and welcome traders, but only on their own terms. The two most important issues were limiting settlement to pre-existing French forts and opening a trade in ammunition—two demands that clashed with the vision that colonists like the Black Boys held for the West. Native leaders were trying to shape the imperial regime in this region to meet their wishes, much as the Black Boys were doing in their own region. But the two visions were completely incompatible. Croghan and others, like Gage and Johnson, recognized the problem and hoped to avoid a collision of these two competing visions by restraining the colonists—if they could only figure out how.

British Headquarters
New York City

Fall 1765

In late September, as summer turned to fall, Croghan's work in winning the peace appeared done. He packed his bags and headed out on the cool waters of the Great Lakes, his destination New York. It had been a remarkable turn of events in a very short period. The Indians who wished Croghan smooth travels thought they had achieved the independence they sought by fighting Pontiac's War. The war now seemed like a success. They had fought to reject British policies intended to make them a subservient, conquered people. During Croghan's meetings, he had accepted the Indians' terms. Indians had, in effect, shaped the contours of the British Empire in their region to meet their expectations, just as the Black Boys were trying to shape imperial institutions to meet theirs.

William Johnson was thrilled as soon as news of Croghan's success arrived at Johnson Hall. He dashed off a report to his superiors in England boasting of Croghan's "important transaction" that "obtain[ed] possession of that important settlement." But Johnson also recognized the message that the Native leaders were sending to the British about what this "possession" meant, noting to his superiors that while the British had secured an "alliance," Pontiac had made "a strong reservation of the rights to the lands about them." Johnson knew that maintaining this coalition was the key to the Empire's stability, so he advised that Indian relations needed to be put "under the management of prudent persons"—people like himself and Croghan. He also used Croghan's triumph to scold imperial officials for the lack of adequate funding coming from London, warning the Board of Trade that his department needed to be "properly supported otherwise the whole may fall to the ground." With Johnson acknowledging the importance of this alliance and the terms by which it had to be "cultivated and cherished," Pontiac and the western Indians had navigated their own political crisis and achieved a new level of independence. Now Johnson needed to make sure he had the means to maintain what Croghan had achieved.[12]

Croghan, for his part, reveled in his victory. His task had been to win over hostile Indians. Peace, it was hoped, would provide the British Empire with a new level of independence. A stable West would free the

Crown from costly wars and military expenses at a time when the debt weighed heavy on imperial administrators. Little did Croghan know, however, that as he returned to colonial society, the political movement his journey had sparked on the frontiers was then achieving its own level of independence and was threatening to undo everything he had accomplished.

Fort Loudon
Conococheague

November 1765

As peace appeared to be taking hold in the West, in the Conococheague near Fort Loudon the tensions between colonists and the Empire still simmered. Lieutenant Charles Grant received the brunt of the colonists' wrath. He grew more insulated as the summer turned to fall and, in turn, more paranoid. He heard rumors that his performance had become the butt of jokes in elite circles back east and that Thomas Gage considered him incompetent. Worse was John Penn, who, sources told Grant, openly embraced the Black Boys and threatened to arrest Grant if he entered Philadelphia—an officer in the British Army who was guided only by his duty! Grant, sitting remote on the frontiers, disconnected from the people mocking him and unsure of his own performance, believed it all.[13]

In September, as Croghan was wrapping up his meetings with Indian delegations near Detroit, Grant wrote a plaintive letter to his superior, Thomas Gage, in which he defended himself from these insults. "I am conscious to myself of having acted according to the best of my capacity and without any other Motive than to give assistance to those distressed, I will therefore Enumerate every action that I think my Enemies (who are Numerous) can take hold of and humbly submit them to your Excellency as the properest judge," he began. Grant then refuted every charge the Black Boys leveled against him and took affidavits from local settlers attesting to his own performance. It was a desperate plea from an isolated man. It was, it turned out, entirely unnecessary. Everything Grant had heard, Gage assured him, was "only rumour." Gage let the insecure officer know that he "always considered [Grant] the Sufferer, and . . . blameless in . . . Conduct."[14]

Grant's situation seemed to be improving on other fronts. In an attempt to cut costs, Gage planned to shutter Fort Loudon along with other smaller forts later in the fall. The idea was that these small forts along the communication line were no longer needed in a time of peace. Gage instead wanted to centralize troops in larger, more strategically important places, like Detroit, Fort Pitt, or the seaports. Grant and his men were to be reassigned to Fort Pitt, where they would join other troops. The new assignment surely came as a welcome change.[15]

Word of Grant's impending withdrawal, however, made the issue of the colonists' confiscated guns all the more pressing. When Grant alerted local justices about his imminent departure, the Black Boys, still smarting over Grant's seizure of the arms, made their move. On November 16, as the troops were preparing to leave, intelligence arrived that James Smith had sent out three parties of men along the roads to seize Grant and McGlashan. Grant decided to stay in the fort, hoping to wear out his hunters.[16]

At about 7:00 p.m., the Black Boys, frustrated that they couldn't capture their quarry, descended again on Fort Loudon to try to scare their game into the open. Thus began the second siege of Fort Loudon. Grant and his soldiers got their first hint that something was afoot when they heard "hooting" coming from the woods, a sign that the Black Boys were using James Smith's training. The troops hunkered down for what they expected would be a night of harassment. As evening fell, the Black Boys launched a barrage of gunfire that lasted until sunrise. At daybreak, as the shooting slowed, Grant watched as more men joined the Black Boys. The besiegers' newly enlarged numbers made them more confident in their defiance. Rather than hide behind trees, the Black Boys stood in the open and blocked all roads to the fort. As night fell on the frontier fort again, the Black Boys lit the sky with another continuous volley.[17]

The shooting stopped as dawn broke. The Black Boys sent a message to Grant demanding the release of the nine guns that Grant held. Here is where the story gets confusing. Grant had always claimed that his hands were tied because he had no orders to return the guns. It turns out, however, that Gage had given Grant permission in early October to release the guns, preferably to a local justice, contingent on Governor Penn's written approval. In other words, Gage had created a legal process under which the guns could be transferred from imperial and military control to colonial and civil care. The problem was that even though Gage's orders gave Grant a way to save face—he would relinquish control of the arms by giving them to another official, thereby never acknowledging they were illegally held—it did require John Penn to act before he could get rid of the troublesome items. Grant, however, never received any word from Penn, so he continued to hold the guns.[18]

As Grant prepared to leave in early November, he tried to hand over the items to local colonial authorities. Evidence suggests that he reached out to local justices two days before the siege to see if they would hold the guns until the governor made his desires known. The justices appear to have rejected this offer, in part because they considered the guns illegally held. If they accepted the guns, they would become complicit in the affair. As far as they were concerned, they thought the guns should be returned directly to their owners without delay. Moreover, they knew that if they held the guns while waiting for Penn's word, then they could easily become the target of harassment, and without a fort or a regiment of the Black Watch to protect them, they surely would be unable to fend off the Black Boys' torment. Ultimately, unable to secure their custody according to his orders, Grant refused to release the weapons. His decision made the Black Boys all the more anxious to recapture them before troops carted them to Fort Pitt with the rest of their supplies.[19]

At 10:00 a.m., after receiving Grant's refusal to relinquish the arms, the Black Boys unleashed a daylight barrage on the fort. The fire was the strongest yet. Some shots lodged in the ramparts, while others penetrated the stockades, forcing the soldiers to take cover. Grant realized that he "had but little ammunition" and decided to hold his fire until the Black Boys launched an assault. The troops followed Grant's orders, crouching behind walls and under furniture, cowering under the onslaught of the colonial militia. During it all, the British troops held steadfast except for one sentry, who, after being nearly hit three times, offered a single defensive shot. At 1:00 p.m. a delegation headed by William McDowell, a justice of the peace who had managed to avoid alienating either side, approached the fort to mediate.[20]

"If you let me have the arms, they will remain in my house till such time as the governor would give orders about them," McDowell promised Grant.[21]

Grant, "much fatigued for want of sleep for two nights and two days before, owing to the rioters firing on the fort," finally gave in. He knew that if he refused, a full-blown battle might result, one that he feared he could lose. Grant opened the doors of the fort and negotiated a truce with the colonists that ended the rebellion. He made McDowell sign an agreement that he would hold the guns until Penn made his wishes known. But he also called on James Smith to end his harassment. Smith, knowing the guns were finally about to be transferred to civilian authorities and that Grant was about to leave anyway, agreed, signing a contract that bound him to pay an astronomical £500 to Grant if he was to "interrupt or insult any person or persons hereafter."

Grant, believing that the guns were "as safe with Mr. McDowell, as if I had taken them to Fort Pitt" and with Smith personally liable for any more assaults, finally handed over the property he had seized in March and watched the Black Boys disperse.[22]

Two hours later, troops from a neighboring fort arrived to help Grant evacuate Fort Loudon. Upon their arrival, they discovered that their mission had changed: they were now reinforcements to aid a defeated regiment. They provided Grant with moral support, helped his wearied troops pack their belongings, and then escorted Grant and his men west toward Fort Pitt. In the Black Boys' eyes, even though this was a planned departure, Grant's march bore the hallmarks of a retreat.[23]

The Black Boys' sense of victory increased when John Penn interceded a few weeks later. Penn sent a letter to William Smith and another justice that essentially blamed Grant for the troubles. While he ordered the justices to quell the "turbulent spirits" of the Black Boys, he also saw "no Reason that there should have been so much Formality used in returning [the guns] to the Owners, after the General had given Orders to his officers to deliver them up." Grant, Penn was implying, had escalated tensions by continuing to put unnecessary rules on the guns' return. And Penn made it clear that he took the side of the gun owners. It was, he wrote, "His Honours pleasure, that they be forthwith returned to their respective owners." With Fort Loudon evacuated, the guns returned, and Penn hamstrung by politics in the East, the Black Boys had achieved a new level of independence just as imperial officials basked in the glow of their successful dealings in Indian Country.[24]

Chapter 8

·—•—·

The Elusive Peace

1766–1768

Fort Oswego

July 4, 1766

Twelve years to the day after George Washington's battle at the forks of the Ohio River, which started the decade of war on the frontiers, Pontiac arrived at Fort Oswego, a British installation on the eastern shores of Lake Erie in western New York, to cement the peace he had made with Croghan through a more formal treaty with Sir William Johnson. When Pontiac entered the fort, he brought along representatives from the Potawatomis, Hurons, and Chippewas, groups that had fought to keep the British out of the Illinois Country. Hugh Crawford, the merchant who had traveled up to Fort Chartres in early 1765 only to be chased out, served as Pontiac's personal escort for the trip, a position Johnson had given Crawford at Croghan's urging. Crawford, it was hoped, could further cement his personal relationship with Pontiac, an investment that would pay dividends as traffic increased on the "open road" that would soon connect Indian Country to the British Empire.[1]

Since Croghan's departure the previous fall, Pontiac's prominence in Indian Country had grown greater. But tensions still lingered among Native groups who were wary at the prospect of peace, and some Native groups became suspicious of Pontiac's close relations with the British. Some even suggested he had become an agent for Great Britain. Before leaving Detroit with Crawford, for instance, Pontiac got into a brawl with other Indian chiefs about policy amid rumors that Pontiac was in the employ of Great Britain. Meanwhile, Pontiac was still suspicious of Great Britain's imperial intentions, which became clear as his entourage made its way to Oswego surrounded by the British military. At a pit stop at Fort Erie, near modern-day Ontario, for instance, they heard gunfire, which caused Pontiac to take cover out of fear that he had been led into a trap to murder him. The gunfire turned out to be nothing more than soldiers shooting fowl. But Pontiac's encounter with his peers in Detroit and with the British on the banks of Lake Erie reflected a situation that continued to be unstable as fear and distrust remained.[2]

At his meeting with Johnson, however, these anxieties were put aside. Johnson produced the peace pipe that Pontiac had given Croghan in Detroit, lit it, and shared it with others, a ritual to show that the war was now over. Johnson then used words to back up his actions.[3]

"I have opened the Gate, and made the Road, clear, smooth and easy for you," he announced.[4]

Johnson followed with a series of promises meant to assure Pontiac of Great Britain's commitment to coexistence on the Indians' terms. There would be, he said, a continued free and peaceful trade between Indians and Great Britain. He promised that the men assigned to oversee Indian relations in the new territory would be "men of honor and probity" who would "prevent abuses in trade, to hear your complaints, and such of them as they can not redress they are to lay before me." To show Great Britain's dedication to good communication, he pledged to send interpreters as well. As an even greater sign of imperial commitment to mutual respect, he offered to send blacksmiths to "repair your arms and implements." Johnson ended by asking that Pontiac and the other Indians forgive the violence of the frontier inhabitants and by reassuring him that the British Empire did not approve of these rash individuals' actions.[5]

Pontiac responded with enthusiasm. Promises of free trade, including arms and ammunition, showed the reciprocity that Indians had expected at the close of the Seven Years' War. Pontiac, "speak[ing] in the name of all the Nations to the Westward whom I command," extended his hand to Johnson in a sign of friendship. But he was also unwavering about his understanding of the relationship between Great Britain and the Indian groups in the Illinois Country. Colonists and other traders could not "straggle thro the woods," he reminded Johnson, but instead had to be confined to forts, where their actions could be watched. This was the realization of the vision Pontiac had long held, a contained and restrained British Empire that served Native interests.[6]

As the council drew to a close, both sides realized that that their visions were compatible and agreed to an alliance. Pontiac thanked Johnson for his promises and vowed to keep peace with the groups he oversaw. Johnson gave out four presents, reported by one historian to be silver medals for the chiefs to take home. Etched into each medal was a record of the peace they had just cemented: "a pledge of peace and friendship with Great Britain, confirmed in 1766." With these final gestures, the imperial vision of a stable Indian Country bound to the British Empire through trade and diplomacy had, much like Pontiac's vision of a restrained British presence, been realized—at least in theory.[7]

British Headquarters
New York

1766

From his perch in New York City, Thomas Gage saw the frontier rebellion in Pennsylvania as a minor squabble amid a new, triumphant moment for the Empire. To celebrate Croghan's success, he invited the proud diplomat to his headquarters for a private dinner. At the meeting, he soothed Croghan's anxiety about the destroyed goods, casting Croghan's potential illegal activity as a petty event that no longer concerned him. In fact, he confided to Croghan that he thought the root cause of the whole uproar was provincial politics in Pennsylvania, not the actions of Croghan or the traders, and that he was growing tired of John Penn's ineffectiveness.[8]

Gage's general outlook changed dramatically after Croghan's return. In the optimistic words that he wrote in November, unaware that the Black Boys were preparing to lay siege to Fort Loudon, the British Empire in North America sat "in perfect harmony with all the nations throughout the continent." The promise of peace finally let him address long-simmering policy concerns. As he observed to his superior in London, the military posts in North America were "scattered and divided, over this vast continent," an inefficiency that he worried might become a vulnerability should war break out again. Indians could more easily capture small forts, as Pontiac's War had shown, than well-fortified garrisons like Fort Detroit and Pitt. Centralizing his troops at large installations also gave him greater maneuverability if danger should arise. It also saved money. With peace in the offing, Gage could now, he noted to one of his British superiors, "take into consideration the multiplicity of forts . . . and to abandon as early as possible in the spring, as many of them shall be adviseable to abandon; in order to lessen expences, and to be able to collect a few of the troops, so widely dispersed, over an immense tract of country."[9]

By 1766, Gage had delivered on his promise, shuttering many small forts like Fort Loudon and reallocating his forces to a few important installations. By 1767, for instance, there were no forts in at least five colonies, and Pennsylvania, which had five forts in 1764, had only one in 1767 at Fort Pitt, the gateway to the West.[10]

Gage's superiors in London, especially Secretary of State Henry Conway, were pleased with the turn of events. Administrators across the ocean, whether Parliamentarians passing new revenue acts on the colonies or high-level appointees managing land regulations, continued to feel the weight of the national debt and directed men like Gage to reduce costs and streamline operations. Conway, for instance, responded to Gage's proposed fort closings with a ringing endorsement, declaring it "very advantageous," especially since the posts were a cost the Empire was "scarce able to bear."[11]

In this situation, Gage's approaches to peace and cost-cutting worked hand in hand. As he noted after learning of Croghan's success in November 1765, the treaties "presaged our future tranquility" in North America—but he also cautioned, "if we take pains to preserve it." A key part of his peacekeeping efforts was to show formerly hostile Indians that the British had the good intentions they promised around the treaty fires by reducing their military presence in the West, something that also, conveniently, reduced Gage's overhead expenses. But Gage didn't want to hand the regulation of trade completely over to colonial governments or make the West vulnerable to anarchy with the removal of posts. Instead, he wanted to continue the military's role in overseeing trade by limiting it to the large posts he retained.[12]

Ironically, even while Gage's plans called for greater centralization of power in specific locations, it also meant reducing the overall presence of imperial government and military force on colonial frontiers at the very moment when more of it was needed to curtail movements like the Black Boys. As Gage complained, "The reins of government are too loose to enforce an obedience to the laws" on colonial frontiers. But that problem wasn't just Gage's. He expected colonial governments to fill the governing void in these regions. If a colony couldn't keep up its end of this bargain, however, that could undermine the stability Gage sought for North America and the peace that Johnson had cemented.[13]

Pennsylvania Frontier

1766–1768

Meanwhile, as imperial visions of the Empire in the West came together and peace seemed at hand, things in the Conococheague got worse. Penn's alliance with frontier people began to crumble shortly after the return of the guns. Reports of William Smith's continued involvement with the Black Boys arrived on Penn's desk in early 1766. He finally had enough with his justice of the peace and recalled Smith's commission in February 1766. Penn also received stern orders from imperial officials to stop colonists from settling on Indian land. And in a rare moment of compromise, he and the Assembly agreed to pass one of the harshest anti-squatting laws ever: any illegal squatters occupying Indian lands could receive the death penalty. This law, it was hoped, would finally reduce the numbers of colonists taking lands in Indian Country, which could breed the same frustration that had led to Pontiac's War.[14]

The tipping point for Penn's break with his frontier colonists came with a brutal mass murder of Indians in 1768. On a cold winter night, Frederick Stump, a Pennsylvanian who had already been cited for squatting on Indian land, his German servant, and some Indians were enjoying the warm hearth of his cabin outside of Carlisle. There was drinking, gambling, and frivolity. Then there was murder. At some point in the night, a drunken Stump killed his Native American companions for reasons that remain unknown. In the sober morning air, he decided to hide his crime. He carted the bodies to a frozen creek, chipped a hole in the ice, and dropped his victims in. But he soon realized that these men probably had close relations in the area who would notice their absence. So he raced to their homes nearby, murdered all the women and children he found, and then burned their cabins down. All along the way, his servant John Eisenhauer helped him do his dirty work. It was a shocking crime.[15]

But what happened next was even more shocking to officials in Philadelphia. Things started out well for the government. After offering a large reward for Stump's arrest, a local militia enticed by the offer of pay found and arrested him. Newly confident officials considered bringing Stump to Philadelphia for trial because many in government circles feared his peers in Carlisle would acquit him. But then things went downhill. Before they could send Stump to Philadelphia, local events overtook them. After Stump had been placed in Carlisle's prison, popular opinion among frontier people began to turn in his favor. Fearing that a trial in Philadelphia would set a dangerous example, they formed a competing militia to spring him from jail. They marched into town, broke into the jail, and hid Stump in the woods, where he and his servant vanished. The militia may have operated under the banner of the Black Boys, because James Smith's memoirs make reference around this time to Black Boys activities of which he disapproved.[16]

John Penn came down hard on the Cumberland County officials. He sent a group of prominent Philadelphians to investigate the jailbreak. They blamed a combination of weak-kneed local justices and overwhelming popular support for Stump. Penn's opposition to Stump and his rescuers broke the alliance between the frontier people and Penn. As George Croghan noted after Stump's rescue, many colonists in the region were heard saying that "Governor Penn has turned

against us [the frontier] and takes part with the Indians," a statement
that confirms that frontier people had earlier felt a bond between themselves and Penn. It also highlights the driving political issue for frontier
people: fear of Indians. The breakdown of the governor's relationship with frontier people, however, meant that Gage's goals of better
law enforcement might be realized. A more forceful governor at odds
with the Black Boys might willingly enact reforms that would keep the
Empire's promises to its Native treaty partners. But it also meant that
colonists, freed from loyalty to their government, could become more
daring and confrontational.[17]

Johnson Hall
Outside Albany

1768

With the treaty at Oswego concluded, William Johnson and others in
charge of managing the Empire knew that their chief problem was no
longer in the Illinois Country. Instead, they turned their eyes to colonists
like Stump who continued to confront Native Americans, often in acts
fueled by a violent hatred that can only be described as racist. They also
threatened to push their settlements onto Native lands, breaking promises Johnson and other imperial officials had made to Native groups.
Johnson, however, had a plan to solve this problem. Since the 1760s,
Johnson had argued that he needed more money and more authority.
Imperial officials were aware of this need. In fact, they had created his
position as Superintendent of Indian Affairs for the Northern District
during the Seven Years' War as a step toward resolving issues aris-
ing from the decentralization of Indian diplomacy. In this new office,
they gave a single person who was responsible to the British Empire,
rather than a colonial government, oversight of diplomacy. Following

the Proclamation of 1763, Johnson called for greater centralization in a proposal to the Board of Trade. His plan required increased funds to keep trade flowing on the open road to Indian Country and more assistants like Croghan who could work closely with Indian groups to make sure they were happy. His proposal contained an additional innovative idea. He wanted to give these deputies the same powers as justices of the peace to regulate trade, therefore taking power away from unreliable local justices like William Smith and placing it in imperial hands. While colonists were likely unaware of this plan, and certainly would have opposed it, Johnson's plan received a warm welcome by the Board of Trade in 1764. The Board agreed with Johnson that the delegation of Indian trade and diplomacy to each colony was "one great cause of the distracted state of Indian Affairs."[18]

But then the penny-pinching began. High imperial officials in London worried about the costs of Johnson's expansive powers. He acknowledged the costs and proposed a tax on the Indian trade to fund his new measures, but administrators an ocean away weren't sure about its applicability. After postponing a decision for years, the Board of Trade ultimately granted colonial governors the powers to regulate their local trade—something they had originally rejected and something Johnson feared would incite the same intrigues and conflicts that had led to war earlier. But it seemed to make the most financial sense to decision-makers an ocean away.[19]

After coming to terms with this decision, Johnson developed an alternative solution. As colonists continued to press into Indian lands, threatening the peace accords Johnson had negotiated, he decided to draw a clearer boundary between colonial settlements and Indians. Since war had muddled the implementation of the original Proclamation Line of 1763, Johnson wanted a new treaty to establish a clear border that could also be a reset for Indian groups in the Greater Ohio Region. A new line that separated colonists from Indians, Johnson thought, would provide the stability that the frontiers of North America so desperately needed. The Board of Trade agreed and, in 1767, gave him permission to negotiate a treaty to establish a new border.[20]

On October 12, 1768, William Johnson convened a grand council at Fort Stanwix, then the heart of Iroquois Country and what is today Rome, New York. His plan was to use clear natural boundaries as a way to make a line more enforceable. For three weeks, Johnson and Iroquoian representatives negotiated. Finally, they agreed to use the Ohio River as the new boundary in the West. Land to the south and east of the Ohio River (West Virginia and Kentucky today), some of the most promising areas Croghan had scouted during his voyage, were now open to British settlements. The areas to the west and north of the river (Ohio and Illinois) remained Indian Country. Using the Ohio River as a line of demarcation reflected the imperial vision for a porous border necessary to promote trade and peace. While the river was a convenient boundary to separate colonial settlements from Indian Country, it was also a waterway for goods and people to flow on and across.[21]

There were, however, two convoluted stories hidden behind the clear border drawn on a map. First, there was the absence of important signatures on the treaty that created this line. Shawnee and Delaware representatives had attended the conference along with the Iroquois, but they refused to acknowledge the new line's southern and western borders, claiming it intruded on their sacred ancestral homeland. Johnson chose to ignore their claims to the territory, and he had good reason. The British Empire had long privileged the Iroquois over these other groups. They saw themselves in the Iroquois: a rising imperial power that had conquered territorial rivals. They considered the Delawares and Shawnees deferential subsidiaries to the Iroquois, much as imperial officials saw the colonies. Johnson had ingratiated himself with the Iroquois, even living with a prominent Iroquois woman, and it was with them that he had the most influence. But even if Johnson could justify his exclusion of the Delaware and Shawnee, it was a poor political decision. Like the colonists challenging the British Empire on the frontiers and in the seaports, these other Native groups felt excluded from the political process, and this resentment would breed unrest.[22]

Second, there was the issue of land speculation. The Crown had offered land in place of cash as a way to repay traders and military officers who were owed back pay for their service in the Seven Years' War. The land payments operated like a futures market, with people buying and selling shares of land that no one fully possessed, with some, like George Washington, buying up massive amounts in anticipation that the Empire would eventually open the territory for settlement. Soon some of these large owners combined to form land companies that planned to develop the land and sell or rent it to new colonists for a hefty profit. The Treaty of Fort Stanwix confirmed many of these patents, creating a potential windfall for many speculators.[23]

William Johnson and his trusted deputy George Croghan were among those enjoying the most benefit. Croghan personally received 200,000 acres, making him one of the largest landowners in all of British North America. Croghan's grant was, as usual, built on shady dealings. Croghan had long claimed that he had purchased 200,000 acres from the Iroquois in the late 1740s, but this private sale was unrecognized by all colonial governments because individual colonists weren't allowed to make direct purchases of land from Indians. According to imperial regulations, Native groups could only sell land to colonial governments at official treaties; then the colonial governments could resell the land to colonists through a process run by land offices, government surveyors, and the like. At Fort Stanwix, Johnson wanted to reward his trusted agent for his good service, so he used the Treaty to turn his illegal private purchase into a legitimate one. During the Treaty negotiations, Iroquois representatives reaffirmed their previous sale to Croghan, and by making it part of the treaty they validated the terms (or so Croghan hoped). The Iroquois also had advised the King that if he refused to recognize Croghan's lands, then Croghan should "get as much from the King somewhere else, as he fairly bought it."[24]

Some historians have faulted Johnson for these grants, arguing that he put profit before peace. But others say that the grants to certain colonists were necessary to win over the support of colonial elites and the governments they ran. The Crown had promised the lands, and Johnson was simply putting an end to the uncertainty about them. Moreover, Johnson's grant to Croghan, while appearing to be a gift of favoritism, was meant as a form of compensation. Johnson also anticipated that this land would be sold and developed someday, so giving control of that future to people he trusted (like Croghan) or to organized outfits (like the land companies owned by traders and military officers) gave him some control over expansion. This top-down, public-private development of western lands was the same tactic the United States' federal government adopted later, in the 1790s, as well.[25]

The compromises Johnson made, however, doomed the stability of his boundary line. First, the Board of Trade rejected Johnson's grants to speculators, arguing that they betrayed the imperial plan to limit settlement and that they would interfere with Indian claims. Nonetheless, competing land companies, empowered by the temporary grants, jostled for a foothold, hoping to reverse that decision. Squatters, meanwhile, challenged the companies' rights and ignored imperial boundaries, leading to a further breakdown of authority in the region. And, of course, the porous boundary between Indian Country and the colonies that was essential to the British Empire's stability led to more violent encounters between colonists and their Indian neighbors. The creation of the boundary line, which Johnson hoped would satisfy the colonists, only made the West's problems worse—and in the case of the land grants, created new ones.[26]

Chapter 9

———◦•◦———

Disintegration

1769

Bedford, Pennsylvania

The Conococheague

September 1769

O n September 28, 1769, sensational news appeared in the *Pennsylvania Gazette*. The Black Boys were patrolling the highways near Fort Pitt and harassing traders again. Worse, their "principal ringleader," James Smith, was accused of murdering an innocent man on the road outside Bedford, a bustling frontier town between the Conococheague and Fort Pitt. The article reported that local officials feared that vigilantes were gathering to free Smith from their jail, so the government transported him to a more fortified jail in Carlisle for trial. The report was right. A group formed to rescue him but failed. Later newspaper accounts, however, informed eastern readers that the situation had taken a turn for the worse. It appeared that Smith had no need of a rescue because a local jury was ready to acquit him.[1]

As with so much else that surrounds the Black Boys, details of the crime are clouded by the retaliatory accusations of those who opposed Smith and those who supported him and his Black Boys. The truth vanished in the smoke of gunfire on that September day. But we can piece together the general outlines of the murder and the events surrounding it. These fragments show that the imperial crisis on the frontiers of the British Empire was continuing.[2]

The story of James Smith's murder trial begins sometime in August 1768. As fear of an Indian war increased after the Stump murders, a group of former Black Boys began inspecting traders traveling along public roads once again, possibly trying to limit the flow of ammunition in anticipation of war. There was something different about this group's behavior, however, as Smith distanced himself from them, claiming to disapprove of their actions. Perhaps they aided in Stump's rescue, but there's no confirming evidence. In any case, outside of Bedford on August 16, this new group destroyed items they considered contraband. Three weeks later, on September 9, magistrates in Bedford arrested two men suspected of raiding traders' goods and sent them to a local fort for safekeeping.[3]

Many people worried that the government was making examples of the detained men. Smith sprang to action when he learned of the arrests, believing the men, like the guns before, had been unlawfully seized and held. They were, he said, held "in confinement by arbitrary or military power"—words similar to the ones colonists in the seaports used to describe new imperial policies that housed troops in their cities and created new admiralty courts that abolished the right to a trial by one's peers for those accused of smuggling oceanic trade.[4]

Smith hatched a plan to free the men. It was so daring that he told no one about it, not even the loyal supporters who followed him into action. First, he raised a small company of his most trusted men, about eighteen in all. Then he recruited William Thompson, "a man whom [he] could trust and who lived there [Bedford]," to act as a spy.[5]

As Smith and his band traveled on the public roads to Bedford in the middle of the day, they displayed their determination to raid the fort. "We told those whom we met, that we were going to take the fort," Smith later recounted. Soldiers at the fort soon heard of Smith's boasts, and while they increased their guard, they also "made game of the notion of eighteen men coming to rescue the prisoners." But Smith's bragging hid his real plan from plain view. As the guards laughed at his bravado, he was lulling them into a false sense of security. Experience had taught him that small, swift groups held tremendous power in the irregular warfare fought on American frontiers if they kept the element of surprise, and Smith still had a surprise in store for Fort Bedford.[6]

As the sun set, Smith and his crew camped in an open field along a river about fourteen miles from Bedford. Because the encampment was far from town, the fort's commandant figured that Smith would start the raid late the following day. Smith's men also thought that was the plan. But Smith knew otherwise. Part of his plan was to hide in plain sight "by stealing a march." At eleven o'clock at night, he roused his men and told them it was time. They shuffled through the woods at about five miles per hour, meeting Thompson at a secret location outside the fort in the early morning hours.[7]

"Is the gate open?" Smith asked.[8]

"It's shut, but they will open it as usual at daylight, as they apprehend no danger," Thompson confided.[9]

Armed with this information, Smith planned his next move. At daylight, as the gates opened and the soldiers were just waking, he would strike. Smith sent Thompson back to the area to continue his scouting, while he and his men hid along the muddy banks of a river about a hundred yards from the fort. As the sun began to warm the dewy ground, a dense fog blanketed the area, giving Smith and his men even greater cover.[10]

Thompson soon appeared through the mist with word that the

gates had opened and that the three morning guards were busy enjoying their "morning dram." Smith knew now was the time to strike.
He told Thompson to go ahead of them, enter the fort as he usually
did, and stand near the store of guns. Smith and his men would follow
close behind him. They would grab the boozy guards while Thompson
seized the weapons during the commotion.[11]

Shielded by the morning haze, Smith and his men scrambled to
within yards of the fort before the sentinels noticed them. By that time,
it was too late. The sentries offered two weak warning shots before
being overrun by the Black Boys. Within minutes, the fort had capitu-
lated. The Black Boys found one of the blacksmiths and "compelled"
him to break their friends out of their chains. Then they left. Looking
back on the event in 1799, Smith felt there was something momentous,
even revolutionary, in what the Black Boys accomplished that autumn
day. It was, Smith wrote with pride, "the first British fort in America
that was taken by what they [the British] called American rebels."[12]

Smith's escapade once again made colonists in the region bolder.
Men calling themselves the Black Boys continued to search travelers
on the road. Robert Callender, the head of the cargo that had spurred
the first Black Boys assault in 1765, was still plying his trade, and in late
September he learned that the Black Boys were targeting him again.
Callender made a different decision this time. Instead of forging ahead,
as his men had done in 1765, he went straight to the authorities, who
sent men out to end the Black Boys' harassment. They arrested three
suspected Black Boys, but James Smith couldn't be found. Later that
day, a traveler ran into Smith on a small side road outside of Bedford and, knowing he was wanted, raced back to Bedford to alert the
authorities. The magistrates, thinking Smith's obscure route indicated
complicity with the Black Boys, sent out another crew to capture him.[13]

Within hours, an innocent man would lay dead, and James Smith
would be in irons. But what caused this deadly turn of events is uncer-

tain. A close reading of the accounts, however, suggests that Smith's claim to innocence may be true. We know that the men from Bedford confronted Smith about his intentions and that Smith claimed he was on his way to survey some land he had recently purchased—a claim many questioned at the time and that cannot be validated. In any case, Smith's pursuers rejected his explanation. Instead, they drew their pistols and demanded he surrender or he "was a dead man."[14]

Smith took their threat seriously and was ready to defend himself. When Robert George, one of his assailants, "snapped" his pistol at Smith (that is, he pulled the trigger on his unloaded gun in an attempt to intimidate Smith), another of Smith's foes cocked his weapon, grabbed one of Smith's traveling companions named Johnson to use as a human shield, and looked ready to shoot at Smith. Smith backed off and aimed his rifle at the men. In a flash, two guns went off; one was Smith's, the other belonged to his assailant. When the smoke cleared, a man named Johnson, who by all accounts was a random traveler who had simply joined Smith for company somewhere along the road, lay bleeding. He would soon be dead.[15]

In the confusion that followed, Smith's attackers slapped chains around his wrists and brought him to the Bedford jail. Then the finger-pointing began. The men accused Smith of firing the fatal shot. Smith said his rifle was aimed elsewhere. The Bedford magistrates, who were no friends of Smith, held an inquest composed, Smith later said, of his personal enemies and allies of the traders. They quickly indicted Smith, accusing him of "willful murder."[16]

Government officials in Bedford knew that the Black Boys had the ability to organize a successful rescue and that such an attempt was likely since the government now held their "ringleader" in chains. Deciding that their jail was too weak, they deported Smith to the stronger jail in Carlisle, using the cover of darkness and traveling on back roads and small paths to avoid discovery. The jailors knew the value of their new prize and placed "heavy irons" on Smith's hands and feet to prevent him from getting away.[17]

The strong irons were a smart move. The Black Boys were convinced that their leader would be a victim of a phony trial because, as Smith later recounted, "the government was so enraged at me." On September 23, the Black Boys appeared in the streets of Carlisle, prepared for yet another assault on a government stronghold, although this time without their leader. Instead, their mission was to do what Smith had done for them: free a prisoner they felt was being held illegally. Soon after the Black Boys arrived, rumors of a larger group marching toward the jail reached Carlisle, with some jailors speculating that more than three hundred people were descending on the town to save Smith. These groups felt that Smith "would not get a fair trial" and therefore needed their support to free him.[18]

The attempted rescue put Smith in a difficult position. He knew he could easily escape, but a jailbreak would imply guilt. Sure, he could disappear into the North Carolina woods and start a new life as he had warned Charles Grant he could, but Smith was now a leading figure in the region and would give up much by having to start all over again. Even if he could live free in the backwoods of another colony, accusations of murder would eventually find him because this world was still very small. Instead, Smith put his faith in the court system. In fact, he had rejected some of his early behavior, writing that after seizing Grant both sides "got out of the channel of civil law entirely," something he came to regret. From the episode he had learned "of the absolute necessity of the civil law to govern mankind." Therefore, when the Black Boys approached the Carlisle jail on September 23 ready to spring their leader, Smith promised the sheriff he wouldn't flee and asked to have the irons removed from his wrists so he could convince his men to disband. The sheriff, apparently convinced that he had no other choice, agreed.[19]

"Withdraw from the jail, and return in peace," Smith commanded. And they did, and Smith's jailors kept the irons off for the rest of his incarceration.[20]

Smith's behavior revealed some of the principles that guided his leadership. As he became more prominent, he also became more thoughtful. Having learned from his earlier action, Smith now wanted to strengthen the legal system, not weaken it. Of course, part of his decision-making was probably based on knowing that he had strong support from his peers who would sit on the trial jury. But still, his desire to be tried showed that he wasn't simply a lawless frontiersman and that the frontier people weren't an unthinking, lawless mass. Indeed, their previous inspection activities and the legal arguments used to justify it all show their desire for order within frontier society. It's just that the Black Boys wanted that order to reflect *their values*, not those of an unfeeling eastern elite or an imperial government that seemed to ignore their concerns. They wanted to control local legal institutions in order to make laws that matched their own beliefs.

As James Smith languished in prison, William Smith was again using his connections and knowledge of the law to rescue his brother-in-law through legal means. William Smith claimed that the initial inquest on the body was hastily and partially done. Insisting that a more thorough autopsy and investigation could produce forensic evidence that proved Smith's innocence, he called on the coroner, William Denny, to re-investigate. Giving in to the pressure, Denny convened a second coroner's inquest that was composed of men William Smith would later describe as those "whose candour, probity, and honesty, is unquestionable." Of course, the party opposed to the Black Boys had a different opinion: the new group, they complained, was "composed chiefly from people about Fort Loudon and from the Great Cove"—home, they noted, to Smith's greatest allies. William Smith also appears to have played some role in the proceedings, something else Smith's opponents noted was "uncommon."[21]

While holding a second inquest on a body was unusual for the time, what truly distinguished this investigation was the attempt to use forensic science to prove Smith's innocence. After digging up the dead man's body, the investigators discovered new evidence. The bullet hole in his shirt showed signs of gunpowder around its edges. The previous inquest had ignored, or been unaware of, this detail. The second investigation took new testimony that paid particular attention to the distance people stood from the victim. One of the key witnesses was an enemy of Smith's who, nonetheless, testified under oath that Smith was standing about twenty-three feet from the murdered man when he fired. The new jury then conducted its own experiment to determine Smith's guilt or evidence. They re-created the scene and fired a rifle at a shirt exactly twenty-three feet away two times, once with the wind to the shooter's back and once in his face. In both cases, no gunpowder residue appeared on the target. The report therefore concluded that the fatal shot must have come from someone closer to Johnson, most likely Smith's assailant who fired his pistol. Although already indicted by a grand jury, Smith could use this new information as evidence in his trial.[22]

These new findings, however, did little to ease Smith's predicament. Once the judges convened the official trial in Carlisle, it was clear that the government planned to make an example of him. The presiding magistrates refused to admit certain evidence, tried to intimidate the jury, and otherwise "severely prosecuted" Smith. Smith knew his fate was uncertain. William Smith expressed the concern when he said, "The proceedings against Smith were truly unlawful and tyrannical, perhaps unparalleled by any instance in a civilized nation." Newspapers reported on the controversial case, and many Pennsylvanians anxiously awaited news of the jury's verdict. James Smith, probably with help from William, developed a strong defense. First, he argued that he had fired in self-defense, which was corroborated by Robert George's testimony that he had in fact snapped a pistol at Smith. That, along with "strong presumptive [evidence]," combined to make a compelling case. In December, four months after his arrest, the jury announced Smith "Not Guilty." Smith walked away from Carlisle a free man.[23]

The decision so shocked the judges that, before releasing Smith, they told the large audience who had assembled to hear the verdict that none of the jurors "should ever hold any office above a constable" because they clearly had failed to maintain the law. The crowd ignored the judges' directive. Many jurors went on to serve in high elective offices. Smith himself was elected to be a county commissioner of Bedford the very next year. It seemed that Smith, the enemy of the colonial government, still had the strong support of his neighbors. In fact, as Smith and his supporters were learning, if they focused their energy at the ballot box, rather than on rebellions, they could elect men like Smith to local offices and find better ways to assert their views through institutions of government. It was a powerful principle that many people throughout the colonies were starting to accept.[24]

Ignoring the instruction of powerful judges appointed by the governor, springing men from jail, and electing enemies of the colonial government to local offices were all signs that the colony's frontiers were asserting their own political independence. Through it all, James Smith maintained his prominence, and the Black Boys movement began to take over more local government institutions as Smith and his supporters served on various bodies. By the 1770s, securely in control of their local governments, people like Smith were poised for even more radical action.

County Courthouse
Carlisle, Pennsylvania

December 14, 1769

After publishing several articles on Smith's murder trial, many of which carried heated opinions, only a brief notice of his acquittal appeared in the December 14 edition of the *Pennsylvania Gazette*. The report also included the conviction of Cornelius Donnahy for murdering William King, a fellow colonist. While Smith's acquittal wasn't what his opponents wanted, the process it took alongside Donnahy's conviction showed that law still functioned on the frontier.

The *Gazette* also carried news of another verdict in Carlisle that day. And it was one that showed the darker side of the movement for independence on the frontiers. Peter Read was acquitted of the murder of an Indian man—and not just any Indian. Read had shot Young Seneca George, the son of one of the most respected Native American leaders in the region who was a close ally and friend of the colony. Earlier, in July, Young Seneca George was traveling down the Susquehanna River with friends on a fishing expedition. At some point, they set up a small camp on the shores of the river as a base of operation. One night, a canoe appeared on the water, this one carrying colonists. The Indians on the shore saw a man stand in the rear of the colonists' boat and raise a long object. A shot rang out from the canoe, and Young Seneca George slumped, killed instantly by a rifle shot.[25]

The government, primarily through the governor, took its usual methods to address Native American alarm at the violence by holding treaties and providing diplomatic condolences. Officials also began to worry that this murder, combined with Stump's murderous rampage, might tip the fragile peace back into war. So they were determined to prosecute the murderer, both to show Indians that Pennsylvania could protect them and to send a message to colonists that perpetrators would be severely punished. The problem, as Read's acquittal made clear, was that local juries were inclined to protect their neighbors and reinforce local prejudices about Indians.

Officials in charge of managing the frontiers and keeping the peace recognized this form of protest and knew the challenge it posed. A common refrain began to appear in the writing of colonial and imperial officials. Colonists considered Indian murderers, they noted to one another, as doing a "meritorious act." As John Penn wrote of his own people, "No jury in any of our frontier counties will ever condemn a man for killing an Indian. They do not consider it in the light of murder, but as a meritorious act. This is unfortunate but I know of no remedy." The Virginia governor agreed, writing, "I have found by experience, it is impossible to bring anybody to justice for the murder of an Indian, who takes shelter among our back inhabitants. It is among those people, looked on as a meritorious action." Thomas Gage agreed, too, observing, "All the people of the frontiers from Pennsylvania to Virginia inclusive, openly avow, that they will never find a man guilty of murther for killing an Indian."[26]

The use of popular justice to enforce local values and to challenge the policies of distant governments was widespread in the years before American independence. Colonists in seaports used friendly juries to protect smugglers who broke the hated trade regulations Parliament placed on them. Frontier communities used the same tactics around issues dealing with defense and the Indian trade. Even though the issues were different, the colonists' intent was the same. In the seaports and on the frontiers, colonists wanted their actions to show the government what they believed was appropriate policy. And the more ignored they felt, the more they looked to themselves for solutions.[27]

As a nation, we often cast the words and actions of the Sons of Liberty and the regular colonists who took to the streets to challenge

British officials as defiant demonstrations of patriotic zeal against an arbitrary government—and they were. But when we look west, to the murder and apparent mayhem taking place there, historians and the layperson alike tend to see a society trending toward anarchy and lawlessness. One historian has recently argued that the frontier regions returned to a raw state of nature in which civil society collapsed, only to be rebuilt with the Revolution. That argument ignores the words of the frontier rebels themselves, who also saw their behavior as defiant acts of patriotism. As the Black Boys' song demonstrated, they believed they served the interests of their fellow colonists by fighting Indians and that corrupt officials and traders were the truly disloyal individuals whose pursuit of self-interest failed the public good and poorly served the Crown. Some Black Boys even called their roaming band of men the Loyal Volunteers, since in their view they were providing the type of protection the King promised to all of his subjects.[28]

In addition, the Black Boys showed a level of sophistication that was anything but anarchical, and in some respects was superior to the Sons of Liberty. Where the Sons of Liberty benefited from the close and well-knit society of urban living, these frontier rebels had to organize a movement across a much larger territory with difficult terrain and scattered populations. In 1765, for instance, the Black Boys organized inspection programs that stretched two hundred miles from the Susquehanna River to Fort Pitt, indicating a level of coordination that the Sons of Liberty still lacked. And while the British Empire struggled to obtain revenue from its North American colonists, the Black Boys successfully raised funds from their neighbors to support their operations.

Moreover, and most important for our story, is that the ideas behind this frontier movement were more radical than what the eastern rebels were doing at this point. The Sons of Liberty aimed to stop new laws and regulations from taking effect. They were trying to maintain the status quo by *preserving* their liberties. The Black Boys were certainly upset with their colonial government, but they were equally angry at imperial policies that seemed to betray the fundamental promise the Empire had made to its subjects: the right to be free from fear so they could enjoy their British liberty. The fear of Indians had become so profound and pervasive among frontier people that their view of Indians had turned, as evidenced by Stump and others, into a violent racism that aimed to exclude Native Americans from the protections of government. Their actions therefore were attempts at redefining who belonged to the Empire and who didn't. As George III stated in his Proclamation of 1763, the Empire gave Indian allies the same legal protection as any British subject.

Frontier colonists rejected this idea. Instead, through their words and deeds they implemented their own sense of who were members of the Empire and who were outside of it—essentially, who could receive the protection of Great Britain and who could enjoy liberty. They were attempting to create a new state on the frontiers, one that formed a new civil society based on the exclusion of Indians—something that seems highly uncivil to modern readers today. Revolution and race thus intermixed on the frontiers of America to fuse into a movement that upset the stability of Empire. As long as the Black Boys persisted, imperial officials would be unsuccessful in their attempt to integrate Native Americans into the Empire and maintain peace on North America's frontiers.

Cahokia
Indian Country

April 20, 1769

With Pontiac's peace, the power struggle in the Illinois Country seemed to be over, and Charlot Kaské had lost. Kaské tried to rally groups for a final assault on the British, a last-ditch attempt to maintain his relevance, but he couldn't muster enough support. Recognizing his weakening power, Kaské retreated further into the interior of North America with his family and remaining supporters. No written record exists of where he went or what he did. Pontiac, meanwhile, had established himself as the chief representative of the Indians in the West to Great Britain. No longer a fearsome military leader, he was now a smooth, determined diplomat.[29]

At first, Pontiac's vision seemed successful. Immediately following the peace at Oswego, stability returned to Indian Country. The British, for the most part, kept up their promises, and Indians enjoyed trade. But as time passed, British colonists continued to push further west. And violence, like the murder of Young Seneca George, became widespread on the borders between the British colonies and Indian Country. While Native Americans around the Great Lakes avoided such direct violence, many knew of it and worried about their future. Their faith in Great Britain and the promises it had made to them began to wane.

Ironically, peace also weakened Pontiac's stature. War united different Indian groups, but peace meant that a unique leader like Pontiac was now unnecessary. Pontiac, nonetheless, continued to travel throughout the region, a respected warrior hoping to reclaim his position. Controversy rather than power seemed to attach to him. The creeping hand of British colonization that many Native groups felt also undermined him.

Some Native leaders even saw him as a burden that they wanted to get rid of. These rivals seized their opportunity on April 20, 1769, when Pontiac visited an Indian village near Cahokia, modern-day St. Louis. Although the details of what happened are murky, Pontiac was found in the village's street with his head bashed from a club and bleeding from a mortal stab wound. A Peoria warrior, it was said, committed the deed to avenge Pontiac's supposed assault on his uncle years earlier. Perhaps, some historians have speculated, the insult occurred at the brawl outside of Detroit in 1766 before Pontiac left for his treaty at Oswego. Even though Pontiac had tried to unite Indians in forceful defense of their homeland, first through military means and then through diplomacy, his murder at the hands of a competing group in 1769 signaled the ongoing strife in Indian Country as Native peoples, like British colonists, struggled with the world remade by the Seven Years' War.[30]

Chapter 10

———•———

Imperial Failure

British Headquarters
New York City

1772

Thomas Gage became more cynical and frustrated as order on the frontiers and seaports appeared to disintegrate. By the early 1770s, he had had enough of the Americans. His former optimism about North America's future, which had led to leniency toward colonists, had changed into pessimism so deep that Gage now scorned all colonists. His dour mood made him re-think his entire approach to the colonies, including the troublesome seaports. As he saw rebels growing ever bolder, Gage concluded that the Empire had acted with too much weakness in the 1760s when it should have shown strength. The way he saw it, Parliament's decision to cancel the Stamp Act and subsequent Townshend Duties should have won appreciation from colonists. Instead, these signs of kindness had, Gage noted, only encouraged the unruly Americans to become "more daring and licentious." By the 1770s, he had changed his accommodating approach. "Nothing can be done but by forcible means," he wrote, so he sent troops into the cities to assert imperial strength.[1]

In the West, Gage also attempted to compel colonial obedience to the Crown, but he tried a different approach. Whereas he wanted to expand imperial power in the cities in order to crush the growing resistance, in the West he wanted to remove it in order to leave colonists without the reassuring presence of the British military. Only then, he felt, would the colonists appreciate how important the Empire was to them. Therefore, in 1772 he ordered the evacuation of Fort Pitt, the strongest symbol of imperial authority in the area. Gage had considered abandoning Fort Pitt for years, but he kept it staffed because of its link to the Illinois Country. By 1772, however, its usefulness as a waypoint no longer existed as Fort Detroit rose in significance, which made the installations along the Ohio and Mississippi Rivers, like Fort Chartres, less essential to trade and imperial plans. Now imperial officials told Gage it was time to follow his earlier instincts.[2]

Indeed, Fort Pitt's existence may have even hindered the Empire's plans for peace. Fort Pitt, Gage worried, gave unruly colonists the confidence that they could murder Indians and that the British military was there to defend them. Without it, however, they would be forced to behave. As he explained to his superiors, "The Indians at their backs, will always keep them quiet." He almost wished for a conflict between colonists and Indians, figuring such an event might force colonists to be more obedient. If frontier settlers "force the Savages into Quarrells by using them ill," Gage wrote, "let them feel the Consequences, we shall be out of the Scrape."[3]

Gage's new strategy wasn't a novel idea. Such a tactic had been suggested throughout the imperial crisis on the frontier. Virginia's governor, for instance, wrote to Gage in 1766 advocating just such a policy. Virginia, like Pennsylvania, experienced a series of Indian murders that went unpunished. That colony's governor, Francis Fauquier, got so frustrated that he suggested, "Perhaps leaving them [colonists] to the mercy of Indians may be the best if not the only way to restrain them." At the time, Gage, still hopeful of achieving peace through different means, rejected the idea.[4]

Gage's orders to raze Fort Pitt received a warm welcome among Indians living in the region. Croghan let his superiors know that "I don't find that the Indians are any way uneasy att the Troops being removed." David McClure, a minister traveling deep in the Ohio River valley on an evangelical mission, was with a group of Indian warriors when news arrived that the troops were leaving Fort Pitt. In his journal he recorded the "joy" the Indians showed at the news. They also told him of their "extreme resentment at the encroachments of the white people, on their hunting ground, and extending their settlements to the Ohio." For Native Americans in the region, the removal of this symbol of European power and sovereignty meant that they had achieved a new level of independence in the Ohio Country.[5]

But the response among colonists was much less enthusiastic. When David McClure returned to Fort Pitt soon after observing Native responses to the fort's coming closure, he stood with the other colonists and watched as British troops dismantled the fort. One afternoon, he came across an officer supervising operations. Their exchange revealed the nature of the crisis of empire on the frontiers.

"What's the reason of your destroying the fort, so necessary to the safety of the frontier?" McClure inquired.

"The Americans will not submit to the British Parliament, and they may now defend themselves," the officer replied. His answer, evoking parliamentary power and the rights of protection owed to loyal subjects, also showed that the frontiers factored into the imperial crisis in the same way as the seaports did. These disparate regions were considered alike in the thinking of men like Gage and his subordinates.[6]

The problem was that Gage's new plan to force colonists into submission failed to generate the deference he expected. In fact, it had the opposite effect. The abandonment of Fort Pitt only confirmed colonists' worst suspicions about their imperial overseers, leaving them further disillusioned with the British Empire. The officer's exchange, versions of which circulated throughout the region, proved to frontier people that the Crown was breaking the foundational contract between subject and monarch. The King's fundamental duty was to provide protection to his subjects on the frontiers, in exchange for which they offered their loyalty. By removing his protection, the King left his subjects on the frontiers feeling unprotected.

While Gage and others hoped this sense of vulnerability would make colonists feel a renewed obligation to the Crown, in truth, it only galvanized the frontier people's opinion that the Crown was betraying them. As Benjamin Franklin warned imperial officials in a caustic editorial published in a number of newspapers, if imperial officials wanted to "strengthen an opinion that you are unfit to govern [colonists]," they should "send armies into their country . . . but instead of garrisoning their forts on their frontiers with those troops to prevent incursions, demolish those forts, and order the troops into the heart of the country."[7] With the departure of British troops in 1772, frontier colonists now knew that they could only depend on themselves and that the Empire was, as far as they were concerned, a paper tiger that refused to provide the protection they demanded. As a result, frontier colonists asserted even greater independence. Indeed, those on the frontiers were independent of the Empire well before those in Philadelphia decided to declare their independence in 1776.[8]

Redstone Creek
Near Fort Pitt

1772

Like Johnson and Gage, George Croghan knew the nature of the imperial crisis on the frontiers. He, however, proposed a very different solution to control increasingly independent frontier people. By the 1770s,
Croghan had resigned from the Indian Department, moved west to a
small community near Fort Pitt, and taken on a new project. As was
usual with Croghan, he hoped his plan would enrich himself and serve
the Empire's interests. His idea was to create a new colony in the West
called Vandalia in the area of modern-day West Virginia. A colony
entirely located in the West, he thought, was the only way to establish
the stability and order the Empire was so desperately trying to find.
To get his plan moving, he convinced many of the elite former officers
and traders who felt that the Empire owed them for their service in
the Seven Years' War to join in this bold venture. Basically, he wanted
to create a massive land company—a conglomerate of all competing
ones—that would have a royal colony attached to it.[9]

 Croghan came up with a way to strengthen his prospects by giving
shares in the colonial venture to some of the most influential men in
England. These included several members of the King's Privy Council
and Thomas Walpole, the nephew of one of the most important prime
ministers in British history and a leading Parliamentarian in his own
right. Vandalia also had American advocates stationed in England,
including Samuel Wharton, formerly of Baynton, Wharton, and Morgan, the trading firm whose goods the Black Boys had destroyed, and
Benjamin Franklin, who had been sent to London to lobby for the interests of the colonies. Wharton himself had relocated to London to seek
compensation for the traders whose businesses were hurt by war.[10]

At first, it looked like Croghan's strategy was destined for success. In 1772, at about the same time the British evacuated Fort Pitt, the Privy Council, which was stacked with new shareholders in Vandalia, quickly approved of the colony—a truly remarkable decision. Unfortunately for Croghan, the victory was short-lived. Soon counter-claimants took the company to court, arguing that it didn't have rights to the land, and a change of administration rescinded the approval of the new colony.[11]

Croghan's scheme has often been cast as an eighteenth-century insider-trading scam. But this view misinterprets the world in which Croghan lived. He was simply operating within an imperial system in which financial interests and public policies went hand in hand. He was also operating in an empire that was increasingly outsourcing colonial efforts to private entities—such as the East India Company in India, which was a corporation that took over many of the responsibilities of governance on the Indian subcontinent. Like Croghan's Vandalia project, the East India Company's largest stockholders included many prominent officials and Parliamentarians.[12]

Characterizing Croghan's motives as simple profit-seeking also ignores the reason behind his action. Croghan's plan for winning supporters shows how well he understood human nature. He knew that the best way to induce people to stay committed to such a bold venture was to promise them lucrative rewards. He gave shares to wealthy friends because he wanted the most elite men in the Empire to be invested in the colony's success. These men who possessed political power, and not the hardscrabble frontiersmen, would create a stable social order.

No one at the time had a problem with the theoretical idea of Vandalia or its governing structure. Instead, the colony's real problem was its location. Imperial officials had long debated the merits of a new interior colony and, except for that temporary decision in 1772, decided that it undermined the interest of the Empire. In contrast, the East India Company, stationed halfway around the world, served the Empire's

mercantilist goals because it held a monopoly on the much-sought-
after tea produced in India. But imperial officials worried that Vandalia would turn colonists away from oceanic trade with their mother
country. A new colony, these strategists in London theorized, would
lead new settlers to spread out across the continent, which would cause
their colonial seaports to become manufacturing centers that refined
the colony's raw materials, rather than shipping hubs, thereby under-
mining the Empire's mercantilist foundation. An inland colony was,
the London-based officials feared, a recipe for American independence
at the very time they were trying to make colonists more dependent on
Great Britain.[13]

Croghan heard the arguments and disagreed. He felt that these
distant bureaucrats misunderstood American life, and he let them know
it. He warned them that their fears of American independence would
come to pass if they *refused* to create Vandalia. An inland colony, he
argued, would instead save their mercantile empire. In a private letter to Samuel Wharton, who was lobbying for the cause in London,
Croghan outlined his argument. He claimed that colonists were land
hungry and that by having access to a new colony they would continue
to lead a dispersed, agricultural lifestyle that exported natural resources
and imported manufactures. If the Crown rejected Vandalia and limited the colonists' settlement to the east, however, people would crowd
together on the seacoasts, thereby increasing the amount of free labor
available and encouraging urban growth and manufacturing. He wrote
to Wharton in 1771 in the rough spelling of a self-educated eighteenth-
century man:

> I know some there are who pretended to Say People [seated] so far
> from the Sea Must [Naturally] Manufacture themselves, which is
> hurtful to the Commerce of Great Britain, Butt there those that
> say so know little of the policy of Americans, whose predominant

passion is to realise an estate and as its easily gott Labour will be always high, as No Man that can obtain [property] for himself, will Labour for another, itt must apear to Every person the Least acquainted with America that Confining the Kings Subjects within the old Colonys must soon ablidge [them] to make every thing they can for thire own use, which [they] will not think of if they have Liberty to [obtain] property att a Distance.[14]

Croghan's arguments made little headway in 1772. But he persisted. Finally, in the spring of 1775, as shots were exchanged between colonists and redcoats on the Lexington Green outside Boston, the Privy Council approved of Vandalia. They postponed implementing it, however, until "after hostilities, which had then commenced between Great Britain and the United Colonies, should cease." Needless to say, when those hostilities ended eight years later, the Privy Council could no longer pursue the project.[15]

Whitehall
London, England

1770s

Croghan's collapsing plan for an interior colony and the reasons for its ultimate failure reveal a key but often overlooked origin of the imperial crisis. While affairs in North America were in a constant state of flux following the end of Pontiac's War, politics in England were equally unsettled. Perhaps the most pressing issue was the economic instability that affected the entire Empire, including Great Britain, which in turn affected politics and policy-making. The economic downturn of the 1760s affected both sides of the Atlantic. In England, it hit workers and laborers especially hard. They soon took to the streets to protest. In the

1770s, food riots rocked Great Britain. Hungry Britons filled the streets, blaming Parliament for their misery and complaining that politicians paid attention to wealthy merchants and large landowners while ignoring the poor and struggling. The looming national debt, the policies it drove, and the limitations it placed on government actions, only made these matters worse.

A charismatic Londoner named John Wilkes became the symbolic leader of those in England who were protesting the British Parliament's exclusionary nature. He won election to Parliament in 1764, but he was refused a seat because warrants for his arrest were issued after he published a pamphlet attacking the current political order. Parliament's rejection of Wilkes only strengthened his position among his supporters. After being exiled for uttering insulting words about George III's mother, Wilkes triumphantly returned to London in 1768, a champion of the lower classes. His determination to challenge those in power also made him a hero for colonists calling for the same reforms. "Wilkes and Liberty" soon became a battle cry for the Sons of Liberty and even inspired the renaming of colonial towns after him.[16]

The wealthy classes in England, meanwhile, didn't survive the economic pressures unscathed. Parliament levied new taxes on them to help cover the rising costs of managing the Empire. By 1768, rich Britons were among the most heavily taxed in the world, and they liked to point out that colonists were among the least taxed. They demanded a reduction in their rates, arguing that the heavy burden drained the home economy. But they didn't need to take to the streets. Instead, they lobbied their friends in Parliament and convinced them to slash their taxes. Parliament offset these cuts with the Townshend Duties, a tax on certain items shipped to the colonies.[17]

Amid this turmoil, the leadership in British government was going through its own form of chaos. In 1762, soon after George III began his reign, he appointed his former tutor, a controversial Scotsman named

Lord Bute, as his prime minister. Among the many inflammatory things Wilkes wrote that got him exiled was that Bute and George's mother were secret lovers and that Bute had used this relationship to win his prominent position in George's government. Wilkes wasn't the only one who criticized the prime minister, although his complaints were the most scandalous. In truth, Bute had a prickly personality that won him few allies in Parliament, and George III soon realized that he had to replace his friend if he was going to be an effective king.[18]

In 1763, George III appointed George Greenville, an experienced administrator with a deep knowledge of the Empire's colonial holdings, as Bute's replacement. Greenville's short but consequential term included the passage of both the Sugar Act and the Stamp Act. Opposition to these acts came from many corners on both sides of the Atlantic, but some of the most effective came from British merchants connected to the colonies who complained the new taxes impeded their already struggling businesses. Combined with the protests of colonists in the seaports, Parliament had little choice but to repeal the acts, a decision that undermined Greenville's agenda. But, more important, Greenville had a falling out with the King over some petty matter, which led to his removal in 1765. Lord Rockingham, who built a coalition government of moderates, followed him. Rockingham, however, couldn't maintain his alliances, and his administration collapsed within a year. William Pitt was appointed his successor in 1766. Pitt was a wildly popular politician credited with winning the Seven Years' War as secretary of state and more recently as a champion of colonial rights. Pitt, now in the twilight of his life, suffered from health problems that drained his energy. Instead, his Cabinet members ran the government. After Charles Townshend, his chancellor of the Exchequer (the treasury), passed a series of unpopular duties in 1767, Pitt was removed from office. He was replaced in 1768 by another moderate, the Duke of Grafton, who was younger and more energetic, if also a little unprepared for the position. Grafton's ministry lasted for just over two years, when Lord North succeeded him in 1770. North would finally bring stability to the home government, holding his position until the end of the American War of Independence.[19]

As a result, from the end of the Seven Years' War in 1763 until 1770—seven crucial years for an empire trying to enact reforms— Great Britain went through six different administrations. The changes led to delays, backpedaling, and inefficiencies that made it difficult to carry out a coherent policy toward North America. This instability in the imperial center deepened the governing crisis on the frontiers and made the crisis in the seaports worse.[20]

When trying to explain the cause of this volatility, one issue recurs: a large national debt that crippled administrators and Parliamentarians alike and drove their unpopular and ineffective policy-making. From the Molasses Act and King's Proclamation in 1763 to the Townshend Duties and the decision to allow colonial governments rather than official agents to regulate the Indian trade, Parliament and imperial administrators wanted to make the Empire more cost efficient and connected. Whether it was a policy of restraining settlement at the Appalachian Mountains or an attempt to raise revenue on specific trade goods, imperial officials were trying to limit the costs of their North American holdings and raise revenue to help fund whatever operations they had to maintain there. Managing the national debt also caused economic uncertainty at home in England, leading to high taxes, riots in the streets, constant changes in administration, and a vocal opposition party that undermined unity at the very time when it was needed most. Debt therefore led to the fracturing of the Empire.

To appreciate just how important debt was to this imperial crisis and just how central the costly frontiers were, consider the following chain of events. In 1763, George III issued a proclamation halting colonial expansion because of the cost associated with an enlarged empire in North America and to prevent costly wars. Two years later, Parliament passed a Stamp Act intended to raise revenue to help cover the burden of maintaining a small military presence on the frontiers that would provide protection to colonists and enforce imperial policy. The Stamp Act enraged people in the cities, but its original purpose had more to do with the need to fund troops in North America than the need to raise revenue on colonists. In the years that followed the Stamp Act's failure, Parliament tried new measures, all with an eye toward raising revenue to offset the steep price of their colonial possessions.

Due to these policy failures, Thomas Gage and William Johnson—both of whom wanted to establish British authority in the western regions and maintain peace through a more forceful regulation of colonists—were stymied by a lack of funds. As George Croghan complained to Benjamin Franklin, days after he returned from his successful Detroit expedition in 1765, the Empire could reach a new level of prosperity and peace if it strengthened the Indian Department, but he feared Parliament would fail to act because of the costs of such a reform. "The principle objection, to the proper regulation of the Indian Department, is, I am told, the expence," he wrote to Franklin, hoping that his colleague might convince officials across the Atlantic to rethink their policies. Croghan rejected the excuses coming from the imperial center. What could be more important—and cost effective—than securing the interior of North America through a strong bureaucracy, Croghan wondered.[21]

Policymakers in Great Britain, meanwhile, could point their fingers at unruly colonists as the reason for their inability to fund what the frontiers needed. In 1773, the secretary of state, the Earl of Dartmouth, rejected William Johnson's requests for greater financial support of the Indian Department because it required new revenue, which, he explained, would have required the "interposition of the authority of the Supreme Legislature [Parliament]." As he noted in his wry reply to William Johnson, "the unhappy prejudices which have so long prevailed in the colonies on this subject" left him, and the Empire more generally, unable to act. For those trying to govern the new empire, then, the crises on the frontiers and in the seaports were connected, even if the colonists themselves didn't yet recognize this.[22]

Boston

Griffin's Wharf

December 1773

The story is a familiar one.

On a cold December night in 1773, a band of men dressed in Indian garb, whooping and hollering in imitation of Indian raids, boarded the *Dartmouth*, a merchant ship moored on Boston's Long Wharf. Their target was clear: tea. The formerly popular staple of colonial consumption had become poisonous to Patriots opposed to imperial policies that they felt were meant to subjugate them. The Americans tore open wooden chests and dumped 90,000 pounds of the leaves into Boston Harbor, destroying an estimated £9,000 worth of merchandise—a figure comparable to the Black Boys' destruction of goods on Sideling Hill. Tea had come to symbolize the principle that fed revolutionary fervor in the seaports: taxation without representation. Much like the Black Boys did in their attack, the Tea Party left non-offensive trade goods on the ship undisturbed, sending a signal to imperial officials that the Patriots weren't lawless ruffians bent on the destruction of property but political protesters whose actions were controlled and intentional. This action in New England sparked a chain reaction that would unite Americans disillusioned with the Empire on the frontiers of North America with those in its seaports. It is an overlooked outcome of this otherwise well-known story.[23]

The immediate cause for the Tea Partiers' discontent was a recent law in which Parliament reduced the cost of British tea in an attempt to shore up the shaky finances of the East India Company, possibly the most important business concern in the British Empire. Following the Seven Years' War, as the British Empire expanded its grasp on the Indian subcontinent, its financial problems forced imperial officials to adopt a new form of colonization. Rather than create costly colonies with their own governing bureaucracies, they outsourced the effort to the East India Company, a private company that also functioned as an arm of empire. It had its own military, a governor, and policing powers. It also had a monopoly on the sale of tea, which was the main source of funding for its operations.[24]

The problem the company faced in the 1770s was that even with a monopoly, the price of its tea was higher than the price colonists paid for tea smuggled in from competitors, like the Dutch. Colonial dislike of East Indian tea took on a political significance after the Townshend Duties of 1768 placed a special luxury tax on colonists who wanted to purchase the item. Its high price combined with a series of organized boycotts meant that by 1773, tons of tea (an astounding 18,000,000 pounds) sat piled high in British warehouses, rotting and sending the Company to the brink of financial ruin. If Parliament refused to act, then the collapse of the East India Company meant that the Empire would begin to crumble in the Far East. To make matters worse, many wealthy Britons owned shares in the Company, so their fortunes were tied to its rise or fall. Those managing the Empire realized that the Company was too important to fail.[25]

Parliament passed the Tea Act in 1773 to save the Company and preserve the Empire's interests in India. Through a series of new regulations on tea and tax benefits designed to help the East India Company, the Tea Act promised to cut the price of East Indian tea, making it, Parliamentarians hoped, more palatable to colonists in North Amer-

ica. The law reflected yet another attempt by Parliament to better integrate the global empire by connecting its interests in India to consumers
in North America.[26]

There were two reasons for the colonists' anger at a law that was
meant to lower the price of the popular item. First, the law contained a
hidden tax. Through a convoluted system of tax rebates offered to the
East India Company, Parliamentarians were able to lower the price
of tea while also maintaining a consumption tax on it. To those who
drafted the law, the proposal seemed like a win-win. The cheap tea
would entice colonists to accept a tax levied by Parliament, something
they had angrily opposed until now, while also providing a financial
benefit for the struggling company. Patriot leaders, aware of Parliamentary tricks, worried that regular colonists might turn out to be the
rational economic actors that Parliament believed they were.[27]

The second problem colonists had with the Tea Act was the way in
which Parliament strengthened the East India Company's monopoly
on the tea trade. Before the act, the company exported its tea to London, where it was auctioned off wholesale to bidders, some of whom
were colonial merchants. As British officials analyzed the system, they
realized that the bidding system might artificially inflate the cost of
tea. To combat this inflation, they decided to end the auctioning practice and gave the East India Company the power to name certain
merchants as its official tea traders, thereby cutting out a number of
colonial merchants. Again, a desire for greater efficiency and cost-
cutting drove the policy. Colonial merchants, however, disagreed,
claiming that it was wrong for the government to give the East India
Company the right to pick winners and losers in the tea trade. The
previous system, they argued, was much more fair because it was open
to all merchants, while this one seemed to favor a select few. Merchants
in the seaports, especially Boston, accused members of Parliament of
enriching themselves at the expense of colonists, echoing the charges

colonists on the frontiers had earlier aimed at Indian traders and the governments that seemed to encourage them.[28]

Many in Parliament considered the destruction of tea in Boston Harbor to be tantamount to the destruction of Crown property. Unlike in the past, they decided to respond with force. As Thomas Gage noted in a report to imperial officials after the Tea Party, it was past time for such action. These troublesome Americans, he advised his superiors, "will be Lyons, whilst we are Lambs but if we take the resolute part they will undoubtedly prove very meek." Parliament then passed a series of ordinances known by colonists as the Intolerable Acts but officially titled the Coercive Acts because they established severe penalties aimed at Boston to force the colonists into obedience. The law placed new limits on town meetings in Massachusetts, the main form of colonial governance in Massachusetts since the colony's first settlement. Colonists believed these public forums were a key way they preserved their liberty. Imperial officials, in contrast, saw these gatherings as too democratic and worried that a radical minority used the forums to stir up greater trouble. Further, Massachusetts governor Thomas Hutchinson was recalled and replaced by Thomas Gage. The commander-in-chief would now also serve as a military governor of the colony. Most upsetting of all, the act shut the port of Boston to all trade, a policy that most colonists viewed as an act of war. The point of these acts was to do the thing Parliament had refused to do up until now: exercise strong imperial power, as the act's title implied, to coerce subjects into compliance.[29]

Although the treatment of Boston was the part of the legislation that received the most attention, another act that was passed alongside the ones focusing on seaports reinforced the belief that the Empire refused to serve the interests of colonists on the frontiers. Parliament gave the newly acquired Canadian government control over the American interior, figuring that the top-down command structure of this government, with a military governor at its head, was more suited to the needs of the West. Granting such power to the colonists' former enemy, French Canada, confirmed their worst fears.

Rather than crush the colonists' resolve, their acts strengthened their will. In fact, the response finally connected the urban crisis with the frontier one. As naval ships descended on Boston Harbor and General Gage assumed the governorship, Bostonians began reaching out to their neighbors for help. The Sons of Liberty sent Paul Revere on a mad dash down the East coast to alert their supporters to the acts' content. Riding by horseback, Revere left Boston on May 14, stopped at New York City, and arrived in Philadelphia on May 19, covering three hundred miles in five days—a remarkable feat on eighteenth-century roads. News of the Intolerable Acts shocked even the most moderate men. Shutting Boston's port with a naval blockade, appointing a military governor, and suspending town meetings seemed like acts of war to many colonists. As Revere raced down the eastern seaboard, British subjects loyal to a common Crown became transformed into American Patriots united in a common cause.[30]

Soon Committees of Correspondence formed throughout the colonies, dotting the countryside from Massachusetts to Georgia, including one near the home of the Black Boys. James Wilson, a Pennsylvanian from Carlisle who would go on sign the Declaration of Independence, helped mobilize the effort. In a rousing speech, he explained that these Committees formed a "chain of freedom" in which "every individual in the colonies who is willing to preserve the greatest of his blessings, his liberty, has the pleasure of beholding himself a link." Counties throughout Pennsylvania formed militias and hosted Committees of Correspondence, all of which were integrated into a network that tied the frontier to Philadelphia and beyond. James Smith served as a chairman of one of these new bodies. The long-term goal of these new colonial institutions was to coordinate a uniform resistance in towns and cities. Soon volunteer militias formed to assist the Committees in their work, serving as an unofficial but very persuasive arm of coercion.[31]

The first order of business for James Smith's frontier Committee was to raise support for Bostonians, a sign that this frontier outpost recognized its place as a link in the vast chain of resistance that now bound Americans together. Smith's Committee declared that the Coercive Acts aimed to "reduce [Bostonians] to a more wretched state of slavery than ever before existed in any state or county." The act, if carried out, "would strip them of the rights of humanity, exposing lives to the wanton and unpunishable sport of the licentious soldiery, and depriving them of the very means of subsistence." They therefore announced their readiness "to oppose it with our lives and fortunes," a willingness to bear arms and even die for their fellow Americans that showed their newfound bond with their eastern countrymen. The affection these Committees expressed toward their Boston colleagues showed that the British subjects who composed them and who previously felt little connection to other colonies were turning into something else—American citizens. It was a momentous step in the history of the American Revolution.[32]

In 1774 and 1775, then, colonists in the East came to the same conclusion about the Empire that those in the West had reached already. What united these two groups was a common feeling that the British Empire no longer served them and that they could rely only on themselves for protection. As colonists from the frontiers raised money and supplies to support their distant colleagues in Boston, and as aid began to stream to this port from the American interior rather than from across the Atlantic Ocean, colonists were constructing the bonds necessary to unite a nation. In fact, the belief that the king had turned on his people became a central part of the formal Declaration written two years later. Those in the East had felt this disregard—even open hostility—with the Coercive Acts, while those on the frontiers had felt it with the removal of all forms of protection. As Thomas Jefferson wrote, the thirteen British colonies were justified in their rebellion because "[the King] has abdicated Government here, by declaring us out of his Protection and waging War against us."

Chapter 11

Revolution

The Old Order

1776

Historians have long debated the significance of the American Revolution. Some have argued that it wasn't particularly revolutionary after all. They claim that political leadership changed little—Thomas Jefferson and George Washington, for instance, belonged to the colonial elite before the Revolution broke out. Others point out that property still stayed in the hands of the few. Still others argue that with slavery intact, this revolution was no radical act at all. But if we look to the West, toward the frontiers of North America, which were then based around Fort Pitt, American independence does appear to be a truly revolutionary event. On almost every measure, colonial life was upended and replaced by something new. The result remade the West.[1]

To appreciate the dramatic changes to the North American landscape, let's begin with the fate of James Smith and the Black Boys' rivals: William Johnson, Thomas Gage, George Croghan, Pontiac, the Quakers, and John Penn.

Sir William Johnson made good Indian relations his life's work, especially with the Six Nations Iroquois. Johnson was so important to the British Empire that he received a baronetcy. By 1774, however, Johnson saw his vision crumbling alongside his authority. The colony of Virginia was engaged in a bitter conflict with the Shawnees that would result in Virginians pushing the boundary he established at Fort Stanwix further west. Sitting outside of Albany, he could do little to stop it. In July, he suffered a fatal stroke. His son John inherited his father's office and good intentions, but he was swept aside by the American Revolution. During the war, John joined with the Iroquois, who were led by William Johnson's Iroquois brother-in-law, and a leading Mohawk, Joseph Brant, to try to defeat the American cause. They fought well, but their fortunes were tied to the larger war effort. When the British Army surrendered, both the Iroquois and John Johnson sought protection in Canada. The revolutionary government of New York, meanwhile, seized the Johnsons' palatial home and abundant lands outside of Albany and sold them. John Johnson spent the rest of his life in Canada, where he continued to manage Indian relations for the much smaller British Empire. Joseph Brant and many of the Iroquois suffered the same loss. New York seized most of their land, and the leaders were forced to relocate to Canada.[2]

Thomas Gage suffered a much more ignoble defeat. In 1763, he was on the fast track to high imperial office. After replacing Jeffery Amherst as commander-in-chief of North America, he had two concerns: establishing the authority of the British Empire on its frontiers and maintaining the peace. As Pontiac's War wound down, he was confident that he could accomplish both aims. But then the colonists on the frontiers and seaports began to upset his well-laid plans by refusing to obey the imperial policies he was supposed to implement. He had to shift his focus from managing the frontiers, opening the Indian trade, and maintaining strong diplomatic outreach to Indian groups to controlling what were supposed to be loyal subjects who seemed intent on upsetting the grand plans of the British Empire. Instead of overseeing the Empire's slow and steady growth in North America, Gage was overwhelmed with riots and rebellions and witnessed its fall. By the 1770s, his confidence had turned to cynicism.[3]

In April 1775, as he watched colonists grow ever more defiant in the face of the Coercive Acts, Gage worried that their boldness was rapidly turning into militancy. On April 18, he ordered a regiment of British Regulars to travel into the Massachusetts countryside under the cover of darkness to secure weapons held in a depot in Concord. Prominent Patriots in Boston soon learned of this secret mission, and they sent Paul Revere on another journey to alert fellow colonists of impending danger. Some historians have speculated that Gage's wife, the American-born Margaret Kemble, was the colonists' secret source for the leak. In any case, colonial militias in Lexington and Concord stood ready to confront the redcoats in the early morning of April 19. The battle was the first in what would become an eight-year struggle, the longest war Americans fought until Vietnam in the twentieth century.

Thomas Gage, however, would spend most of the war in England, far away from the potential glories of battle. Following the British defeats at Lexington and then Bunker Hill, Gage was recalled, an embarrassing end to a formerly promising career. Worse, rumors of his wife's indiscretion still persist. Worse still, when Great Britain feared a French invasion in 1778, the Army called on the formerly disgraced Jeffery Amherst rather than Thomas Gage to organize a defense of the homeland.[4]

George Croghan remained true to form—which is to say he stayed loyal to his own self-interest—throughout the imperial crisis. His main concern was getting recognition of the enormous grant of land he had received at the Treaty of Fort Stanwix. At the start of the American Revolution, he kept his home near Fort Pitt, but rumors of loyalism followed him wherever he traveled, probably based on his reputation as a person with unclear motives. Pressured by Patriots on the frontiers, he left his home near Fort Pitt and sought shelter in Philadelphia, where he tried to clear his name and receive clear title to his land from the Continental Congress.[5]

Croghan's efforts were unsuccessful, largely because no one was concerned with him anymore. The man whose home was so important in 1765 that it appeared on maps of the colony died penniless and unnoticed outside of Philadelphia in 1782. There was no announcement of his death in any newspaper, and the location of his grave was unknown to historians until the late twentieth century, when it was discovered in St. Peter's churchyard in Philadelphia. The Revolution had rendered him irrelevant. His previous importance came from the patronage of Sir William Johnson and the good relations with Indians that brought him wealth through trade. At the time of his death, Patriots were in the midst of overthrowing the imperial system that had given Croghan his prominence, and his influence declined alongside the Empire he had served. It was a dramatic fall for a man whose rise had been meteoric.[6]

Then there was Pontiac, the Indian chief whose war began the crisis on the frontiers and whose transformation to peacemaker was supposed to end it. An assassin caused his death in 1769. But the spirit of resistance would remain alive and reappear in pan-Indian movements aimed at asserting Native sovereignty and stopping the forces of colonization. Most notably, it reappeared in 1812 when Tecumseh, a Shawnee, organized groups in the same region Pontiac did to defend their homeland.

In 1763, these four men were the most powerful figures in North America, especially on the frontiers of the British Empire. They were empowered to usher in an era of peace by transforming the frontiers from violent areas defined by fear to stable zones that brought prosperity. But the American Revolution displaced each of them. When we look at the fate of these individuals and consider that one definition of a revolution is a fundamental change in political leadership, then we can say that in the West, revolution was nearly complete.

Meanwhile, in Pennsylvania itself, the Revolution overthrew the old colonial order—although in a way that reflected its own peculiar politics. The Quaker elite who had been the target of the Black Boys' anger, and John Penn, the frontier people's former ally, received vastly different treatment during the war. Accusations of secret and self-interested dealings with Indians that frontier people had leveled at Quakers during the imperial crisis inflamed revolutionary passions in Philadelphia. In 1776, the drafters of the new revolutionary government for the state gave the frontier counties equal representation, a demand by those areas dating to 1763. That meant that frontier representatives now outnumbered eastern ones. The drafters did so because they realized the frontier areas were the most opposed to the old order and the most supportive of radical, revolutionary action that targeted the old elite.[7]

The revolutionary frontier government enacted many of the sentiments put forth by the Black Boys. In 1777, for instance, the government suspended *habeas corpus* (the right to challenge the legality of a detention) in order to seize twenty Quakers suspected of carrying on a secret correspondence with the British, and held them in Winchester, Virginia, for several months. When Congress debated the move, the Paxton Boys were cited as a historical example that justified such strong action. James Lovell, a Congressman from Massachusetts, argued that Quakers deserved their treatment because of their past displays of disloyalty to and cruelty to their own people. Indian relations were the means by which they demonstrated this tyranny. He recalled that "old Israel [Israel Pemberton, a trader called the King of the Quakers because of his influence] and the tribe in general turned out armed when scandalous oppression had stirred up the Paxton Boys."[8]

Lovell not only sided with the Paxton Boys but indicted the Quakers for oppressing them—for causing them to act, for "stirring" them up. That Lovell, a Congressman from Massachusetts, would offer this interpretation of the Quakers' political actions shows just how widespread these once local perceptions had become during the Revolution. With Congress meeting in Philadelphia alongside Pennsylvania's revolutionary government (which itself was now dominated by the frontier counties that had produced the Paxton Boys and Black Boys), and because members from each institution regularly mingled with one another, such a view of Quakers became accepted by all. Pennsylvania's particular frontier politics had become nationalized.[9]

Even those stationed as far away as France shared this view of Quakers. Ralph Izard, a South Carolinian who served in the U.S. diplomatic corps during the Revolution, wrote a letter in 1778 discussing the benefits of representative governments. He wrote that no form of government better served the people's interest or protected their liberty than a democratic one. There was one exception to this rule, however: Quaker Pennsylvania. There the "ridiculous spirit of Quakerism" had created the only Assembly he knew of that was "disapproved by the people at large." The general impression in the governing bodies of the new nation was that Quakers as a whole were not pacifists and neutrals, but tyrants with a history of undercutting the interest of the people through their ill-spirited dealings. This idea, voiced first among Pennsylvania's self-described frontier inhabitants, now shaped national opinion.[10]

The story of John Penn is far different. While Quakers languished in Virginia, Pennsylvania's revolutionary government allowed Penn to live on country estates in Philadelphia's present-day Fairmount Park and in New Jersey. At one point, he even took an oath of allegiance to the revolutionary government. After the Revolution, Pennsylvania paid the Penn family £130,000 for its remaining land in Pennsylvania— better treatment than most expatriated loyalists received. John Penn left to travel in Europe after the Revolution but eventually returned to live in Philadelphia, dying there in 1794. Thomas McKean, an ardent revolutionary, was one of his pallbearers, and his body was interred in the altar at Christ Church. As his treatment suggests, outside of the colonial Assembly and the Quaker Party elite, the governor was never quite as unpopular as his opponents would have liked. Indeed, of all those holding a leadership position before the Revolution in this story, he suffered the least.[11]

The New Order
Independence Hall
Philadelphia, Pennsylvania

1776

While these figures fell from power, James Smith and his Black Boys continued their rise. In the years after his acquittal, James Smith took on a more public and active role as the Revolution changed Pennsylvania's political landscape. He served on various boards, continued to lead vigilante militias, and took an active hand in mobilizing official protest movements in the wake of the Tea Party. In July 1776, Smith reached new prominence when he was elected to serve in the Provincial Convention, a temporary body that was formed to write a new constitution for Pennsylvania. In these roles, Smith became a central player in the frontier revolution, making sure its values shaped the course of events.[12]

The story of the Provincial Convention that Smith attended in 1776 begins in the East but ends in the West. As events pushed colonists

closer to independence, revolutionary elements in Philadelphia became
frustrated with the uncooperativeness of the ruling Quaker Party and
with moderate men in powerful positions, many of whom attained
wealth and status through trade and colonial political appointments.
As these power brokers created more roadblocks to revolution, radicals
in Philadelphia who wanted the colony to take stronger actions against
imperial policies began leveling charges of inaction, conservatism, and
self-dealing at the same people whom those on the frontiers had long
criticized.[13]

With the colonial government committed to maintaining the status
quo, these urban revolutionaries, probably a minority in their own communities, knew that they needed allies to accomplish the overthrow of
the colonial order. They turned west to find what they sought. Through
a series of controversial political maneuvers (some of which were organized by Bostonian John Adams, who was then residing in Philadelphia
to attend the Continental Congress), angry revolutionaries in Philadelphia brought the colonial Assembly to its knees. They formed militias
and extralegal committees, and used their growing power to pressure
moderates to become more radical, while the Continental Congress
pressured the Assembly to act to their liking. By the summer of 1776,
the Assembly could no longer seat a quorum, as moderates and loyalists
were pushed out and radicals who had been elected to serve refused to
sit in the body. Instead, the various independent committees in the city
and beyond, most of which took orders from the Congress, seized the
political authority that the Assembly had formerly exercised.[14]

In July 1776, shortly after the Continental Congress declared thirteen colonies independent states, the revolutionaries in Philadelphia
called for a convention to write a new state constitution to fit the pressing problems of the times. They also did something remarkable: they
gave up their own political power. Rather than weighting representation in the convention toward the East, as it had been during the colo-

nial era, they gave equal representation to every county. By doing this, they gave a large majority to these westerners. They did it because they knew the West opposed the Quakers as strongly as they did, and that western dominance could limit the influence of any moderates who tried to preserve some elements of the old constitution.[15]

When residents of Westmoreland County voted, they sent James Smith to represent their interests. Although there is little evidence of the debates that went into the Convention—as one of its chroniclers noted, "mystery has and apparently always will surround the making of the Constitution of 1776"—we can sense the influence of frontier ideas about the old Assembly. Experience, rather than political theory, drove the delegates crafting the new constitution. As one uneducated but opinionated delegate shouted at an adversary in the midst of the debate, "You learned fellows who have warped your understandings by poring over musty old books, will perhaps laugh at us; but, know ye, that we despise you."[16]

Such attitudes echo the ones James Smith and his Black Boys had expressed as early as 1765. At the time, they were fringe opinions in colonial society, the views of a frontier people who had little real political power. A decade later, they were the foundations for a new constitution that would govern the state. And while we don't know exactly what the frontier delegates like Smith did during the framing of the government, we know that they had significant influence on it. One of Smith's fellow frontier delegates, John Moore, was assigned to the most important committee: the committee to write "a declaration of rights." The committee drafted a bill of individual rights—a concept that continued to influence constitution-making in the new nation— that listed the liberties Pennsylvanians should expect under their new government. One of the sixteen declarations was that "government is, or ought to be, instituted for the common benefit, protection and security of the people, nation or community; and not for the particular emolument or advantage of any single man, family, or sett of men." The language shows the merging of easterners' political beliefs with those of the frontier people. Their mention of a "family" reflects the complaints that people like Franklin had leveled against proprietary rule, while the reference to a group of men ("sett of men") is a clear critique of the colonial government that frontier people believed had failed them and instead served wealthy traders and the Quaker elite.[17]

More important, the declaration completely upended the basis of government. Under the colonial system, the Crown was sovereign, and all power descended from the monarch. It was a hierarchical system that applied in the military, in the government, and in society. The new revolutionary constitution of Pennsylvania was based on a very different principle: popular sovereignty. In this version, power emanated from the people. As the Declaration of Rights announced, "All power being originally inherent in, and consequently derived from, the people; therefore all officers of government, whether legislative or executive, are their trustees' and servants, and at all times accountable to them." The constitution represented a transformation from a monarchical society to a democratic one. It was a principle that frontier people had acted on during the imperial crisis as they realized that the King and the political system he oversaw failed them. Through rebellions like the Black Boys', frontier people drew political power away from the British Empire and placed it in their own hands. With the new constitution, they were institutionalizing what they had already achieved in unofficial practice.[18]

The changes the Pennsylvania constitution made to most legal officers shows just how thoroughly this frontier revolution shaped this new American state. Before and after the Revolution, justices of the peace were the most important local officeholders because they enforced the law. Under the old system, the governor, whose power descended from the Crown, appointed such officeholders. During the imperial crisis,

this structure came under pressure, especially on the frontier. As official policies conflicted with local sentiments, justices of the peace had
to either adapt to meet community beliefs or face harsh punishments.
Justices like William Smith and John Armstrong who frustrated colonial and imperial officials because of their concern for the popular voice
became the norm.

The revolutionary constitution made official this new basis of
authority. These formerly appointed officeholders became elected in the
new government, meaning that neighbors now elected the people who
would enforce the law. Under this new system, local communities could
nullify laws by electing justices of the peace who refused to enforce
unpopular legal codes. While the constitution gave the state government some ability to oversee these officeholders, the essence of the new
system made law enforcement more democratic. This shift represents
more evidence of how revolutionary the American Revolution was for
those on the frontiers. It overturned the very foundation of the law,
moving it from the Crown to the people. This change was the natural
outcome of a constitution written by frontier people who had resented
seeing the law serve the interests of colonial and imperial elites at the
expense of the frontier people.[19]

Such radical changes affected other parts of the new government.
The formerly powerful legislature that frontier people accused of protecting eastern interests in the colonial era looked far different after
1776. Philadelphia and the original eastern counties, which had sent
twenty-six representatives for most of the colonial era, now sent six
each, making their total representation twenty-four. The eight newer
western counties also sent six each, giving them forty-eight representatives, or twice as many as the easterners. Moreover, as the frontier
people had long complained, the colonial government had no way to
address geographic expansion. The new constitution included a clause
that reflected their devotion to rule by the people. After declaring that

"representation in proportion to the number of taxable inhabitants is the only principle which can at all times secure liberty, and make the voice of a majority of the people the law of the land," the new constitution required the state to conduct a regular census to make sure that representation matched populations. Because most people believed that the frontier counties were the fastest growing, this was a grant of future power to westerners.

The change in voting requirements was even more dramatic. In the colonial era, a man needed £50 of property or acreage to qualify to vote. Even though this wasn't as much of a burden as requirements in other colonies or in Great Britain, it still limited the ability to vote, leaving somewhere between a quarter and a half of the free male population ineligible. The old policy reinforced frontier complaints that the government was run for and by the elite. The new constitution removed all property restrictions on voting for white men. Even as this helped the small artisans in Philadelphia, it also empowered the laborers, small landowners, and squatters on the frontiers. All told, the new state represented a significant shift of political power from East to West, a change crafted by those who attended the convention, the majority of whom were westerners. As one historian quipped, "The backcountry delegates no doubt headed home pleased with a job well done."[20]

James Smith was one of those satisfied representatives, and his constituents seemed happy with the constitution he helped draft. They were also impressed with the half a ton of rifle powder and ton of lead he carried back to them, a gift from the state that was meant to show these frontier people that their new government would meet their military needs—the very thing the British Empire had been so unwilling to do. In the fall elections, Smith's neighbors elected him to the new Assembly as one of their inaugural representatives. As James Smith returned to Independence Hall in 1777 with forty-seven fellow frontier representatives, the frontier revolution took hold.[21]

The Frontier Revolution

1777–1783

War, however, drew James Smith away from politics. One day in 1777, as he was working in the legislature in Philadelphia, a boisterous band of backwoodsmen came storming through the streets. "My old boys," as he liked to call the Black Boys, were heading to the front lines in New Jersey to fight the British, and they wanted him to lead them again. Smith had always believed that his destiny was on the battlefield, and now he wasn't about to be denied the greatest fight of his life. He petitioned the legislature for a leave of absence so he could use his skills where they were most needed. The legislature happily agreed.[22]

In this new battle, Smith applied the same guerilla tactics he had used to harass traders. His men marauded roads near Princeton, searching for British troops in the days following George Washington's decisive victory there. Before long, Smith was claiming that his troops had killed or captured more enemy soldiers than he had men under his command. But then a serious illness left Smith incapacitated. By the time his health returned in Burlington, New Jersey, his men had moved on.[23]

Smith refused to be slowed. After he recovered, he returned to Philadelphia to petition the Pennsylvania government to recognize his guerilla-style warfare. He proposed to return to Fort Pitt, raise another band of men, train them in his style of fighting, and then rejoin Washington to fight the British. He convinced his audience to back his plan, but the legislators lacked the authority to make such a decision without the approval of George Washington. They therefore sent a remarkable letter to Washington, reproduced below, and sent Smith to Washington's headquarters in Morristown to plead his case. The letter shows just how much the revolutionary state had changed into a frontier state. Under the British, the colonial legislature mostly ignored frontier people. Now the new revolutionary assembly actually promoted their cause.

Sir,

Application has been made to us by James Smith Esqr. of Westmoreland, a Gentleman well acquainted with the Indian Customs, and their manners of carrying on war, for leave to raise a Battalion of marksmen expert in the use of Rifles, acquainted with the Indian method of fighting, to be dressed intirely in their fashion, for the purpose of annoying and harrassing the Enemy in their marches and encampments. We think 2 or 300 Men in that way might be very useful. Should your Excellency be of the same Opinion and direct such a Corps to be formed, we will take proper measures for raising the men on the frontiers of this State, and follow such other directions as your Excellency shall give in this Matter.[24]

Smith marched out to Washington's headquarters to make his case, but Washington was less receptive to Smith's plan. He questioned "the scheme of white men turning Indians," but he thought so highly of Smith that he offered him an appointment as a major of a regiment of riflemen. Smith, however, refused. His "old boys" were gone, and he disliked the idea of working under someone. Instead, he headed back to Fort Pitt, where he planned to raise his own militia and defend his home from Indian attacks.

Smith's neighbors welcomed his return. While the many frontier men who enlisted in the Continental Army became sharpshooters who helped Washington ultimately win against the British, their war service also meant that they left their homes open to invasion. As war with Great Britain dragged on in the East, Indian groups in the West who had initially stayed neutral started to think that a British victory would give them a better chance to secure their rights. The shift of Indians into the British fold intensified frontier people's sense of fear and once again brought war to their homes. As one of James Smith's friends wrote to Washington in the spring of 1778, "The Indian war could not have broke out at a more unfortunate period many of our best Marksmen are in the service. we parted wth most of our Guns for the use of the Army, at a time when they were much wanted in the Camp, we deprived ourselves of the means of defence for the service of our Country and we hope that *now* when we are in such imminent danger of distruction."[25]

With the return of hostilities on the Pennsylvania frontier, James Smith put the plan Washington rejected into action. And in the process, he unleashed a frontier revolution defined largely by offensive actions against Native groups. In 1778, he led a ranging party, scalped at least four Indians, and launched raids on their settlements. At one point, he led a war party of four hundred men deep into Indian Country, exceeding his orders "in quest of Indians." Smith and men like him on the frontiers continued to receive support from the Pennsylvania government with its many frontier representatives. Indeed, the government appointed a lieutenant in every county to oversee operations, and every county was divided into districts overseen by sub-lieutenants. The pacifistic Quaker colony Smith had grown up in had changed into a modern military state, and frontier people like James Smith were receiving the aid of government that they had long sought.[26]

Smith's western forays during the war foretold his own future and that of the nation he helped establish. During the American War of Independence, frontier people still saw Native Americans as their chief enemy, and the new states were willing to act more forcefully against Native groups than the British Empire was willing to do. Smith's ranging party, for instance, received material support from Pennsylvania.

After peace, governments encouraged the continued settlement of western regions through new development schemes. Rapid expansion, rather than restraint, defined the new American nation, a striking contrast to the British Empire's policy for the West. After the war ended, Smith, along with thousands of other American citizens, enacted this change. Smith and others streamed south and west, settling on the fertile lands Croghan noted with such optimism during his voyage in 1765. Before the Revolution, this land was firmly in Indian hands by British decree, but the success of the Revolutionary War had transformed the region.

Here, too, James Smith helps us see just how complete this revolution was in the West. After settling on new lands in Bourbon County, Kentucky, Smith helped draft the first state constitution for Kentucky and served in its early legislature. The creation of a new state founded on democratic principles reflected the fulfillment of the frontier revolution. With the power of government in their hands, frontier people were able to take a more offensive stance toward Native groups and, through both warfare and land deals, encourage a rapid expansion onto Indian lands. By obtaining more land and removing Indians as perceived threats to their ambition, they had achieved the independence they sought. Indeed, this frontier revolution was more remarkable than the eastern one we know so well, because it affected two revolutions simultaneously: one that overthrew the British Empire, and the other that ignored Native American claims to land.

A revolution in government allowed both to succeed. Colonists on the frontiers saw in their colonial and imperial governments unrepresentative institutions that excluded them from policymaking and failed to serve them. They lived in constant fear of war and felt that their governments cared little for their problems. During the American Revolution, frontier people seized the reins of power and remade governments to suit their needs. For those in the West, this democratic revolution meant a fundamental change in frontier policy. As one frontiersman writing about Indian policy in the new nation in 1792 noted, "The best defense is offense."[27]

James Smith followed this line of reasoning in his memoir, published in Kentucky in 1799. He recounted his experiences as an Indian captive, as leader of the Black Boys, and as a revolutionary war soldier. But beyond woodsy anecdotes, Smith declared the real reason for his memoir in his introduction: "Experience has taught the Americans the necessity of adopting their mode [of warfare], and the more perfect we are in that mode, the better we shall be able to defend ourselves against them, when defence is necessary." Smith saw his memoir as a military treatise on Indian customs meant to be read by Americans so they could better understand their enemies. Though presented in an argument of self-defense, his book was based, as was his life, on the idea that American citizens and their governments should continue to expand westward and remove Indians from their lands, through force and violence if necessary, to make room for the growing country.

Indeed, Smith's book reflects the logic of expansion that would define the future of the new nation. Alongside advice for fighting wars, he gives detailed descriptions of the productive potential of the land he saw in the Ohio River valley and beyond. In this way, his memoir served as an intelligence report and promotional tract for future settlers in Kentucky, as well as a guide for how to wage war with Native Americans—something he clearly viewed as an inevitable result of American expansion. In the lines of Smith's memoir, then, fear of Native Americans mixed with a desire for more productive land controlled at the time by Native people. It was a combination whose logic produced the roadmap for America's history in the West in the years that followed.

Smith wasn't alone in his views. Many Americans shared both a fear of Native American groups as enemies and a deep desire for more land. In the years that followed, the logic of these two beliefs made forceful Indian removal a justified course of action to many settlers who lived on war-torn frontiers. With the backing of a government responsive to their demands, these newly minted citizens marched west in search of new and better land. As they pressed forward, they transformed Indian Country into new territories and states. They often secured this property by waging wars with defensive rationales that looked like offensive ones to Native Americans. A democratic revolution carried out by frontier people empowered them to address their fears and achieve their economic dreams. The result: an expansionary, landed empire that the British had previously tried to avoid. This change in political power came at a price, however: a vicious cycle of wars in the West, and the often questionable expropriation of Indian lands.[28]

Viewed from the West, then, the story of the British Empire's fall and the United States' rise fails to fit with the stories of the American Revolution we know so well. But this western tale is, nonetheless, essential to understanding the nation and its founding. On the one hand, the story tells of a people throwing off a government that they thought served them poorly and putting the power to determine their future in their own hands. And the democracy they helped to build was—and still is—a radical idea that can be a powerful force for positive change. But on the other hand, their victory came at a cost for those who were excluded from the revolutionary society, and that story should be told as well. Few events better capture these complex origins of American independence than the struggle for control of the American frontier. Indeed, the story of the Black Boys is as important as any other because the legacy of these revolutionaries persists in the cultural DNA of the nation they helped to found.

Epilogue

---•——

Legacies

Fort Loudon

Present Day

On a clear but cool day about a decade ago, I found myself standing inside Fort Loudon, the site of the Black Boys' Rebellion. My trip came as a welcome surprise, a respite from the monotony of academic life. Earlier, I had emailed the local Fulton County Historical Society to see if they might hold some otherwise unknown documents on the Black Boys. They responded that they did not, but a representative invited me to visit the area so I could see the area myself and share with them what I had learned of the rebellion.

The opportunity was too good to pass up. I hopped into my old Jeep and traveled three hours west on the Pennsylvania Turnpike, a road that runs parallel to Forbes Road, now Highway 30. I thought of the pack trains that used to travel the rough roads to Pittsburgh, especially as I raced through tunnels carved out of mountain ranges that would have tested the toughest of horses. I arrived at my destination in the evening. Coming from the light-polluted city, I was unused to the depth of the darkness that greeted me. It felt like the frontier. Much to my delight, my host's home was all the more appropriate—an early-nineteenth-century farmhouse. Its stone facade, brightened by candles in the windows to welcome its guests, made me feel like an eighteenth-century traveler, someone like George Croghan approaching the evening's resting place after a long day of wearying travel.

My time in the region was enlightening. Indeed, it sparked my desire to write this book. I traveled over the same mountain passes that the redcoats, Black Boys, and traders did. I visited places they stopped at, including a tavern-turned-home in McConnellsburg that may have been part of the rebellion, and I met local residents still talking about the Black Boys. I even saw the unexpected: the birthplace of James Buchanan, the president before Abraham Lincoln, whose general inept-itude in office had pushed the country toward civil war. He was, much to my surprise, born a few miles from Fort Loudon at the base of a mountain that, I suspect, was the site where McGlashan and the Black Boys first clashed on that March night. Seeing the physical geography, including a hike along the base of Sideling Hill, gave me a much deeper understanding of the events that took place more than 250 years ago.

It was during my stop at Fort Loudon that I began to realize the lasting significance of the events of 1765. The fort itself was a testament to a community determined to preserve its connection to the American Revolution. Several years ago, I was told, a local resident fascinated with the story of James Smith spearheaded an amateur archaeological excavation of the area. To their surprise, they discovered the postholes from the fort, showing an outline of its walls. The find was so impres-sive that the state government decided to help re-create the fort. Fort Loudon, to my twenty-first-century eyes, appeared small and insignif-icant. Its walls are barely higher than a basketball hoop, and I'm sure that with a few friends I could easily breach them. For those who care about it, however, its size belies its enormous importance. Its presence gives this small community in the middle of Pennsylvania a chance to make a direct connection to events that transformed the world. In fact, more than a few residents told me that the American Revolution started here, and they wished more people knew that. I think they are more than a little right.

A shrine to James Smith stands just outside the fort's wall in a white farmhouse. It sits elevated on a slight incline, staring down at the fort, much as the Black Boys did during their two sieges. Inside the house one finds a mannequin decked out in the Black Boys uniform and ephemera relating to James Smith's life, including a reproduction of a portrait done of Smith much later in life.

Smith's portrait is only of his upper body. He wears a plain white shirt with a red scarf tied around his neck, and a black jacket with gold buttons. Most important is the large hunting frock hefted over his shoulders. It's the defining article of clothing for an American frontiersman.

Smith's choice of clothing says a great deal about the man he became. He wears the clothing of the establishment—a white shirt, a standard black jacket, and a rich red scarf are what one expects to see among the lawyers and merchants. The white shirt and jacket therefore reflect Smith's role as a legislator and community leader. The red scarf, however, tells a different piece of his story. It was the color of the handkerchiefs that Smith's regiment wore in Pontiac's War as a way to distinguish themselves from others; and the Black Boys may have used that strategy as well. Over that, Smith wears a hunting frock ornamented with white, yellow, and blue fringe, an emblem of a frontiersman and something likely worn by soldiers from that area throughout the American Revolution. The portrait, then, tells much of the story of Smith's life.[1]

Yet, if you didn't know Smith's particular story, he looks remarkably unassuming. He has classic male-pattern baldness, which suggests he may have been bald during the rebellion itself. His stare carries no real expression. The red handkerchief might even convey a sense of plainness, since most wealthy individuals preferred white, often silk, cravats to colored ties (colored ties being a sign that the owner needed to hide damage and soil). He appears simple and even strangely modern. Unlike what one sees in portraits of George Washington or John Adams, if you look just at his face, he resembles someone you might encounter on the streets leaving work at five o'clock or in church on Sunday.

Without knowing Smith's story, one might think that the portrait shows James Smith mellowed and restrained with age. But that would be wrong. In 1793, Smith, then in his late fifties, shot a man over a contested election. He killed the man and won the election. In 1812, at age seventy-seven and a year before his death, he stayed true to the prediction that he was destined to be a warrior: he joined the United States' military effort against the Shawnee leader Tecumseh in his unsuccessful pan-Indian uprising that was reminiscent of Pontiac's War. The portrait of this seemingly ordinary, almost anonymous, frontiersman masks Smith's true character—unless you look closely at his dark eyes, which carry a strange combination of intensity and mischief. If you look close, you might even notice a smirk. A careful observer might get a sense of looking at someone who knew he mattered.[2]

What really struck me that day, however, occurred inside the fort's walls. A youth group happened to be camping at the fort. When my host introduced me to the kids as a historian studying the Black Boys, their chaperone, a sturdy man whose build would have suited the demands of an eighteenth-century frontier, gave an impromptu lecture about the Black Boys' Rebellion. He recited names and dates with a precision far greater than I ever could. But more important, he made clear to his captive audience that the Black Boys' Rebellion was about the right to bear arms. Elite easterners and the British military had conspired to take away the frontiersmen's guns, and James Smith and his boys laid siege to Fort Loudon to protect their right to have those guns. They succeeded and helped establish a basic right of the new nation. As the leader spoke, I realized that the wide-eyed kids before him weren't his only audience; so was the eastern academic who was intruding on his territory.

The speech delivered at the fort reminded me of a truth about history—one that usually goes unsaid, although everyone who practices it knows it to be true. There are facts, which some people find boring and are mostly uncontested, and then there are interpretations, which is what makes history exciting and alive. The most convincing interpretations combine facts to explain not only what happened but why it happened. In so doing, a historian gives an event meaning.

Here in this interpretative gray area, the debate about the truth of the past occurs. I have to admit, the youth group leader's explanation of the Black Boys wasn't all wrong; like all fact-based history, it did have an element of truth. The Black Boys did see the seized arms as their lawful private property illegally taken by their government. James Smith did help write the revolutionary constitution in Pennsylvania that contained the declaration "That the people have a right to bear arms for the defence of themselves and the state." These are words that the nation's Bill of Rights would echo, whose meaning we still debate today.

But as I traveled through the region, thinking about the speech I'd heard, I realized that the Black Boys' Rebellion had a larger, truer, and more relevant story to tell than the one offered by the local resident inside the fort. His feelings toward the East—the sense of ignorance and disregard he thought those in the state and federal capital and in the financial centers held toward people like him—bred contempt for government in the modern day that resembled the feelings the Black Boys had in their time. In fact, the political divisions and social tensions between rural and urban America have always been a major part of the nation's politics, except for that brief moment in 1776 when East and West collaborated to accomplish something many people thought impossible.

Consider the history of the people who formed the Black Boys in the years that followed the American Revolution. As soon as peace was settled with the British in Paris in 1783, the bonds between East and West began to fray as Americans formed parties that divided along regional lines. With peace, those in the countryside, many of whom had fought as enlisted soldiers or in local militias, felt ignored once again. Many veterans struggled to make ends meet, and the pay they received from Congress turned worthless in an inflationary spiral that plunged the nation into a recession. Speculators in the east soon snapped up the worthless bonds of frontiersmen and bought large tracts of land in newly opened western areas. Veterans were left with little, while wealthy easterners appeared to control the nation's wealth. With the passage of the U.S. Constitution and the creation of the federal government, something frontiersmen generally opposed, many people felt that this new document undid the accomplishments of the Revolution and returned the nation to the hierarchical, elitist ways of the British Empire. It seemed to some that the revolution they had fought for had simply replaced British aristocrats with eastern American ones.

In 1794, after the federal government passed a tax on whiskey, something that westerners figured would hurt them more than anyone else, they rebelled just as they had done in 1765. The very region the Black Boys operated in became one of the central hubs for opposition activities. Alexander Hamilton, under the command of President George Washington, decided that the federal government, then based in Philadelphia, needed to show its dominance by suppressing the rebels in Pennsylvania—a sign that unlike the British Empire, this new nation had the force necessary to compel its citizens into compliance. A large militia composed of regiments from the eastern areas marched west ready to confront their fellow citizens. The so-called Whiskey Rebels, facing a force larger than they could have anticipated, petered out. But while the rebellion may have been squashed, the sentiments that fueled it remained and infused partisan politics. In fact, at about the same time, Hugh Henry Brackenridge, one of the most observant reporters on the American frontier, predicted that the fibers knitting this new nation together were so fragile that "the time will come when the Western country will fall off the Eastern, as North will from the South, and produce a confederacy of four."[3]

The suspicion of—even hostility toward—the federal government continued as men like James Smith traveled down the Ohio River to establish new communities. The farther they traveled from the new capital of Philadelphia, the more distrustful of its motives they became. It's no surprise that when Thomas Jefferson and James Madison, the most vocal opponents of a strong federal government in Philadelphia, searched for allies to help them protest its overreach, they knew they would find sympathetic ears on the frontiers. With their help, Democratic-Republican Societies formed throughout western areas to oppose the policies coming from the East and formed the backbone of the first party system. When the Federalists passed the Alien and Sedition Acts in 1798, frontier people offered the strongest opposition. James Smith's new state legislature, for instance, passed the Kentucky Resolves—the famous declaration of states' rights that inspired James Calhoun and other southerners in the postwar period to make nullification arguments for laws affecting slavery.

The role of the frontiers in shaping American politics continued in even more concrete ways throughout the nineteenth century. The first frontier president, Andrew Jackson, fought the Second National Bank, accusing it of serving the elite interests of easterners at the expense of the frontiersmen. He destroyed the bank and distributed the financial power of the central bank throughout the country by empowering smaller, local banks, believing that individual communities were better equipped to serve their citizens than a centralized and distant institution. He also oversaw Indian removal, declaring as justification that "it will incalculably strengthen the southwestern frontier and render the adjacent States strong enough to repel future invasions," a sentiment that echoes the demands of frontier people during the American Revolution. It's no mistake that his strongest supporters came from those living along the trans-Appalachian frontier, the descendants of the Black Boys.

In the 1850s, as the country fractured over the issue of slavery, the attitudes that drove the Black Boys helped divide the nation further. James Buchanan, the president born in the shadow of the Black Boys' Rebellion, showed how the suspicions of eastern governments that was so strong in rural areas could merge with southern attitudes that favored slavery. Buchanan may not have been the most vocal proslavery figure, but he was the most important for defending slavery on the eve of the Civil War. His concerns were like those that drove the Black Boys. He worried that eastern abolitionists were causing disunion by trying to force the federal government to interfere in internal matters of individual states. He refused to use executive power when necessary, mainly because his disdain of the federal government made him unwilling to go against his strong belief in a limited executive. His loathing of a northeastern elite and what he saw as meddling activists probably reflected his cultural origins near Fort Loudon, rather than a devotion to the south or slavery. After war broke out, Confederates eyed the area in which the Black Boys had operated a century before, figuring that

the people there were still sympathetic to the south's complaints of easterners intruding on their livelihoods for their own personal gain. The
Confederates made several raids on the area, stories retold to me on my
visit, but the Union was able to push back the invaders.

And then there was the man I met in the fort, criticizing the eastern
elite who he feared ignored his beliefs and dismissed his needs—a living
legacy of this cultural pattern.

Author's Note

R eaders will notice the use of dialogue in certain sections of the
text, something not usually found in works of history. I chose this
technique for several reasons, mainly because I decided it was the
best way to tell the story while also maintaining historical accuracy.

In fact, inspiration for the use of dialogue came from the sources
themselves. While this book relies on a range of sources (including the
work of other historians, printed material, and manuscript correspondence) to tell the story of the Black Boys, Pontiac and his allies and enemies, and imperial agents like George Croghan and William Johnson,
one type of source in particular added color and encouraged the use of
dialogue: depositions and treaty minutes. The constant clashes between
the Black Boys and imperial officials resulted in many legal depositions. Likewise, negotiations between diplomatic officials representing
the British Crown and Native American groups often took the form of
exchanges of dialogue. These records provided detailed and often ver-
batim accounts of conversations between people.

Reading these items gave me such a close feeling for people's inter-
actions that I felt compelled to tell this story. The sources "spoke" to

me, and I wanted to convey the same sense of action that I felt in the archives. Dialogue became a way to do that. In fact, I began to understand why Neil Swanson in the early twentieth century wrote a fictionalized account of James Smith in *The First Rebel*. The sources are among the most extensive and riveting that I have encountered, and they lend themselves to dramatic retelling. In my case, I didn't want to write historical fiction, but I did want my history writing to be as engaging as possible. I therefore considered transforming passages from original sources into exchanges of dialogue.

Still, as a traditionally trained historian, I found experimenting with the use of dialogue in a work of history, rather than a work of historical fiction, to be a little unsettling. I soon adjusted to it because it seemed to promote clearer writing and do full justice to the story. Indeed, I think the use of dialogue makes the confrontations and relationships between the various actors more realistic and gives readers a better way to experience the historical period. Still, I faced several dilemmas along the way that challenged me as a historian trying to tell a true story.

First, did I trust the sources enough to turn reports of conversations between people into dialogue? Ultimately, having read countless depositions and other reports on both sides, I trusted the depositions to be accurate, particularly when multiple depositions, or other sources, included similar phrasing. I therefore felt it acceptable to use dialogue as I did, making sure to footnote full quotations from which the dialogue originated.

After making this decision, I occasionally faced a second, technical problem: changes to tenses and pronouns. If, for instance, Charles Grant told of a conversation that he had with Smith, he would speak in the past tense for his verbs and use the third person and past tense for summaries of what Smith said. This presented me with a harder decision than the question of trust. If I changed a tense or a pronoun, a future historian might use that quote directly as if the original source had said it. Ultimately, I decided that this book was about storytelling, and in a small number of cases I made minor changes to tenses and pronouns to better suit the use of dialogue. In these cases, I provide a full quotation of the original source in the footnotes, and note the type of change I made in the text.

For those interested in this dilemma, here are two examples in which the use of dialogue presented me, as a historian writing a work of history, with problems. Both are from Chapter 4.

Example 1

"Where are you going?" McGlashan asked them.

"Hunting," they answered, staring at McGlashan and his men as if they were targets of the hunt.

"If you are hunting us, you should find us better game," McGlashan replied before ordering them to clear the road.

This passage comes from depositions that Sergeant Leonard McGlashan gave after confronting the Black Boys. The exact text of the deposition that I have revised is: "I asked them where they were going, they answered that they were going a hunting; I told them that if they were hunting us that they should find us better game, and commanded them to clear the road for the Kings Troops which they would not do, until I was oblidged [*sic*] to order my party to fix their bayonets, the sight of which procured me and my party a clear passage to Fort Loudon."

As you can see, I changed the dialogue from the source to reflect the first person and present tense that was surely spoken. The content is for the most part the same as recounted by McGlashan, with a slight editorial change for narrative flow, noted in the following by italicized text: "if they were hunting us that they should find us better game" became "If ~~they~~ *you* ~~were~~ *are* hunting us ~~that they,~~ *you* should find us better game." Most likely, in a spoken exchange the "that" that I deleted wouldn't have been used, and its inclusion in the deposition reflects the way "that" serves to retell a story to another person. If anything, it's possible that "then" would have been used instead of "that" in the exchange, but I would rather remove a super-fluous word than add words I don't know were spoken. Historians remove unnecessary and awkward words from quotations regularly, although they often note it with an ellipsis—a technique that doesn't work for dialogue. Similarly, historians change tenses and the like in quotations but note those changes by placing the revised word in brackets—another technique that doesn't work well for dialogue. Therefore, I made the changes as I did and chose to note them in the footnote.

Example 2

"What do you mean appearing with such a mob before the King's fort," Grant asked Smith.

"I came to demand the prisoners," Smith replied, and threat-ened to rescue them if Grant tried to move them to the jail in Carlisle for trial.

"Suppose they were sent to Carlisle and escorted by the King's troops. What would you do?" Grant asked.

Smith's answer showed the growing resolve of the frontier people.

"We would first fire over the soldiers, and if they would not give up the prisoners, then we are determined to fight the troops. We would sooner die to a man than let them prisoners go to jail," he warned.

This dialogue is taken from a deposition of Lieutenant Charles Grant. Grant recounts the dialogue he had with Smith, but I've edited it to reflect a first-person dialogue in the present tense. The exact text of the original source reads:

> He, the said James Smith, came and acknowledged that he was the man that headed said party. I asked him what he meant by appearing with such a mob before the King's fort? He said that he came to demand the prisoners which I had at that time in custody and that he understood they were to be committed to Carlisle gaol. I asked him what he wou'd do suppose they were sent to Carlisle and escorted by the King's troops? He made answer, that his party should first fire over the soldiers and if they would not give up the prisoners upon that, they were determined to fight the troops and die to a man sooner than let them prisoners go to gaol.

As you can see, the dialogue in Example 2 reflects the source almost perfectly. Aside from the changes involving pronouns and tenses, I made some stylistic adjustments to reflect the natural course of dialogue. The most substantive change, for purposes of readability, had to do with placing the question about what Smith would do if the prisoners were sent to Carlisle. My line reads: "Suppose they were sent to Carlisle and escorted by the King's troops. What would you do then?" The alternative would have been: "What would you do suppose they were sent to Carlisle and escorted by the King's troops?" The alternative is awkward, and not likely the way a verbal exchanged occurred. Similarly, for style purposes, "we would die to a man sooner than let them prisoners go to gaol" became "we would die to a man *sooner* than let them prisoners go to *jail*."

A historian's job is to be true and accurate to the past *and* to share his or her research with a wider audience through publication and other means. I don't think my decision to use dialogue in the way that I have has affected the book's historical accuracy, since the quotes repeat what was reportedly originally said, changing only the tenses and not the substance of the text. In fact, I think their use has improved my ability to convey this history to readers. I hope that this Author's Note, along with notations in the footnotes, will provide sufficient caution for historians about the need to consult original sources for material before using anything themselves. Perhaps this Author's Note and the book more generally can also promote a discussion about the writing of history, its potential and limitations, and the different styles historians can use in writing for different audiences. Had this book been published for a purely academic audience, I probably wouldn't have used this technique (I didn't for my first book, *Frontier Country*, for precisely this reason), but I believe *Frontier Rebels* is a better book because of the decision.

———•———

Finally, writing a book is rarely a solo endeavor. All authors owe a debt of gratitude to the people who facilitated their books' publication. The inspiration for *Frontier Rebels* came from three sources. One was my first book, *Frontier Country: The Politics of War in Early Pennsylvania*. I came across the story of the Black Boys, Pontiac, and the imperial crisis while researching that book. But because it was my first book, and one targeting a specialized audience of colonial historians, it focused almost exclusively on Pennsylvania and its political history from its founding through the Revolution. I was interested in the political problems that developed through territorial expansion. Therefore, only the Black Boys' story made it into that book in any substantive way, and even then, in only a very brief way. But as I wrote that book, the outlines of *Frontier Rebels*, a more story-driven book that takes a wider focus on the crisis of the empire in the West, crystallized. Conversely, the argument I developed in *Frontier Country* influenced my argument in *Frontier Rebels*, and all those who helped me craft that book had an influence on this one, including especially Bob Lockhart at Penn Press.

The second source of inspiration came from my engagement with non-academic history enthusiasts. I began this book when I was on the faculty at Williams College. In the classroom, I found students who wanted to learn history and were excited to read, but they preferred shorter books (certainly a phenomenon not unique to undergraduates). When I searched for a book that could examine the imperial crisis on the frontier of North America, I could never find one that suited the story I wanted to tell and fit the students' needs. So I decided to write a book that might be suitable for a classroom assignment for courses on early American history, and especially the American Revolution. I want to thank those students for their inspiration.

At the same time, I have always been engaged with public history—that is, working with teachers, history enthusiasts, library and museum professionals, and others involved in conveying history to non-academic audiences. Their enthusiasm for history was infectious, and when I spoke of the Black Boys and the imperial crisis, many people expressed a fascination with this untold story and a desire to learn more about it and the era more generally. I hope that *Frontier Rebels* speaks to their passion for history and furthers their engagement with the past.

The last source of inspiration came from the David Library of the American Revolution, which provided me with a space to write this book. The grounds of the Library, combined with its immense hold-ings, made it a writer's paradise. I am indebted to the David Library for its support of this project and of my career more generally. Williams College, likewise, offered me a year-long sabbatical that allowed me the time to write. I deeply appreciate the support of both institutions.

Several individuals provided important guidance throughout the process. Michael McDonnell and Woody Holton both read early drafts and offered important advice and much-needed corrections. The manuscript is stronger because of their critiques, and any remaining faults are my own. Dan Guzy, Paul Douglass Newman, and Christopher Pearl read later drafts and provided additional advice that strengthened the manuscript before it headed to production. I especially thank Chris for pointing to additional sources and sharing his knowledge of the Black Boys, and Dan Guzy for offering critical advice and sharing his wonderful maps. Dan and I share some friendly disagreements about how to interpret the significance of the Black Boys, but his research is superb and I am indebted to him for help with data points included on the map of the Black Boys' Rebellion. Gary Nash also provided helpful feedback near the end of the project, which allowed me to further refine the work and its argument. Alexis Smith provided me with excellent advice on the manuscript and helped me learn more about the Ohio River valley and its politics.

Keith Thomson, former executive officer at the American Philosophical Society, read the first draft of the manuscript. His support of the project was instrumental in its publication. After sharing some of his own insights on the early American west, he put me in touch with his agent, George Lucas. George likewise helped me polish the manuscript and guided me through the ropes of shopping a book and selecting a publisher. I especially thank George for introducing me to Maria Guarnaschelli at W. W. Norton. Even before signing a contract, she gave me sage advice and offered a close reading of the manuscript that reassured me that Norton was the right place for the book. Her assistant, Nathaniel Dennett, subsequently proved to be a strong supporter who has helped marshal the book through production. Melanie Tortoroli arrived late in the process, but she has guided the manuscript across the finish line. Her editorial insight has strengthened key parts of the manuscript, and she has been a wonderful supporter of the book.

Abby Shelton, my assistant at the APS, helped in all matters, including (but not limited to) editorial, technical, and administrative support. Her suggestions have strengthened the book, and her work has helped me in innumerable other ways. Other colleagues at the APS have made my non-writing work life fulfilling. I especially thank Bob Hauser, Linda Jacobs, Merrill Mason, Annie Westcott, and John Wolfe, and those in the Library who make it one of the finest research libraries in America, especially Brian Carpenter, Marian Christ, Anne Downey, David Gary, Charlie Greifenstein, Val Lutz, Earle Spamer, and Scott Ziegler. I am particularly indebted to Bob Hauser, the Society's current Executive Officer. Bob dedicated several days to reading the manuscript amidst a whirlwind of other events. It was a Herculean effort, but his editorial critique improved the manuscript throughout.

Last but certainly not least, Laura and my children continue to brighten my life, and they have inspired me to write, especially as my children become older and more interested in history. But there is an irony there. My only regret with the publication of the book is the hours I spent in front of the computer instead of spending time with them.

Notes

———•———

ARCHIVES

APS   American Philosophical Society
HSP   Historical Society of Pennsylvania, Philadelphia, PA
PHMC   Pennsylvania Historical and Museum Commission, State
           Archives, Harrisburg, PA

PRINTED SOURCES

IHC   *Collections of the Illinois State Historical Library*
Pa. Archives *Pennsylvania Archives*
PCM   *Minutes of the Provincial Council of Pennsylvania*
WJP   *Papers of Sir William Johnson*

PREFACE: THE CRISIS OF EMPIRE

1. The best distillation of the Stamp Act Crisis is Edmund Morgan, *The Stamp Act Crisis: Prologue to Revolution* (1953; repr., Chapel Hill: University of North Carolina Press, 1995), quotation from 307. For the evolution of this movement from protests to something more, see Pauline Maier, *From Resistance to Revolution: Colonial Radicals and the Development of American Opposition to Britain, 1765–1776* (New York: W. W. Norton, 1992). For those who

see taxes as a sensible way of managing the Empire's new debt, see Eliga H. Gould, *The Persistence of Empire: British Political Culture in the Age of the American Revolution* (Chapel Hill: University of North Carolina Press, 2000) and *Among the Powers of the Earth: The American Revolution and the Making of a New World Empire* (Cambridge: Harvard University Press, 2012), 105, and Lewis Gipson, *The Coming of the American Revolution, 1763–1775* (New York: Harper Torchbooks, 1962).

2. See Maier, *From Resistance to Revolution*, and Maier, "Popular Uprisings and Civil Authority in Eighteenth Century America," *The William and Mary Quarterly Third Series* 27, no. 1 (January 1970): 3–35, for an analysis of the forms of protest the colonists adopted. For an overview on the policies the Empire took toward the West, see Gipson, *The Coming of the American Revolution*; Colin Calloway, *The Scratch of a Pen: 1763 and the Transformation of North America* (New York: Oxford University Press, 2006); and Jack Sosin, *The Revolutionary Frontier, 1763–1783* (New York: Holt, Rinehart and Winston, 1967); and especially Jack Sosin, *Whitehall and the Wilderness: The Middle West in British Colonial Policy, 1760 to 1775* (Lincoln: University of Nebraska Press, 1961).

3. Neil Swanson, *The First Rebel: Being a Lost Chapter of Our History and a True Narrative of America's First Uprising against English Military Authority* (New York: Farrar & Rinehart, 1937). The novel was the basis for an early John Wayne film, *Allegheny Uprising* (1939). Historians have noted the presence of the Black Boys with greater frequency in recent years, though there is still no sustained study of them. For more scholarly takes, see Eleanor Webster, "Insurrection at Fort Loudon in 1765: Rebellion or Preservation of Peace," *Western Pennsylvania Historical Magazine* 47 (1964), 5–39, and Stephen Cutcliffe, "Sideling Hill Affair: The Cumberland County Riots of 1765," *Western Pennsylvania Historical Magazine* 59 (1976), 39–54. For the most recent studies, see Gregory Evans Dowd, *War under Heaven: Pontiac, the Indian Nations, and the British Empire* (Baltimore: Johns Hopkins University Press, 2004), 204–11; Patrick Griffin, *American Leviathan: Empire, Nation, and Revolutionary Frontier* (New York: Hill & Wang, 2007), and Terry Bouton, *Taming Democracy: "The People," the Founders, and the Troubled Ending of the American Revolution* (New York: Oxford University Press, 2007). Edward White, *The Backcountry and the City: Colonization and Conflict in Early America* (Minneapolis: University of Minnesota Press, 2005), discusses James Smith, the leader of the Black Boys, extensively.

CHAPTER 1: SETTING THE STAGE

1. The best work on the Seven Years' War is Fred Anderson, *Crucible of War: The Seven Years' War and the Fate of Empire in British North America, 1754–1766* (New York: Vintage, 2000), especially 505–506 for the peace treaty and its significance. For a discussion of European visions of the West, see Paul Mapp, *The Elusive West and the Contest for Empire, 1713–1763* (Chapel Hill: University of North Carolina Press and the Omohundro Institute, 2011). This and the following paragraphs are based largely on these works.

2. For the details on Washington's orders, see Jason Farr, "The Unlikely Success of a Provincial Surveyor: George Washington Finds Fame in the American Interior, 1749–1754," in Edward Lengel, ed., *A Companion to George Washington* (West Sussex: Wiley-Blackwell, 2012), Chapter 2. For the best biographies on Washington during this era, see Douglas Southall Freeman, *Washington* (1968; repr., New York: Simon & Schuster, 1995); Ron Chernow, *Washington: A Life* (New York: Penguin Books, 2010); Robert Dalzell and Lee Baldwin Dalzell, *George Washington's Mount Vernon: At Home in Revolutionary America* (New York: Oxford University Press, 2000); Joseph Ellis, *His Excellency: George Washington* (New York: Alfred A. Knopf, 2004); and Peter Henriques, *Realistic Visionary: A Portrait of George Washington* (Charlottesville: University of Virginia Press, 2006); Anderson, *Crucible of War*, 1–73.

3. Anderson, *Crucible of War*, 453–56, 505–6, 515–17.

4. For discussions of the debt and its influence on policy-making, see Edmund Morgan, *Stamp Act Crisis* (1953; repr., Chapel Hill: University of North Carolina Press, 1995), 21–40; Richard Middlekauff, *The Glorious Cause: The American Revolution, 1763–1789* (New York: Oxford University Press, 2005), 53–73; Thomas Purvis, "The Seven Years' War and Its Political Legacy" and Peter D. G. Thomas, "The Greenville Program, 1763–1765," in *A Companion to the American Revolution*, Jack P. Greene and J. R. Pole, eds. (West Sussex: Wiley-Blackwell, 2003), 112–22; Anderson, *Crucible of War*, 560–71, 644–47; Robert Wright, *One Nation under Debt: Hamilton, Jefferson, and the History of What We Owe* (New York: McGraw-Hill, 2008), 34–39; Jack Sosin, *Whitehall and the Wilderness: The Middle West in British Colonial Policy, 1760–1775* (Lincoln: University of Nebraska Press, 1961), especially 79–98. The actual budget numbers fluctuate in many of these accounts. I have relied on the United Kingdom Public Spending website for the numbers I use, accessible

here: http://www.ukpublicspending.co.uk/year_spending_1764UKmn_14
mcln#ukgs302 (accessed July 21, 2018).

5. For the best work on the colonial economy, see John Menard and Richard
McCusker, *The Economy of British America, 1607–1789* (Chapel Hill: Institute
of Early American History and Culture at the University of North Carolina Press, 1985), especially 51–90. See also Thomas Purvis, *Revolutionary
America, 1763–1800* (New York: Facts on File, 1995), 37–122, especially 84–
85 for data on iron-making. For the consumer revolution, see T. H. Breen,
*The Marketplace of Revolution: How Consumer Politics Shaped American Inde-
pendence* (New York: Oxford University Press, 2004), 1–194. For a shorter
discussion of this transformation, see Jack P. Greene, "The Origins of the
New Colonial Policy, 1748–1763," in Greene and Pole, *A Companion to the
American Revolution*, 101–11.

6. By the 1760s, colonists became well aware of this unfavorable balance
of trade. See, for example, Daniel Dulany, *Considerations on the propriety of
imposing taxes in the British colonies for the Purpose of Raising a Revenue by Act
of Parliament* (Annapolis, MD: Jonas Green, 1765), 44. Historians have
recently challenged the notion that the colonies operated at a serious deficit. Many have shown that there were various forms of trade that colonists
did not consider, such as ship-building and the carrying trade with Caribbean, that made the deficit much smaller than they often assumed. See
especially Menard and McCusker, *Economy of British America*, 83. While
these revisions to the balance-of-trade deficit appear accurate, the impressions at the time are more relevant, since these beliefs are what drove
individuals' actions.

7. See, especially, Breen, *Marketplace of Revolution*, 1–194, and "'Baubles of
Britain': The American and Consumer Revolutions of the Eighteenth
Century," *Past and Present*, no. 119 (May 1988): 73–104.

8. For fears of French success, see *Pennsylvania Gazette*, May 9, 1754.

9. The best accounts of Pennsylvania's experience in particular are Matthew
Ward, *Breaking the Backcountry: The Seven Years' War in Virginia and Penn-
sylvania, 1754–1765* (Pittsburgh: University of Pittsburgh Press, 2004) and
Peter Silver, *Our Savage Neighbors: How Indian War Transformed Early America*
(New York: W. W. Norton, 2008). The creek's name has several different
purported origins. For the Black Boys as the source of the creek's name,
see William Henry Egle, *History of the Commonwealth of Pennsylvania: Civil,
Political and Military from Its Earliest Settlement to the Present Time* (Philadel-

phia: E. M. Gardner, 1883), 376, and Sherman Day, *Historical Collections of the State of Pennsylvania* (Philadelphia: G. W. Gorton, 1843), 120, 125. For a contemporary eighteenth-century account of the creek's origins, see John Ewing Memorandum Book, Pennsylvania Historical and Museum Commission (hereafter PHMC), State Archives, Harrisburg, PA. In 1784, John Ewing was sent to survey the southern boundary of Pennsylvania and traveled along the communication line created during the Seven Years' War that ran from Philadelphia to Fort Pitt. In his journal, he recounts how Bloody Run got its name: "John Paxton keeps a Tavern at ye Warriors Mt or Bloody Run; so called from the Murder of a Number of People sent to Scout Provisions to Mr. Buchanan who was surveying ye Roads to Bedford in ye Year 1755." Unlike the other possible sources of the creek's name, Ewing's was written twenty years after the war, and its chronological proximity to the event makes it the most accurate in my thinking.

10. For examples of this fear, see the Diary of Rhoda Barber, Historical Society of Pennsylvania (hereafter HSP), and for the sentries aiding farmers, see John Armstrong to General Forbes, Carlisle, July 9, 1758, *Pennsylvania Archives* (hereafter *PA Archives*), First Series, 3:448. Quote from [James Burd?] to [?], Fort Augusta, Dec. 28, 1756, Edward Shippen Thompson Collection, PHMC.

11. Anderson, *Crucible of War*; for celebrations, see 373–74.

12. For discussions of this, see Morgan, *Stamp Act Crisis*, 21–40; Lewis Gipson, *The Coming of the Revolution, 1763–1775* (New York: Harper Torchbooks, 1962), 1–84, especially 55–68; and Sosin, *Whitehall and the Wilderness*, especially 3–51 and 79–98.

13. The best account of the Empire's attempt to order the West, and the problems it caused, is Sosin, *Whitehall and the Wilderness*, especially 52–78. Fred Anderson also provides an excellent analysis of the creation of these new policies and their reception in the colonies in *Crucible of War*, 453–690. Timothy Shannon, *Indians and Colonists at the Crossroads of Empire: The Albany Congress of 1754* (Ithaca, NY: Cornell University Press, 2000), 220–26, details Johnson's appointment. His book also provides a wide perspective on the Albany Plan and imperial reform efforts.

14. "The Royal Proclamation, October 7, 1763," *The Avalon Project: Documents in Law, History and Diplomacy*, Lillian Goldman Law Library, Yale Law School, http://avalon.law.yale.edu/18th_century/proc1763.asp (accessed April 17, 2018). For an essay that examines imperial intent with this Proc-

lamation and subsequent plans, see Daniel Richter, "The Plan of 1764: Native Americans and a British Empire That Never Was," in Daniel Richter, *Trade, Land, and Power: The Struggle for Eastern North America* (Philadelphia: University of Pennsylvania Press, 2013), 177–201. For more on the Proclamation and its wider context, see Colin Calloway, *The Scratch of a Pen* (New York: Oxford University Press, 2006).

15. Sosin, *Whitehall and the Wilderness,* especially 52–98 and 181–210; Calloway, *Scratch of a Pen,* 92–111; Anderson, *Crucible of War,* 557–690; and Richter, "The Plan of 1764."

16. Morgan, *Stamp Act Crisis,* 21–40, Purvis, "The Seven Years' War and Its Political Legacy," and Thomas, "The Greenville Program, 1763–1765," in *A Companion to the American Revolution,* Greene and Pole, eds., 112–22.

17. Morgan, *Stamp Act Crisis,* 54–74, Thomas, "The Greenville Program, 1763–1765," and "The Stamp Act Crisis and Its Repercussions, Including the Quartering Act Controversy," in *A Companion to the American Revolution,* Greene and Pole, eds., 118–33. Stephen Dowell, *A History and Explanation of the Stamp Duties* (London, 1893), 15.

18. Ibid. Morgan estimates the total cost of the North American troops to be £220,000, while Thomas puts the number higher, at £350,000. Thomas's number probably comes from Greenville, which Morgan says includes military expenditures in areas other than North America. Either way, the combined total would have been about £120,000—or about a half to a third of either estimate.

19. For the economic recession, see Gary Nash, *Urban Crucible: The Northern Seaports and the Origins of the American Revolution* (Cambridge: Harvard University Press, 1986), especially 155–59.

20. For the best sustained analysis of Pontiac's War, see Gregory Evans Dowd, *War under Heaven: Pontiac, the Indian Nations, and the British Empire* (Baltimore: Johns Hopkins University Press, 2004), especially 90–105 for more on Neolin. See also Richard White, *The Middle Ground: Indians, Empires, and Republics in the Great Lakes Region, 1650–1815* (Cambridge: Cambridge University Press, 1991), 269–314.

21. Dowd, *War under Heaven,* especially 114–47.

22. The critique of the plan is widespread in the literature, but for summations, see Calloway, *Scratch of a Pen,* 92–111, especially 98–99; Dowd, *War under Heaven,* 177–203, especially 177–79; and Richter, "Plan of 1764," especially 184–87.

23. Dowd, *War under Heaven*, 162–68.

24. William Johnson to the Lords of Trade, August 30, 1764, in Clarence Alvord, ed., *Collections of the Illinois State Historical Library: The Critical Period, 1763–1765* (Springfield: Illinois State Historical Library, 1915), vol. X, pp. 305–8, quotation from 307 (hereafter *IHC*).

25. George Croghan to Thomas Gage, Fort Pitt, March 2, 1765, Thomas Gage Papers, American Series, Clements Library, University of Michigan (hereafter Gage Papers).

CHAPTER 2: THE MISSION

1. Croghan has figured prominently in the historiography of Indian–white relations and trade. Most sources depict him as a very effective trader who won Indian allies early in his career and then later became a rapacious land dealer who tried to maximize his own interests. For the best biographies of Croghan, see Albert Volwiler, *George Croghan and the Westward Movement, 1741–1782* (New York: AMS Press, 1971), and especially Nicholas Wainwright, *George Croghan, Wilderness Diplomat* (Chapel Hill: University of North Carolina Press, 1959). For more recent takes, see the composites drawn in James Merrell, *Into the American Woods: Negotiators on the Pennsylvania Frontier* (New York: Norton, 1999); William Campbell, *Speculators in Empire: Iroquoia and the 1768 Treaty of Fort Stanwix* (Norman: University of Oklahoma Press, 2012); Eric Hinderaker, *Elusive Empires: Constructing Colonialism in the Ohio Valley, 1673–1800* (New York: Cambridge University Press, 1999); Richard White, *The Middle Ground: Indians, Empires, and Republics in the Great Lakes Region, 1560–1815* (Cambridge: Cambridge University Press, 1991); and Gregory Evans Dowd, *War under Heaven: Pontiac, the Indian Nations, and the British Empire* (Baltimore: Johns Hopkins University Press, 2004). My own perspective on Croghan is influenced by these works and others but mostly by my extensive reading of his correspondence.

2. Wainwright, *George Croghan*, 4, and Volwiler, *George Croghan*, 23. There is some evidence that Croghan was born around 1718. See Wainwright, *George Croghan*, 107.

3. Wainwright, *George Croghan*, 5–12.

4. For comparisons between the British frontiers and North America, see Colin Calloway, *White People, Indians, and Highlanders: Tribal People and the Colonial Encounters in Scotland and America* (New York: Oxford University

Press, 2008); and Fintan O'Toole, *White Savage: William Johnson and the Invention of America* (Albany: State University of New York Press, 2005), especially 16–38 for an example of how Irish society may have shaped someone like Croghan. His own lineage is murky, with none of his biographers being able to identify his parents. His extended family, however, is known. Most were traders or otherwise connected to merchant communities in Ireland, England, and North America. His relative, Nicholas Croghan, was a very successful Ireland-based merchant who served as Croghan's Dublin agent and whose son, William, emigrated to America in the 1760s and became a soldier in the American Revolution and an early settler in Kentucky. See John Kleber, ed., *The Encyclopedia of Louisville* (Lexington: University Press of Kentucky, 2015), 233, and Wainwright, *George Croghan*, 260.

5. Wainwright, *George Croghan*, 207 and 260; and Nicholas B. Wainwright, "An Indian Trade Failure: The Story of the Hockley, Trent and Croghan Company, 1748–1752," *The Pennsylvania Magazine of History and Biography* 72, no. 4 (1948): 345.

6. For Croghan practicing subterfuge, see Howard Peckham, *Pontiac and the Indian Uprising* (Princeton, NJ: Princeton University Press, 1947), 47–48.

7. See O'Toole, *White Savage*, for the best recent biography of Johnson. James Flexner's *Mohawk Baronet: A Biography of Sir William Johnson* (Syracuse, NY: Syracuse University Press, 1959) is also noteworthy, especially 7–12 on his early life and extended family. See David Preston, *Texture of Contact: European and Indian Settler Communities on the Frontier of Iroquoia, 1667–1783* (Lincoln: University of Nebraska Press, 2009), for a work that emphasizes Johnson's unique role in maintaining the Iroquois alliance.

8. For Johnson at the battle, see Eric Hinderaker, *A Tale of Two Hendricks: Unraveling a Mohawk Mystery* (Cambridge, MA: Harvard University Press, 2010), 260–66. For his appointment, see Timothy Shannon, *Indians and Colonists at the Crossroads of Empire: The Albany Congress of 1754* (Ithaca, NY: Cornell University Press, 2000), 220–26 and 240, n13; Hinderaker, *Elusive Empires*, 40–43, 146–48; Merrell, *Into the American Woods*, 82; Michael McConnell, *A Country Between: The Upper Ohio Valley and Its Peoples, 1724–1774* (Lincoln: University of Nebraska Press, 1997), 126–27; O'Toole, *White Savage*, 232, and Wainwright, *George Croghan*, 113, for Croghan's appointment.

9. Walter S. Dunn, *Opening New Markets: The British Army and the Old Northwest* (Westport, CT: Praeger, 2002), 118–19, and Wainwright, *George Croghan,* 213.

10. George Croghan to Thomas Gage, Fort Pitt, March 12, 1765, Gage Papers; and Wainwright, *George Croghan,* 213–15.

11. Walter Dunn offers the most exhaustive account of the finances of the mission in *Opening New Markets,* especially 118–21. On the shell company, see Wainwright, *George Croghan,* 217, and the correspondence of Thomas Gage at the Clements Library, especially Thomas Gage to William Johnson, New York, April 15, 1765.

12. These details come from Dunn's analysis of the Baynton, Wharton, and Morgan account books. See Dunn, *Opening New Markets,* 118–22, and Walter Dunn, *People of the American Frontier: The Coming of the American Revolution* (Westport, CT: Praeger, 2005), 165–67.

13. For details on the weather, see Alexander Fraser to Thomas Gage, Fort Pitt, March 4, 1765, Gage Papers. See also Joseph Galloway to Benjamin Franklin, January 23, 1765, http://franklinpapers.org/franklin//framed Volumes.jsp?vol=12&page=025a (accessed April 17, 2018) for details on the departure.

14. Fraser to Gage, March 4, 1765, Gage Papers.

15. Alexander Fraser to Thomas Gage, Fort Pitt, March 4, 1765, Gage Papers.

16. Amherst has been generally blamed for the cuts to the Indian Department. While these charges are largely true, he also had external pressures. In any case, this depiction of Amherst represents the general consensus of historians. For overviews, see Dowd, *War under Heaven,* especially 72–78; White, *Middle Ground,* 248, 256–68; and Anderson, *Crucible of War,* 472–75, which provides a more sympathetic perspective on Amherst's rationale, and 535–53.

17. George Croghan to the Lords of Trade, June 8, 1764, *IHC,* 10:257. I have seen a manuscript copy that deviates slightly from this text in grammar and spelling, though the content and argument are the same. For the manuscript, see Cadwaladar Collection, Series IV, Box 5, page 4. On Amherst's recall, see Anderson, *Crucible of War,* 552–53.

18. For a good overview of Gage, see David Hackett Fischer, *Paul Revere's Ride* (New York: Oxford University Press, 1994), 32–37. For more on the structure of the British Army and its relationship to the aristocracy, see David

Hackett Fischer, *Washington's Crossing* (New York: Oxford University Press, 2004), 33–34.

19. Thomas Gage to Governor James Wright [GA], New York, March 7, 1765, Gage Papers.

20. Thomas Gage to Colonel Henry Bouquet, New York, March 4, 1765, Gage Papers.

21. For more on the nature of Indian–white diplomacy and the type of characters who succeeded, see Merrell, *Into the American Woods*.

22. For the best accounts of this problem, see Jack Sosin, *Whitehall and the Wilderness: The Middle West in British Colonial Policy, 1760–1775* (Lincoln: University of Nebraska Press, 1961), and Colin Calloway, *The Scratch of a Pen: 1763 and the Transformation of North American* (New York: Oxford University Press, 2006). It is also distilled in White, *Middle Ground*, 269–314; Anderson, *Crucible of War*, 453–502; and Dowd, *War under Heaven*, especially 177–85 and 233–36.

23. Gage to Henry Bouquet, [May 1?], 1764, Papers of Thomas Gage, PHMC.

24. Ibid.

25. Ibid. The problem of controlling colonists is rampant throughout the historiography. See especially Patrick Griffin, *American Leviathan* (New York: Hill & Wang, 2007), 46–94, and Sosin, *Whitehall and the Wilderness*, 3–78, 99–127.

26. *The Papers of Henry Bouquet*, ed. Louis M. Waddell (Harrisburg: Pennsylvania Historical and Museum Commission, 1994), 6:768–769.

27. For the best work on Pontiac the man, see Howard Peckham, *Pontiac and the Indian Uprising* (Princeton, NJ: Princeton University Press, 1947), especially the chapter "Early Life." Many of the conflicting accounts used in this section come from Peckham's work, especially 14–17 and 28–29. For the most nuanced perspectives on Pontiac, see White, *Middle Ground*, 269–315, and Dowd, *War under Heaven*. The two best summaries of this historiography are White, *Middle Ground*, 269–71; and Dowd, *War under Heaven*, 5–12.

28. Peckham, *Pontiac and the Indian Uprising*, 14–17.

29. Ibid., especially 47–48 for the Croghan reference.

30. For "war called 'Pontiac's'" see Jennings, *Empire of Fortune: Crowns, Colonies, and Tribes in the Seven Years' War*, 438–54. Recently, a major conference on the conflict at the McNeil Center for Early American Studies used this

name for the war, a title that also appears in various other historians' works.

31. For a similar take on Pontiac, see White, *Middle Ground*, especially 267–314.

32. For discussion of this division, see Peckham, *Pontiac and the Indian Uprising*, 267–69; White, *Middle Ground*, 299–305; and David Dixon, *Never Come to Peace Again: Pontiac's Uprising and the Fate of the British Empire in North America* (Norman: University of Oklahoma Press, 2005), 240–41.

33. For discussion of the theory that Great Britain may have created the idea of Pontiac as a singular leader, see Dowd, *War under Heaven*, 7–9 and 10–11 for Ottawa leadership styles. William Johnson to George Croghan, Johnson Hall, March 9, 1765, *The Papers of Sir William Johnson* (Albany: The University of the State of New York, 1953) (hereafter *WJP*), 11:627–630.

34. See especially White, *Middle Ground*, 269–314, for the view of Kaské's camp. For the quote, see Colin Calloway, *Shawnees and the War for America* (New York: Viking, 2007), 41.

35. For Kaské's growing power, see White, *Middle Ground*, 300–305; Dowd, *War under Heaven*, 217–19; and Calloway, *Scratch of a Pen*, 76.

CHAPTER 3: THE CONVOY DEPARTS

1. Details on his ownership can be found in Walter S. Dunn, *Opening New Markets: The British Army and the Old Northwest* (Westport, CT: Praeger, 2002), 118–19. For the average New England farmer, see Thomas Purvis, *Revolutionary America: 1763–1800* (New York: Facts on File, 1995), 113, and for a full view on colonies, see Alice Hanson Jones, *The Wealth of a Nation to Be: The American Colonies on the Eve of the Revolution* (New York: Columbia University Press, 1980), 224, Table 7.5. For more on Callender's background, see Judith Ridner, *A Town In-Between: Carlisle, Pennsylvania, and the Early Mid-Atlantic Interior* (Philadelphia: University of Pennsylvania, 2010), 51–52, 80, 89.

2. For the best work on the development of southeastern Pennsylvania, see James Lemon, *Best Poor Man's Country: Early Southeastern Pennsylvania* (New York: W. W. Norton, 1976). For Lancaster itself, see Jerome Woods, *Conestoga Crossroads: Lancaster, Pennsylvania, 1730–1790* (Harrisburg: Pennsylvania Historical and Museum Commission, 1979). For the creation of Cumberland County and Carlisle's development, see Ridner, *A Town In-Between*, especially 12–111. For the Mason quote, see Charles

Mason, diary, January 10 and January 17, 1765, MG614, Papers Regarding the Paxton Boys and Conestoga Massacre, LancasterHistory.org, Lancaster, PA.

3. Ridner, *A Town In-Between*, 49. For Croghan's house, see Albert Volwiler, *George Croghan and the Westward Movement, 1741–1782* (New York: AMS Press, 1971), 16–18, and Nicholas Wainwright, *George Croghan, Wilderness Diplomat* (Chapel Hill: University of North Carolina Press, 1959), 9–12. For Croghan's ventures, see also Eric Hinderaker, *Elusive Empires: Constructing Colonialism in the Ohio Valley, 1673–1800* (New York: Cambridge University Press, 1999), 41–43.

4. For the county's creation, see Ridner, *A Town In-Between*, especially 12–43, and Patrick Spero, *A Frontier Country: The Politics of War in Early Pennsylvania* (Philadelphia: University of Pennsylvania Press, 2016), Chapter 4.

5. Ridner, *A Town In-Between*, 12–43.

6. Ibid.

7. For "pioneer," see Ridner, *A Town In-Between*, 101–102, 89–90 for his service and postwar success, and 244, fn 91, for the closeness of Croghan and Callender. Callender is a largely overlooked figure, mostly because many of his papers are lost. He does appear as a prominent trader in most of the above-cited works. In addition to Ridner, see Hinderaker, *Elusive Empires*, 40–43.

8. On horses arriving, see Deposition of Robert Callender, March 28, 1765, Gage Papers. On the plans that went into the transportation, see Deposition of James Maxwell, April 3, 1765, Gage Papers. The hundred horses come from Maxwell's deposition, which says that in addition to the eighty-one horses the Black Boys attacked, another thirty loaded with powder and lead were sent to his father's house. The home being formerly Pawling's was noted in the Black Boys' song reproduced below. The Black Boys referred to this waypoint as Pawlings, but the depositions suggest that it had recently changed hands. For the Pawlings home, see *History of Franklin County, Pennsylvania: Containing a History of the County* (Chicago: Warner, Beers & Co., 1887), especially 559, and *Publications of the Genealogical Society of Pennsylvania* (Philadelphia, PA: March, 1918), 7:15–16. Pawling owned a 745-acre piece of property and a 121-acre one. I suspect the 121-acre plot was the one used because it was the new property and likely further west—the type of property a person would sell or lease to someone else.

9. For evidence of these rumors and the scrutiny of Howe's place as a way-point, see Deposition of Robert Callender, March 28, 176, Gage Papers; Deposition of Robert Allison, April 1, 1765, Gage Papers; and Deposition of William Smith, April 3, 1765, Gage Papers.

10. Quotation from Deposition of Robert Allison, April 1, 1765, Gage Papers.

11. For the best account of the war experience, see Peter Silver, *Our Savage Neighbors* (New York: W. W. Norton, 2008), especially 196–97 for the account of the raid. For the Civil War comparison, see Matthew Ward, *Breaking the Backcountry* (Pittsburgh: University of Pittsburgh Press, 2004), 58 and 268, fn 11. For more on frontiers in eighteenth-century Pennsylvania, see Patrick Spero, *Frontier Country: The Politics of War in Early Pennsylvania* (Philadelphia: University of Pennsylvania Press, 2016).

12. Benjamin Franklin, *Great Britain Considered* (Philadelphia, 1760), 21. For a further expansion of this argument, see Spero, *Frontier Country*, especially the Introduction, Coda, and Chapters 5–7.

13. See especially Spero, *Frontier Country*, Chapters 5 and 6.

14. For a list of the taxables and representation, see Charles Lincoln, *The Revolutionary Movement in Pennsylvania* (Philadelphia: University of Pennsylvania, 1901), 47–48.

15. For larger treatments of this war and its politics, see Spero, *Frontier Country*; David Preston, *The Texture of Contact* (Lincoln: University of Nebraska Press, 2009), James Merrell, *Into the American Woods: Negotiators on the Pennsylvania Frontier* (New York: Norton, 1999); Matthew Ward, *Breaking the Backcountry* (Pittsburgh: University of Pittsburgh Press, 2004); Robert Davidson, *War Comes to Quaker Pennsylvania* (New York: Temple University Publications by Columbia University, 1957); Kevin Kenny, *Peaceable Kingdom Lost: The Paxton Boys and the Destruction of William Penn's Holy Experiment* (New York: Oxford University Press, 2009); and Alan Tully, *Forming American Politics: Ideals, Interests, and Institutions in Colonial New York and Pennsylvania* (Baltimore: Johns Hopkins University Press, 1994).

16. Letter from Edward Biddle to James Biddle, Reading, PA, *Minutes of the Provincial Council of Pennsylvania* (Harrisburg, PA: Theodore Fenn and Company, 1851), 6:705 (hereafter *PCM*).

17. Armstrong quote from Tully, *Forming American Politics*, 157. Letter believed to be from Francis West was first produced in Samuel Hazard, *Hazard's Register of Pennsylvania* (Harrisburg, PA, 1829) 4:309 and reproduced in numerous other accounts.

18. For representative scholarship on the Paxton Boys, see Peter Silver, *Our Savage Neighbors*; Kevin Kenny, *Peaceable Kingdom Lost: The Paxton Boys and the Destruction of William Penn's Holy Experiment* (New York: Oxford University Press, 2009); Brooke Hindle, "The March of the Paxton Boys," *The William and Mary Quarterly* 3, no. 4 (1946), 461–86; Alison Olson, "The Paxton Boys' Pamphlet War," *Pennsylvania Magazine of History and Biography* 123, no. 1–2 (1999): 31–54; and Jack Brubaker, *The Massacre of the Conestoga: On the Trail of the Paxton Boys in Lancaster County* (Charleston: History Press, 2010). See also Spero, *Frontier Country*.

19. For the petition, see *Votes of Assembly*, 8th series, 7:5582.

20. Ibid.

21. Thomas Gage to William Johnson, New York, March 10, 1765, Gage Papers; William Johnson to Thomas Gage, Johnson Hall, March 9, 1765, Gage Papers; Thomas Gage to Colonel Bouquet, New York, March 4, 1765, Gage Papers.

22. Thomas Gage to Henry Bouquet, *Papers of Henry Bouquet*, 6:762, and Thomas Gage to William Johnson, New York, Feb. 25, 1765, Gage Papers.

23. For the imperial plans for the West, see Jack Sosin, *Whitehall and the Wilderness: The Middle West in British Colonial Policy, 1760–1775* (Lincoln: University of Nebraska Press, 1961), 3–180.

24. The best accounts of this new imperial apparatus can be found in many of the above-cited works, but see especially Fred Anderson, *Crucible of War: The Seven Years' War and the Fate of Empire in British North America, 1754–1766* (New York: Vintage, 2000), especially 560–71; Daniel Richter, "The Plan of 1764: Native Americans and a British Empire That Never Was," in *Trade, Land, and Power*, ed. Daniel Richter (Philadelphia: University of Pennsylvania Press, 2013); and Gregory Evans Dowd, *War under Heaven* (Baltimore: Johns Hopkins University Press, 2004), 170–212. The best work on the subject is Sosin, *Whitehall and the Wilderness*.

25. William Johnson to Thomas Gage, Johnson Hall, Feb. 14, 1765, Gage Papers.

26. Thomas Gage to Captain Cochrane in SC, New York, Feb. 25, 1765, Gage Papers; Arthur Dobbs to Thomas Gage, Brunswick, March 11, 1765, Gage Papers.

27. For rumors, see Anderson, *Crucible of War*, 629–630; Richard White, *The Middle Ground* (Cambridge: Cambridge University Press, 1991), 299–305; "Journal of George Croghan 1765," in Israel Daniel Rupp, *Early His-*

tory of Western Pennsylvania: And of the West, and of Western Expeditions and Campaigns (Harrisburg, PA: W.O. Hickok, 1846), 167; Journal of George Croghan, *Collections of the Illinois State Historical Library: The New Regime, 1765–1767*, 11:2; George Croghan to Thomas Gage, March 2, 1765, Gage Papers.

28. William Johnson agreed with this plan. In fact, he seems to have come up with it independently. See William Johnson to George Croghan, March 9, 1765, *WJP* 11:627–30.

29. For its centrality to British planners, see John W. Huston, "The Evacuation of Fort Pitt, 1772," *The Western Pennsylvania Historical Magazine* 48, no. 4 (1965), 317–29. For the numbers of families, see Howard Peckham, *Pontiac and the Indian Uprising* (Princeton, NJ: Princeton University Press, 1947), 280–81.

30. "Crawford's Statement, July 22, 1765,"*IHC*, 10:483–84. For more on Crawford, see Charles Hanna, *The Wilderness Trail or the Ventures and Adventures of the Pennsylvania Traders on the Allegheny Path* (New York: G.P. Putnam's Sons, 1911), 2:373–78.

31. "Crawford's Statement," *IHC*, 10:483–84.

32. Ibid.

33. Ibid. Crawford's official report was delivered in July 1765 in New York.

CHAPTER 4: THE ATTACK

1. For the advertisement, see *Pennsylvania Journal*, March 1765.

2. The basis for this paragraph and the preceding ones come from the following sources. "Contrary to law" and "enable" in Deposition of William Smith, April 3, 1765; Fifty in Deposition of Elias Davison, March 8, 1765; "Blow brains out" in Deposition of Robert Allison, March 10, 1765, Gage Papers. For the report of scalping knives, see *Pennsylvania Journal*, March 21 and March 28, 1765.

3. "Forty-nine" from Deposition of Elias Davison, March 8, 1765, and criticism of route in Robert Allison, April 1, 1765, Gage Papers. Details on uncertainty about the signature from Deposition of William Smith, April 3, 1765, Gage Papers. For more on Davison's attempts to mediate, see *Pennsylvania Journal*, March 21 and 28, 1765.

4. Information on the thirty-six additional horses can be found in the Deposition of James Maxwell, April 3, 1765, Gage Papers.

5. See especially Deposition of Robert Allison, April 1, 1765, and Deposition of William Smith, April 3, 1765, Gage Papers.

6. See especially Deposition of William Smith, April 3, 1765, Gage Papers.

7. See especially Deposition of Elias Davison, March 8, 1765, and Deposition of Robert Allison, March 10, 1765, Gage Papers.

8. James Logan to James Steel, November 18, 1729, in Charles Hanna, *The Wilderness Trail* (New York: G. P. Putnam's Sons, 1911), 1:162. For more on this topic, see Patrick Spero, *Frontier Country: The Politics of War in Early Pennsylvania* (Philadelphia: University of Pennsylvania, 2016), especially page 36. For an autobiography, see James Smith, *An Account of the Remarkable Occurrences in the Life and Travels of Colonel Smith* (Lexington, KY: John Bradford, 1799). For more on Smith, see Gregory Evans Dowd, *War under Heaven: Pontiac, the Indian Nations, and the British Empire* (Baltimore: Johns Hopkins University Press, 2004), especially 205–207; Patrick Griffin, *American Leviathan* (New York: Hill & Wang, 2007), 74–82; and Terry Bouton, *Taming Democracy* (New York: Oxford University Press, 2009). Although I have read these accounts and others cited above that mention Smith, my own impressions of him come largely from reading the primary sources. See Patrick Spero, "Recreating James Smith at the Pennsylvania State Archives," *Pennsylvania History* 76 (2009): 474–83, for my own analysis of his autobiography and its reliability.

9. Smith, *An Account of the Remarkable Occurrences*, 5.

10. For an account of Smith's captivity, see Smith, *An Account of the Remarkable Occurrences*, 5–59. For mourning wars, see especially Daniel Richter, "War and Culture: The Iroquois Experience," *The William and Mary Quarterly*, October 1983, 528–59. The most systematic examination of the experience of captives from these wars is Ian Steele, *Setting All the Captives Free: Capture, Adjustment, and Recollection in Allegheny Country* (Montreal: McGill-Queen's University Press, 2014).

11. Smith, *An Account of the Remarkable Occurrences*, 5, 59–61.

12. Smith, *An Account of the Remarkable Occurrences*, 59–61.

13. The quotes come from Smith, *An Account of the Remarkable Occurrences*, 59–60. I infer that they were the group that accompanied the Highlanders and Bouquet west. For the account of the regiment dressed as Indians, see Arthur Grenfell Wauchope, *A Short History of the Black Watch, 1725–1907* (London: William Blackwood & Sons, 1908), especially 14.

14. For details of the raid, see Deposition of Robert Callender, March 28,

1765; Deposition of Robert Allison, April 1, 1765; Deposition of Robert Brownson, April 3, 1765; Deposition of James Maxwell, April 3, 1765, in the Papers of Thomas Gage, PHMC; Deposition of Elias Davison, March 8, 1765, and Deposition of Robert Allison, March 8, 1765, Gage Papers; John Reid to Thomas Gage, Carlisle, June 1, 1765, Gage Papers. Quote from John Armstrong to George Croghan, March 26, 1765, Cadwalader Collection, Series IV, Box 5, HSP. See also Smith, *An Account of the Remarkable Occurrences*, 60–63.

15. Quotation from Smith, *An Account of the Remarkable Occurrences*, 61.

16. Deposition of Robert Allison, March 8, 1765, Gage Papers.

17. First-person accounts of the raid come from Smith, *An Account of the Remarkable Occurrences*, 111–12; Deposition of Elias Davison, March 8, 1765; and Deposition of Robert Allison, March 8, 1765, Gage Papers.

18. The account of Bloody Run is still living history. On a trip to the region, my guide was sure to point it out and explain its origins. For the Black Boys as the source, see William Henry Egle, *History of the Commonwealth of Pennsylvania: Civil, Political and Military from Its Earliest Settlement to the Present Time* (Philadelphia: E.M. Gardner, 1883), 376. For more on this alternative origin, see note 9 in Introduction.

19. Smith, *An Account of the Remarkable Occurrences*, 61.

20. The preceding dialogue is taken from Smith, *An Account of the Remarkable Occurrences*. The passage reads: "When they saw their pack-horses falling close by them, they called out *pray gentlemen, what would you have us to do?* The reply was, *collect all your loads to the front and unload them in one place; take your private property and immediately retire.*" The only alteration in the text was to strike the "to" from "to do."

21. See Deposition of Elias Davison, March 8, 1765, and Deposition of Robert Allison, March 8, 1765, Gage Papers.

22. For what they found, see Smith, *An Account of the Remarkable Occurrences*, 61–62. For more on the rum, see John Reid to Thomas Gage, June 4, 1765, Fort Loudon, Gage Papers, and Nathan McCulloch to George Croghan, Bedford, March 7, 1765, Gage Papers.

23. The value of the destroyed cargo fluctuated widely, with estimates ranging from a couple of thousand pounds to £30,000. Walter Dunn estimated that the total value of the goods Croghan acquired was closer to £15,000, a number Robert Callender also used in his April deposition. Only a fraction of that was destroyed by the Black Boys. I therefore believe the num-

ber was more in the £2,000–4,000 range. For estimates, see Francis Wade to William Johnson, April 26, 1765, *WJP*, 4:729–30; John Armstrong to George Croghan, March 26, 1765, Cadwalader Collection, Series IV, Box 5; John Penn to Thomas Gage, March 22, 1765, Gage Papers. For Dunn's conclusion that cargo worth £3,000 was destroyed, see Walter S. Dunn, *Opening New Markets* (Westport, CT: Praeger, 2002), 120.

24. For accounts of the reaction to the destruction of goods, see John Reid to Thomas Gage, June 4, 1765, *PCM*, 9:269–72, and Depositions of Leonard McGlashan, especially the second one, *PA Archives*, 4:233–37. On the bribes, see Lt. Charles Grant to Thomas Gage, September 16, 1765, Gage Papers.

25. For a history of the 42nd Regiment, see Wauchope, *A Short History of the Black Watch*, especially 3–21. For more on the Highlanders, including a few references to the Black Watch, see Colin Calloway, *White People, Indians, and Highlanders: Tribal People and Colonial Encounters in Scotland and America* (New York: Oxford University Press, 2008).

26. The account of this pursuit comes primarily from the Depositions of Leonard McGlashan, especially the second one, *PA Archives*, 4:233–37. Moon data come from http://aa.usno.navy.mil/rstt/onedaytable?form=1&ID=AA&year=1765&month=3&day=7&state=PA&place=mcconnellsburg (accessed April 17, 2018).

27. See Depositions of Leonard McGlashan, especially the second one, *PA Archives*, 4:233–37.

28. Ibid.

29. Depositions of Leonard McGlashan, especially the second one, *PA Archives*, 4:233–37. I have updated the dialogue to represent the first person, the present tense, and the narrative flow. The exact text of the deposition that I have revised for narrative flow is: "I asked them where they were going, they answered that they were going a hunting; I told them that if they were hunting us that they should find us better game, and commanded them to clear the road for the Kings Troops which they would not do, until I was oblidged to order my party to fix their bayonets, the sight of which procured me and my party a clear passage to Fort Loudon."

30. Thomas Gage provided an example of this clear understanding of jurisdiction during the Paxton Boys' Rebellion. Gage had a long-running

correspondence with a subordinate stationed in Philadelphia that gave detailed instructions on how the British Army should act. Both agreed that they must defend the Indians, but Gage made it clear that his officer had to work under civil control and not independently. J. Schlosser to Thomas Gage, January 31, 1764, Papers of Thomas Gage, PHMC.

31. For discussions of making an example out of the captured men, see Nathan McCulloch to George Croghan, Bedford, March 7, 1765, Gage Papers, and Thomas Gage to Lt. Col. Reid, New York, June 9, 1765, Gage Papers. Gage used the phrase "exemplary punishment," which was often code for execution.

32. The numbers vary. James Smith said he had about two hundred men in *Account of the Remarkable Occurrences*, 111–12, while contemporaries put it at a smaller number, sometimes more than half as much. For a contemporary estimate, see Thomas Barnsby to Thomas Gage, Carlisle, March 11, 1765, Gage Papers, and Lt. Charles Grant to Col. Bouquet, Fort Loudon, March 9, 1765, Gage Papers.

33. Accounts of the siege can be found in Smith, *An Account of the Remarkable Occurrences*, 111–12, and Lt. Charles Grant to Col. Bouquet, Fort Loudon, March 9, 1765, Gage Papers.

34. The flags of truce come from Smith, *An Account of the Remarkable Occurrences*, 111–12.

35. This dialogue is taken from the Deposition of Lt. Charles Grant, *PA Archives*, 4:220. Grant recounts the dialogue he had with Smith. I have edited it to reflect a first-person dialogue in the present tense, though its content is otherwise accurate. The exact text of the original source reads: "He, the said James Smith, came and acknowledged that he was the man that headed said party. I asked him what he meant by appearing with such a mob before the King's fort? He said that he came to demand the prisoners which I had at that time in custody and that he understood they were to be committed to Carlisle gaol. I asked him what he wou'd do suppose they were sent to Carlisle and escorted by the King's troops? He made answer, that his party should first fire over the soldiers and if they would not give up the prisoners upon that, they were determined to fight the troops and die to a man sooner than let them prisoners go to gaol."

36. For information on the siege, see especially Nathan McCulloch to George

Croghan, Bedford, March 7, 1765, and Deposition of Lieutenant Charles
Grant, *PA Archives*, 4:220–22. For "civil war," see Thomas Barnsby to
Thomas Gage, Carlisle, March 11, 1765, Gage Papers.

37. Deposition of Richard Brownson, April 3, 1765, Gage Papers. The exact
quotation reads: "Hearing a knocking at the door of the said house I
opened it and discovered a number of persons whose faces were blacked
and disguised. That on his asking them what they wanted, they answered
they want the master of the house. This deponent told them he was not
at home and again inquired what their business was, to which they then
made answer we want Croghan's store of powder and lead to be delivered
up to them on sight."

38. For the raid on Maxwell's, see William Trent to Joseph Shippen, March
13, 1765, Shippen Papers, HSP, and the proceedings of the Governor's
Conference, Deposition of Robert Callender, March 28, 1765; Deposition of Robert Allison, April 1, 1765; Deposition of Robert Brownson,
April 3, 1765; Deposition of James Maxwell, April 3, 1765, in the Papers
of Thomas Gage, PHMC. Also John Reid to Thomas Gage, Carlisle,
June 1, 1765, Gage Papers. The note on the Marylanders comes from the
Pennsylvania Journal, March 1765. Most of the traders acknowledged that
they carried powder and lead, although it's unclear if these items were
intended for the treaty or for the trade that was to follow it. For stopping at Maxwell's earlier, see Deposition of Elias Davison, March 8, 1765,
Gage Papers, and Deposition of Robert Allison, March 10, 1765, Gage
Papers.

39. For Croghan's ammunition opinion, see George Croghan to Henry Bouquet, March 12, 1765, *Papers of Henry Bouquet*, 6:766–67.

40. John Armstrong to George Croghan, March 26, 1765, Cadwalader Collection, Series IV, Box 5, HSP.

41. Thomas Gage to Henry Bouquet, New York, March 21, 1765, Gage
Papers.

42. For visits, see William Johnson to Thomas Gage, April 27, 1765, *WJP*,
4:732–33, and Thomas Gage to William Johnson, New York, April 15,
1765. For pretenses, see Thomas Gage to Henry Bouquet, New York,
March 21, 1765, Gage Papers.

43. For Johnson's defense of Croghan, see William Johnson to Thomas
Gage, Johnson Hall, April 27, 1765, Gage Papers. See also a series of letters Johnson wrote to Gage in the *WJP*, 11:687–712. Johnson's loyalty to

Croghan comes out in these letters, even if he advocates for an official and impartial investigation of the matter. For "great inveteracy," see William Johnson to Thomas Gage, Johnson Hall, April 3, 1765, Gage Papers.

44. For the new estimates, see Thomas Barnsby to Thomas Gage, Philadelphia, April 10, 1765, and especially Charles Grant to Thomas Gage, Fort Loudon, May 17, 1765, Gage Papers. For Gage's chastisement of Croghan, see Thomas Gage to George Croghan, April 4, 1765, Gage Papers.

45. For Fraser's anxiety, see Alexander Fraser to Thomas Gage, Fort Pitt, March 4, 1765, Gage Papers. For his mission, see Fraser to Campbell, May 17, 1765, *IHC*, 10:493–94.

46. For his departure, see Henry Bouquet to Thomas Gage, Philadelphia, April 10, 1765, Gage Papers, and George Croghan to William Johnson, March 21, 1765, *WJP*, 11:645–47.

47. For Kaské, see Richard White, *The Middle Ground: Indians, Empires, and Republics in the Great Lakes Region, 1650–1815* (Cambridge: Cambridge University Press, 1991), 301, and Dowd, *War under Heaven*, 217–19, 223–25.

48. For Kaské's early alliance, see Dowd, *War under Heaven*, 217–19.

49. Dowd, *War under Heaven*, 218–19.

50. Indian Council, February 24, 1765, *IHC*, 10:450–51.

51. Ibid.

52. Reply of Aubry in Indian Council, February 24, 1765, *IHC*, 10:452–53.

53. Ibid.

54. Ibid.

55. Ibid.

CHAPTER 5: TRANSFORMATION

1. The best study of Penn and his family is Lorett Treese, *Storm Gathering: The Penn Family and the American Revolution* (University Park: Pennsylvania State University Press, 1992).

2. For more on the support of frontier people, see Patrick Spero, *Frontier Country: The Politics of War in Early Pennsylvania* (Philadelphia: University of Pennsylvania Press, 2016), esp. Chapter 7, and James Hutson, *Pennsylvania Politics, 1746–1770: The Movement for Royal Government and Its Consequences* (Princeton, NJ: Princeton University Press, 1972), especially chapter 3 and 105–107, 129, 168 for specific discussions.

3. For a contemporary critique of proprietary colonies that makes this point,

see Benjamin Franklin, *Cool Thoughts on the Present Situation of Our Public Affairs* (Philadelphia: W. Dunlap, 1764). For more on Penn's founding and its proprietary nature, see Patrick Spero, "Creating Pennsylvania: The Politics of the Frontier and the State, 1681–1800" (PhD diss., University of Pennsylvania, 2009), Chapter 1.

4. For discussions of this alliance, see Spero, *Frontier Country*, chapters 6–8.
5. Ibid.
6. Discussion of the heavy snow is in Davenport to Indian Commissioners, March 27, 1765, Papers of the Indian Commissioners, HSP. For James Maxwell, see, for instance, John Reid to Thomas Gage, June 4, 1765, Fort Loudon, Gage Papers. For his relationship to William Maxwell, see Deposition of James Maxwell, April 1, 1765, Gage Papers. For Armstrong's middle ground, see John Armstrong to George Croghan, March 26, 1765, Cadwalader Collection, Series IV, Box 5, HSP. For his reputation, see Spero, *Frontier Country*, 184, 191.
7. "The Address of the Inhabitants of Cumberland County to the Governor," March 1765, *Papers of Henry Bouquet*, 6:777–79.
8. Ibid.
9. Ibid.
10. Thomas Barton, *Conduct of the Paxton Volunteers*, in Paxton Papers, 267, 278–79, 296–97. Barton is quoting a speech that Lord Carteret delivered in 1739 after rioting in Great Britain.
11. John Penn to William Johnson, March 21, 1765, Albany, Gratz Collection, HSP.
12. John Armstrong to George Croghan, March 26, 1765, Cadwalader Collection, Series IV, Box 5, HSP.
13. The fullest account of Penn's time in Carlisle is found in his letter to Thomas Gage dated June 28, 1765, in the Gage Papers. Other references to his time are in John Armstrong to George Croghan, March 26, 1765, Cadwalader Collection, Series IV, Box 5, HSP; Henry Bouquet to Thomas Gage, March 29, 1765, and Henry Bouquet to Thomas Gage, Philadelphia, April 10, 1765, Gage Papers; Thomas Gage to William Johnson, New York, April 15, 1765, Gage Papers; John Reid to Thomas Gage, Carlisle, June 1, 1765, Gage Papers; and Davenport to Indian Commissioners, March 27, 1765, Papers of the Indian Commissioners, HSP. For Smith's testimony, see Deposition of William Smith, April 3, 1765, Gage Papers, and *Pennsylvania Journal*, March 21 and 28, 1765.

14. For Smith's testimony, see Deposition of William Smith, April 3, 1765, Gage Papers, and *Pennsylvania Journal,* March 1765.

15. For insufficient testimony, see John Penn to Thomas Gage, June 28, 1765, Gage Papers; Governor John Penn to Thomas Gage, June 28, 1765, Gage Papers; and Thomas Gage to Governor John Penn, New York, July 5, 1765, Gage Papers.

16. For "sundry petitions," see John Armstrong to George Croghan, March 26, 1765, Cadwalader Collection, Series IV, Box 5, HSP.

17. For "daring and insolent," see John Reid to Thomas Gage, Carlisle, June 1, 1765, Gage Papers. For "Paxtonians," see Davenport to Indian Commissioners, March 27, 1765, Papers of the Indian Commissioners, HSP. Other references that conflate the Black Boys with the Paxton Boys include William Johnson to George Croghan, April 8, 1765, *WJP,* 11:680–82, and William Johnson to John Penn, April 3, 1765, *WJP,* 11:664–65. For early passports, see Copies of Passports for May 15 and May 20, 1765, signed by William Smith, *PA Archives,* 4:219–20. For the "cloathing" quote, see John Reid to Thomas Gage, June 4, 1765, *PCM,* 9:270.

18. For Smith's early involvement, see Robert Callender to Henry Bouquet, March 11, 1765, *Papers of Henry Bouquet,* 6:764–65.

19. The best account of the Spears attack is in "An Extract of a letter from Colonel John Reid, June 3, 1765," *PCM,* 9:269–70.

20. Ibid.

21. For information on Spears and the clash at Widow Barr's, see Deposition of Henry Prather, July 18, 1765, *PA Archives,* 4:237; Deposition of John Shelby, *PA Archives,* 4:222–23, "Extract of a letter from John Reid, June 1, 1765," *PCM,* 9:269; "Charles Grant to Thomas Gage," August 24, 1765, *PA Archives,* 4:231–32; and Deposition of Leonard McGlashan, *PA Archives,* 4:233–34. McGlashan's deposition was marked by twelve men, presumably the men under his command.

22. Ibid.

23. Ibid.

24. Deposition of Lieutenant Charles Grant, *PA Archives,* 4:220–21, and "Extract of a Letter from John Reid," *PCM,* 9:270.

25. Deposition of Lieutenant Charles Grant, *PA Archives,* 4:220–21.

26. "Croghan's Journal," *IHC,* 11:6–7.

27. Accounts of the treaty can be found in two printed sources. The first is the *Minutes of the Provincial Council of Pennsylvania.* The other is "George

Croghan's Journals," *IHC*, 11:1–64. My estimated numbers come from Croghan's journal in which he lists the Indian leaders attending and estimates the size of their parties. See "Croghan's Journals," *IHC*, 11:10.

28. "At a meeting with the Indians, May 15, 1765," *PCM*, 9:261.

29. Ibid.

30. For details on the exchanges, see William Murray to Thos. Gage, Fort Pitt, May 12, 1765, Gage Papers, and John Reid to Thomas Gage, May 28, 1765, Gage Papers.

31. Thomas Gage to William Johnson, June 3, 1765, *WJP*, 11:762–64.

32. For a description of his orders, see Alexander Fraser to Colonel Campbell, Commandant of Fort Detroit, May 17, 1765, *IHC*, 10:493. Fraser's stay in the region is difficult to piece together. A series of letters he sent to Gage have been lost, and the remaining letters often contain only fragments of stories with the chronology jumbled. The following is my best reading of this correspondence and timeline.

33. For details of harassment and his capture, see Alexander Fraser to Thomas Gage, May 15, 1765, *IHC*, 10:491–92, and especially Alexander Fraser to Colonel Campbell, May 17, 1765, *IHC*, 10:493–94.

34. For "disposed," see Fraser to Gage, May 15, 1765, *IHC*, 10:492. For "ador'd," see Alexander Fraser to Thomas Gage, May 18, 1765, *IHC*, 10:494–95.

35. See Fraser to Gage, *IHC*, 10:492.

36. This account is drawn from Fraser to Gage, May 15, 1765, *IHC*, 10:492.

37. "Die in our defence" is from Fraser to Gage, May 15, 1765, *IHC*, 10:492. "Integrity" is from Fraser to Gage, May 18, 1765, *IHC*, 10:494–95.

38. Fraser to Campbell, May 20, 1765, *IHC*, 10:495–97.

39. Fraser to Gage, May 15, 1765, *IHC*, 10:492.

40. On ammunition, see Fraser to Campbell, May 17, 1765, *IHC*, 10:493. For rumors of support and overflowing shops, see Alexander Fraser to Campbell, May 20, 1765, *IHC*, 10:495.

41. Alexander Fraser to Campbell, May 20, 1765, *IHC*, 10:495.

42. Fraser to Gage, May 26, 1765, *IHC*, 10:515–16.

43. Ibid.

CHAPTER 6: CRISIS

1. "Air on horseback" is from John Reid to Thomas Gage, Carlisle, June 1, 1765, Gage Papers.

2. Information on the seizure is taken primarily from Deposition of Lt. Charles Grant, *PA Archives*, 4:220–22, and John Reid to Thomas Gage, Carlisle, June 1, 1765, Gage Papers. "Shoot the bougar" is from Reid; the rest of the dialogue is from the deposition. Minor changes have been made to make the dialogue flow. The text reads in the original: "I was riding out and about a mile from this post as I was coming home in company with two other men, was wayla'd by five men arm'd, namely James Smith, Samuel Owens, John Piery, and two others, whose names I don't know, all under command of the aforesdaid James Smith, some called out to catch me, others to shoot me, on which I rush'd thro' them and on passing one of them attempt to catch my horse by the bridle, notwithstandg I passed them all, and when they saw that I was out of their hands, one of them fired a gun, whether at me or my horse, I cannot say, at which my horse started into the thicket which occasioned by falling; the rioters then came up to me, made me as they said the King's prisoner, upon which one of them said, 'take the durk of the rascall.' I asked them for what? They said they wou'd let me know that before I wou'd go home. I asked them where they were taking me to? They said they would take me before Justice Reyonald. I ask'd if it would not do as well to go before Justice Smith, being the most convenient? They said that their orders was to bring me before Justice Reyonald."

3. Grant's biography is taken from Paul Pace, "Kilts and Courage, The Story of the 42nd or Royal Highland Regiment in the American War for Independence 1776–1783" (unpublished ms. shared with me via internet exchange). I want to also thank Smith Rebellion 1765 (www.smithrebellion1765.com) for the initial citation and Dan Guzy, *The Black Boys Uprising of 1765: Traders, Troops, and "Rioters" during Pontiac's War* (Mercersburg: Conococheague Institute, 2014).

4. Deposition of Lt. Charles Grant, *PA Archives*, 4:220–22, and John Reid to Thomas Gage, Carlisle, June 1, 1765, Gage Papers.

5. Deposition of Lt. Charles Grant, *PA Archives*, 4:220–22.

6. Deposition of Lt. Charles Grant, *PA Archives*, 4:220–22 for quotation, which reads, "Their commander, James Smith, said that they were as ready for a rebellion as we were to oppose it." Pronouns were changed for purposes of dialogue.

7. Ibid.

8. For Grant's belief that he was not liable to honor the agreement, see John Reid to Thomas Gage, June 1, 1765, Fort Loudon, Gage Papers.

9. For information on the sergeants, see John Reid to Thomas Gage, June 1, 1765, and June 4, 1765, Gage Papers. For Smith's defense, see James Smith to Lieutenant Charles Grant, June 17, 1765, *PA Archives*, 4:229–30.

10. For information on the discovery of the advertisement, see Deposition of Thomas Romberg, September 12, 1765, *PA Archives*, 4:238–39, and The Petition of Thomas Romberg, *PA Archives*, 4:239. The text of the advertisement is in *PCM*, 9:271. What is likely Romberg's copy is in the Gage Papers.

11. See Deposition of Thomas Romberg, September 12, 1765, *PA Archives*, 4:238–39.

12. On Gage demanding action, see Thomas Gage to Governor John Penn, June 16, 1765, *PCM*, 9:267–68. On Penn asking for documents and appearances, see John Penn to William Smith, June 27, 1765, *PCM*, 9:273; John Penn to Justice James Maxwell, June 27, 1765, *PCM*, 9:273; John Penn to Justices of Cumberland County, June 27, 1765, *PCM*, 9:273–74; and John Penn to Charles Grant, June 27, 1765, *PCM*, 9:274. On the inquisition at Fort Loudon, see Deposition of Henry Prather, September 12, 1765, *PA Archives*, 4:237–38; Deposition of Thomas Romberg, September 12, 1765, *PA Archives*, 4:238–39; and Charles Grant to Thomas Gage, September 16, 1765, Gage Papers.

13. Deposition of Thomas Romberg, September 12, 1765, *PA Archives*, 4:238–39.

14. *PA Archives*, 4:237–38; *PCM*, 9:276, 281.

15. For Penn's proclamation, see "A Proclamation," *PCM*, 9:264–66. For its arrival at Fort Loudon, see Charles Grant to Thomas Gage, June 16, 1765, Gage Papers.

16. For the warrant on McGlashan and the verdict, see John Reid to Thomas Gage, June 4, 1765, Gage Papers. On escorts, see numerous Gage letters from June, but especially Thomas Gage to William Johnson, June 30, 1765, Gage Papers; John Reid to Thomas Gage, July 9, 1765, Gage Papers; and John Reid to Thomas Gage, July 15, 1765, Gage Papers, which also mentions the continued harassment.

17. For funds raised, see Charles Grant to Thomas Gage, May 1, 1765, Gage Papers. For Fort Smith, see William Smith to Charles Grant, Fort Smiths, November 14, 1765, Gage Papers and *PA Archives*, 4:244. The printed version in the *Pennsylvania Archives* doesn't identify the recipient of this letter dated "Fort Smith," but the Gage Papers makes clear that

Grant was its intended recipient. The Gage Papers also seems to indicate that William's house was called Forth Smiths, but the printed version has the singular. "Smiths" may represent either a possessive use, as in "Smith's fort," or a plural in recognition of the two Smiths as leaders. I suspect the latter was the case, since William Smith was unlikely to use the possessive in such a way.

18. For Campbell, see James Smith, *An Account of the Remarkable Occurrences in the Life and Travels of Colonel Smith* (Lexington, KY: John Bradford, 1799), 61–62.

19. Song from James Smith, *An Account of the Remarkable Occurrences*, 62–63.

20. See especially Edmund Morgan, *The Stamp Act Crisis: Prologue to Revolution* (Chapel Hill: University of North Carolina Press, 1962), and Pauline Maier, *From Resistance to Revolution* (New York: W. W. Norton, 1992).

21. On the Fort Pitt officer, see John Reid to Thomas Gage, June 7, 1765, Fort Bedford, Gage Papers, and George Croghan to Henry Bouquet, March 12, 1765, *Papers of Henry Bouquet*, 6:766.

22. "Miscreants," "lawless banditti," "traitors," and "exemplary punishment" are in Thomas Gage to Lt. Col. Reid, New York, June 9, 1765; for "rebellion," see Thomas Gage to John Penn, New York, June 16, 1765; for "villains" and "quartered," see John Reid to Thomas Gage, June 4, 1765, Fort Loudon, Gage Papers; for "Seditious," see Henry Bouquet to Thomas Gage, Philadelphia, March 20, 1765, Gage Papers; for "my enemies," see Lt. Charles Grant to Thomas Gage, September 16, 1765, Gage Papers; for "ungovernable people," see John Penn to Thomas Gage, Philadelphia, February 10, 1766, Gage Papers.

23. For others who emphasize the inability of government to control this area, see especially Patrick Griffin, *American Leviathan: Empire, Nation, and Revolutionary Frontier* (New York: Hill & Wang, 2007); David Preston, *Texture of Contact: European and Indian Settler Communities on the Frontiers of Iroquoia, 1667–1783* (Lincoln: University of Nebraska Press, 2009); and Kevin Kenny, *Peaceable Kingdom Lost: The Paxton Boys and the Destruction of William Penn's Holy Experiment* (New York: Oxford University Press, 2009).

24. Lt. Charles Grant to Gen. Thomas Gage, August 24, 1765, *PA Archives*, 4:281; John Reid to Thomas Gage, June 1, 1765, Gage Papers. For "issued no proclamations," see John Reid to Thomas Gage, June 4, 1765, Gage Papers. John Armstrong to George Croghan, March 26, 1765, Cadwalader Collection, Series IV, Box 5, Croghan Correspondence. John Penn to

Thomas Gage, Philadelphia, February 10, 1766, Penn Correspondence, HSP. Gage to Bouquet, March 7, 1765, *Papers of Henry Bouquet*, 6:762.

25. John Penn to Thomas Gage, June 28, 1765, Gage Papers.

26. John Penn to Thomas Gage, June 28, 1765, Gage Papers; [James Burd?] to Joseph Shippen, Fort Augusta, January 19, 1764, Shippen Papers, HSP.

27. John Ross to Benjamin Franklin, May 20, 1765, Papers of Benjamin Franklin, American Philosophical Society, Philadelphia, PA.

28. Benjamin Franklin to John Ross, June 8, 1765, http://franklinpapers.org/ franklin/framedVolumes.jsp?vol=12&page=138a (accessed April 17, 2018).

29. Benjamin Franklin, *Cool Thoughts on the Present Situation of Our Public Affairs* (Philadelphia: W. Dunlap, 1764); http://www.franklinpapers.org/ franklin/framedVolumes.jsp?vol=11&page=153b. For more on Franklin in this moment, see Gordon Wood, *The Americanization of Benjamin Franklin* (New York: Penguin, 2004), and Esmond Wright, *Franklin of Philadelphia* (Cambridge: Harvard University Press, 1988), 141–42.

30. Gage to Conway, May 6, 1776, *The Correspondence of Thomas Gage*, ed. Clarence Edwin Carter (New Haven, CT: Yale University Press, 1931), 1:191.

31. For British officers' use of "country people," see Thomas Barnsley to Thomas Gage, Carlisle, March 11, 1765; Nathan McCulloch to George Croghan, Bedford, March 7, 1765; Lt. Charles Grant to Col. Bouquet, Fort Loudon, March 9, 1765; Thomas Gage to Henry Bouquet, New York, March 21, 1765; Thomas Gage to Capt. Murray at Fort Pitt, New York, March 21, 1765; Thomas Gage to George Croghan, New York, March 30, 1765; Thomas Gage to Capt. Barnsley, Carlisle, New York, April 6, 1765; Henry Bouquet to Thomas Gage, Philadelphia, April 10, 1765; Thomas Gage to William Johnson, New York, April 15, 1765; Thomas Gage to William Johnson, New York, April 21, 1765; Charles Grant to Thomas Gage, Fort Loudon, April 25, 1765; Charles Grant to Thomas Gage, Fort Loudon, May 17, 1765; John Reid to Thomas Gage, June 4, 1765, Fort Loudon; Thomas Gage to Lt. Grant, New York, August 13, 1765, Gage Papers.

32. On the need for more inspectors, see William Johnson to George Croghan, Johnson Hall, April 8, 1765, Cadwalader Collection, Series IV, Box 6, Folder 33, HSP.

33. "Croghan's Journal," *IHC*, 11:24–26.

34. For "finest," see "Croghan's Journal," *IHC* 11:29. For more on Croghan's

dig, see Keith Thomson, *The Legacy of the Mastodon: The Golden Age of Fossils in America* (New Haven, CT: Yale University Press, 2008), 21–23.

35. Cherokees, May 22, 1765, "Croghan's Journal," *IHC* 11:27. Abandoned town, May 16, 1765, and May 23, 1765, "Croghan's Journal," *IHC* 11:24, 27.

36. June 6 and June 7, 1765, "Croghan's Journal," *IHC* 11:30–31. For "thick scull," see Fred Anderson, *Crucible of War: The Seven Years' War and the Fate of Empire in British North America, 1754–1766* (New York: Vintage, 2000), 630.

37. For "inslave," see "Croghan's Journal," *IHC* 11:30, and Anderson, *Crucible of War*, 630–31.

38. For accounts of this standoff, see Richard White, *The Middle Ground: Indians, Empires, and Republics in the Great Lakes Region, 1650–1815* (New York: Cambridge University Press, 1991), 299–305; Anderson, *Crucible of War*, 628–32; and Gregory Evans Dowd, *War under Heaven: Pontiac, the Indian Nations, and the British Empire* (Baltimore: Johns Hopkins University Press, 2004), 217–31. For Kaské's desire to have him burned, see "Croghan's Journal," 40–41. Kaské is the Shawnee Indian he references.

39. "Croghan's Journal," *IHC*, 11:42.

CHAPTER 7: INDEPENDENCE

1. Richard White, *The Middle Ground: Indians, Empires, and Republics in the Great Lakes Region, 1650–1815* (Cambridge: Cambridge University Press, 1991), 296–303, and Fred Anderson, *Crucible of War: The Seven Years' War and the Fate of Empire in British North America, 1754–1766* (New York: Vintage, 2000), 630–31.

2. "Croghan's Journal," *IHC*, 11:42. See also Gregory Evans Dowd, *War under Heaven: Pontiac, the Indian Nations, and the British Empire* (Baltimore: Johns Hopkins University Press, 2004), 229–31.

3. "Croghan's Journal," *IHC*, 11:42. Pontiac's words in the opening conference appear somewhat confused. After asserting Native sovereign rights, he seems to contradict himself by saying the English will be received with open arms when they come to take possession of the territory. I suspect that this final statement was something Croghan recorded poorly or misunderstood. Pontiac earlier in the conference and in subsequent

conferences made it clear that the Indians still claimed ownership of the land. Most likely, Pontiac was telling Croghan the English would be well received in Indian Country but didn't say (or mean to say) that the English would be received with open arms when they came to take *possession*—a right the Indians still claimed.

4. On traveling separately, see "Croghan's Journal," *IHC*, 11:41–42. On Croghan's encounters along the way to Detroit, see "Croghan's Journal," *IHC*, 11:42–43. On the diplomatic negotiations, see "Croghan's Journal," *IHC*, 11:43–52.

5. See especially "Croghan's Journal," *IHC*, 11:39, for sending a delegation ahead of him.

6. "Croghan's Journal," *IHC*, 11:45.

7. Ibid., 11:45–46.

8. Ibid.

9. For Croghan's continued meetings, see "Croghan's Journal," *IHC*, 11:47–52. For mentions of ammunition, see 48–49. For Croghan providing the goods, see 51–52. For extended quote, see 48.

10. "Croghan's Journal," *IHC*, 11:4344.

11. Jane Merritt, "Metaphor, Meaning, and Misunderstanding," in *Contact Points: American Frontiers from the Mohawk Valley to the Mississippi, 1750–1830*, ed. Andrew R. L. Cayton and Fredrika Teute (Chapel Hill: University of North Carolina Press, 1998), 74, and Francis Jennings, *The Ambiguous Iroquois Empire: The Covenant Chain Confederation of Indian Tribes with English Colonies from Its Beginnings to the Lancaster Treaty of 1744* (New York: W. W. Norton, 1984), 44. Jennings emphasizes *uncles* as the traditional term used to form a typical political alliance. By the 1760s, I believe this usage had gone by the wayside in European-Indian diplomacy, even if Indians continued to use such metaphors internally. For Croghan using *children*, see "Croghan's Journal," *IHC*, 11:45.

12. "William Johnson to the Lords of Trade, September 28, 1765," *IHC*, 11:87–90.

13. Charles Grant to Thomas Gage, September 16, 1765, Gage Papers. On the threat of arrest, see Charles Grant to Thomas Gage, August 24, 1765, *PA Archives*, 4:231–33.

14. Charles Grant to Thomas Gage, September 16, 1765, Gage Papers, and Thomas Gage to Charles Grant, October 2, 1765, Gage Papers. Gage did

look into Grant's performance, but Colonel John Reid gave his endorsement. See John Reid to Thomas Gage, September 13, 1765, Gage Papers.

15. For Gage's strategy, see Jack Sosin, *Whitehall and the Wilderness: The Middle
West in British Colonial Policy, 1760 to 1775* (Lincoln: University of Nebraska
Press, 1961), 115–18.

16. For a record of the troops' announced departure, see William Smith
to Charles Grant, November 14, 1765, *PA Archives*, 4:244–45. I believe
this document was written by William Smith after Grant announced his
intention to leave. He approached Smith and other justices to put materiel
in their possession. For an account of the siege, see Charles Grant to John
Reid, November 22, 1765, *PA Archives*, 4:246–47.

17. Charles Grant to John Reid, November 22, 1765, *PA Archives*, 4:246–47.

18. For evidence of this shift in policy, see Grant to Reid, November 22, 1765,
James Smith Obligation and Jonathan Smith Obligation, *PA Archives*,
4:245–46; *PA Archives*, 4:246–47.

19. Ibid., and William Smith to [Grant,] November 14, 1765, *PA Archives*,
4:244–45.

20. Grant to Reid, November 22, 1765, *PA Archives*, 4:246–47; and William
Grant to John Reid, November 25, 1765, *PA Archives*, 4:247–48.

21. Quotation adapted from Grant to Reid, November 22, 1765, *PA Archives*,
4:246–47. The exact passage adapted reads: "They kept firing at the
fort to one o'clock, when Mr. M'Dowell came in, and said, if I would
let him have the arms, that he would give me a receipt, and that those
arms would remain in his house till such time as the governor would give
orders about them, and that the owners would be satisfied whatever the
governor thought proper to do with them."

22. Grant to Reid. November 22, 1765, *PA Archives*, 4:246–47; James Smith
Obligation and Jonathan Smith Obligation, *PA Archives*, 4:245–46. An
important note on these documents: in the *Pennsylvania Archives*, these obligations are dated November 10; but in the Gage Correspondence, the
date is November 18, which would be two days after the November 16
siege began and would make more chronological sense.

23. William Grant to John Reid, November 22, 1765, *PA Archives*, 4:247–48.

24. [John Penn] to William Smith and Justice Reynolds, December 18, 1765,
LCMP, HSP.

CHAPTER 8: THE ELUSIVE PEACE

1. On Crawford's escort, see Howard Peckham, *Pontiac and the Indian Uprising* (Princeton, NJ: 1947), 288, and William Stone, *The Life and Times of Baronet William Johnson* (Albany: J. Munsell, 1865), 2:273–74. On the arrival and additional groups, see William Fowler, *Empires at War: The French and Indian War and the Struggle for North America* (New York: Walker, 2004), 282.

2. For the best overview of these incidents, see William Nester, *Haughty Conquerors: Amherst and the Great Indian Uprising of 1763* (Westport, CT: Praeger, 2000), 253–54. See also Peckham, *Pontiac and the Indian Uprising*, 288–89.

3. The following is taken from John Romeyn Brodhead, ed., *Documents Relating to the Colonial History of the State of New York*, 7:854–67.

4. Ibid., 7:854.

5. Ibid., 7:855.

6. Ibid., 7:858–59.

7. Stone, *The Life and Times*, 2:278.

8. George Croghan to William Johnson, November 18, 1765, *WJP*, 11:967–70.

9. "Thomas Gage to Conway, November 9, 1765," *IHC*, 11:115–16; Gage to Conway, September 23, 1765, *IHC*, 11:85–87.

10. General Distribution of His Majesty's Forces, February 22, 1767, *IHC*, 11:512, and Jack Sosin, *Whitehall and the Wilderness: The Middle West in British Colonial Policy, 1760–1775* (Lincoln: University of Nebraska Press, 1961), 110–13.

11. Thomas Gage to Conway, November 9, 1765, *IHC*, 11:115–16; Sosin, *Whitehall and the Wilderness,* Conway quotes on 110 and 111.

12. Quote from Gage to Conway, November 9, 1765, *IHC*, 11:115–16; Sosin, *Whitehall and the Wilderness,* especially 106–12, 115–19.

13. Quote from Sosin, *Whitehall and the Wilderness,* 109.

14. Ibid.

15. Ibid.

16. Ibid., and James Smith, *An Account of the Remarkable Occurrences in the Life and Travels of Colonel Smith* (Lexington, KY: John Bradford, 1799), 67.

17. Ibid. Quote from George Croghan to Colonel Wilkins, Philadelphia, March 1768, Cadwalader Collection, Folder 29, HSP.

18. Sosin, *Whitehall and the Wilderness,* 74–77, 167, especially 74, fn. 58; Richard

White, *The Middle Ground: Indians, Empires, and Republics in the Great Lakes Region, 1650–1815* (Cambridge: Cambridge University Press, 1991), 351–55; and especially William Campbell, *Speculators in Empire: Iroquoia and the 1768 Treaty of Fort Stanwix* (Norman: University of Oklahoma Press, 2012), especially Chapter 4, 109–38.

19. See especially Sosin, *Whitehall and the Wilderness*, 153–61.

20. Ibid., 122–23, 167–73, and Campbell, *Speculators in Empire*, especially 120–25. Sosin seems to believe land speculators drove much of this policy-making among colonists. But the situation on the ground was also driving Johnson's thinking. Indeed, Sosin himself seems to recognize this, noting that the Board of Trade approved of a new boundary to "alleviate [Indian] apprehensions over unauthorized attempts by the whites." On fear of war, see Patrick Spero, "Creating Pennsylvania: The Politics of the Frontier and the State, 1681–1800" (PhD diss., University of Pennsylvania, 2009), and Patrick Spero, *Frontier Country: The Politics of War in Early Pennsylvania* (Philadelphia: University of Pennsylvania Press, 2016).

21. Sosin, *Whitehall and the Wilderness*, 174–76, and map on boundary. For the best summary of the treaty itself, see Campbell, *Speculators in Empire*, Chapter 5, 139–66.

22. Sosin, *Whitehall and the Wilderness*, 176–79; White, *Middle Ground*, 351–55.

23. For the speculators, see Sosin, *Whitehall and the Wilderness*, especially 128–80, and Campbell, *Speculators in Empire*, 139–66.

24. The Croghan grant is covered in Eric Hinderaker, *Elusive Empires: Constructing Colonialism in the Ohio Valley, 1673–1800* (New York: Cambridge University Press, 1999), 172–73. For a summary of the Croghan grant made shortly after the treaty, see *Journal of the House of Delegates* (Richmond, VA: 1826), 137. In this record, the Virginia Assembly is trying to understand its post-revolution debts, and the status of the various western landholdings is debated. For quotation, see *Early Recognized Treaties with American Indian Nations*, 128, http://earlytreaties.unl.edu/treaty.00007.html (accessed April 17, 2018).

25. For profits before peace, see White, *Middle Ground*, 353. Sosin, *Whitehall and the Wilderness*, especially 172–77, makes a similar argument, though he emphasizes that some of Johnson's decisions may have been made to alleviate the potential objections of Virginians. For an interpretation even more sympathetic to Johnson, see Campbell, *Speculators in Empire*, 163–66.

26. For the lingering debate over who held the most valid claim to this land, see Sosin, *Whitehall and the Wilderness*, 177–79, and especially Chapter 8, 181–210, 227.

CHAPTER 9: DISINTEGRATION

1. The account that follows is based on the articles from the *Pennsylvania Gazette* from September 28 and November 2, 1769; the October 26 post-script to the October 25, 1769, issue of the *Pennsylvania Journal*; and James Smith, *An Account of the Remarkable Occurrences in the Life and Travels of Colonel Smith* (Lexington, KY: John Bradford, 1799), 67–73.
2. Ibid.
3. Ibid.
4. Smith, *An Account of the Remarkable Occurrences*, 67.
5. Ibid. Previously, scholars had questioned Smith's tale, but the October 25 *Pennsylvania Journal* newspaper report, which I have not seen cited elsewhere, provides strong corroboration that Smith rescued the prisoners. For the best discussion of Smith's claim, see Gregory Evans Dowd, *War under Heaven* (Baltimore: Johns Hopkins University Press, 2004), 208–9. For further evidence that the jailbreak occurred, see Christopher Pearl, "'For the Good Order of Government': The American Revolution and the Creation of the Commonwealth of Pennsylvania, 1740–1790" (PhD diss., SUNY–Binghamton, 2013), 312, fn. 11.
6. Smith, *An Account of the Remarkable Occurrences*, 67.
7. Ibid., 67–68.
8. Dialogue is closely adapted from Smith, *An Account of the Remarkable Occurrences*, 67. It is changed to reflect the proper tense. The original reads: "I asked him if the gate was open."
9. This dialogue is also taken from Smith, *An Account of the Remarkable Occurrences*, 67–68. It is changed to reflect the proper tense and punctuation. I have also abbreviated it, cutting words unnecessary for dialogue. The original reads: "He said it was then shut, but he expected they would open it as usual, at day-light, as they apprehend no danger."
10. Smith, *An Account of the Remarkable Occurrences*, 67–68.
11. Ibid., 68.
12. Ibid.
13. See especially "Extract of a letter from Bedford, September 21, 1769," in

Pennsylvania Gazette, September 28, 1765, and *Pennsylvania Journal,* October 26, 1769.

14. The following is based on the *Pennsylvania Gazette* from September 28 and November 2, 1769; the October 26 postscript to the October 25, 1769, issue of the *Pennsylvania Journal*; and Smith, *An Account of the Remarkable Occurrences,* 67–73. Quotations from Smith, *An Account of the Remarkable Occurrences,* 68.

15. Ibid.

16. Ibid.

17. Ibid.

18. Quotations from Smith, *An Account of the Remarkable Occurrences,* 69.

19. Ibid.

20. Ibid.

21. Letter from William Smith dated October 16, 1769, *Pennsylvania Gazette,* November 2, 1769, and Postscript to the *Pennsylvania Journal,* October 26, 1769.

22. Smith, *An Account of the Remarkable Occurrences,* 72–73, quotation from 72.

23. Ibid., 72–73.

24. Ibid.

25. *Pennsylvania Gazette,* October 5, 1769; *Pennsylvania Gazette,* November 2, 1769; *Pennsylvania Gazette,* December 14, 1769. For more on this murder, see especially James Merrell, *Into the American Woods: Negotiators on the Pennsylvania Frontier* (New York: Norton, 1999), 302–15.

26. John Penn to Thomas Penn, September 12, 1766, Penn Correspondence, HSP; Francis Faquier to John Penn, December 16, 1766, *PCM,* 9:349–51. Gage quote is from Alfred Cave, *The French and Indian War* (Westport, CT: Greenwood Press, 2004), 57.

27. For more on popular justice in the East, see Barbara Clark Smith, *The Freedoms We Lost: Consent and Resistance in Revolutionary America* (New York: New Press, 2010).

28. On anarchy, see Patrick Griffin, *American Leviathan: Empire, Nation, and Revolutionary Frontier* (New York: Hill & Wang, 2007).

29. White, *Middle Ground,* 304–305; Anderson, *Crucible of War,* 631–32. For details on the treaties, see "Croghan's Journal," *IHC,* 11:44–52.

30. See White, *Middle Ground,* especially Chapters 10 and 11 for an analysis of the post-independence world, and Dowd, *War under Heaven,* 260–62, for Pontiac's death.

CHAPTER 10: IMPERIAL FAILURE

1. Quotations from David Hackett Fischer, *Paul Revere's Ride* (New York: Oxford University Press, 1994), 37–43. "Forcible means" is in Fischer, *Paul Revere's Ride*, 42. For "daring and licentious," see Fischer, *Paul Revere's Ride,* 37.

2. For the evacuation of the fort, see John Hutson, "The Evacuation of Fort Pitt, 1772," *The Western Pennsylvania Historical Magazine* 48, no. 2 (October 1965): 317–29, especially 320–21.

3. "Indians at their back" is in Fischer, *Paul Revere's Ride*, 43; "we shall be out of the scrape" is in David Preston, *Texture of Contact: European and Indian Settler Communities on the Frontiers of Iroquoia, 1667–1783* (Lincoln: University of Nebraska Press, 2009), 262.

4. Jack Sosin, *Whitehall and the Wilderness: The Middle West in British Colonial Policy, 1760–1775* (Lincoln: University of Nebraska Press, 1961), 109.

5. George Croghan to Thomas Gage, series 4, box 20, folder 7, Cadwalader Family Papers, HSP; David McClure, *Diary of David McClure,* ed. Franklin B. Dexter (New York: Knickerbocker Press, 1899), 85. See Patrick Spero, *Frontier Country: The Politics of War in Early Pennsylvania* (Philadelphia: University of Pennsylvania Press, 2016), Chapter 9, for further discussion, especially 207–9.

6. This exchange is only slightly changed for purposes of dialogue. The original reads: "I asked one of the officers, the reason of their destroying the fort, so necessary to the safety of the frontier. He replied, 'The Americans will not submit to the British Parliament and they may now defend themselves.'" See McClure, *Diary,* 101.

7. [Benjamin Franklin], "Rules by which a Great Empire may be reduced to a Small One," published in numerous newspapers. See, for example, *Pennsylvania Gazette,* December 15, 1773, and *New York Journal,* January 27, 1774.

8. For a further development of this idea, see Spero, *Frontier Country,* especially Chapter 9. See also George Croghan, Box 6, Series IV, Folder 8, Cadwalader Collection, HSP, and McClure, *Diary of David McClure,* 85.

9. For more on Vandalia, see Albert Volwiler, *George Croghan and the Westward Movement, 1741–1782* (New York: AMS Press, 1926; repr. 1971). For details on the arguments and petitions offered for the colony, which do not receive much attention in Volwiler's biography, see the Croghan and Wharton let-

ters in the Cadwalader Collection, Box 5, Series IV, especially petition for
the colony on 4. He argues that a new colony will serve the interests of
settlers, Indians, and the British Empire as well as manufacturers. See also
Sosin, *Whitehall and the Wilderness,* 181–280. For the capital, see Otis Rice,
The Allegheny Frontier: West Virginia Beginning, 1730–1830 (Lexington: University Press of Kentucky, 1970), 77. For the government, see George Henry
Alden, "New Governments West of the Alleghenies before 1780: An Intro-
ductory Study" (PhD diss., University of Wisconsin, 1897), 29–31.

10. Ibid.

11. On early approval of the colony, see Sosin, *Whitehall and the Wilderness,*
181–280, especially 199–206.

12. On the self-interest, see Sosin, *Whitehall and the Wilderness,* which takes
heavy issue with the role of land speculators. For Croghan in particular,
see William Campbell, *Speculators in Empire: Iroquoia and the 1768 Treaty
of Fort Stanwix* (Norman: University of Oklahoma Press, 2012). For the
acceptance of and role for interests in imperial governance, see especially
Michael Kammen, *Empire and Interests: The American Colonies and the Politics
of Mercantilism* (New York: J.B. Lippincott, 1970).

13. Sosin, *Whitehall and the Wilderness,* 128–64, 181–210.

14. George Croghan to Samuel Wharton, November 2, 1771, Ohio, Cad-
walader Collection, Series IV, Box 5, Folder 31, HSP. See also George
Croghan to Board of Trade, Croghan Papers, Cadwalader Collection,
Series IV, Box 5, 4, HSP.

15. Quote from Alden, "New Governments West of the Alleghenies before
1780," 35.

16. For more on Wilkes, see Richard Middlekauff, *The Glorious Cause: The
American Revolution, 1763–1789* (New York: Oxford University Press, 2005),
57–58; Anna Clark, *Scandal: The Sexual Politics of the British Constitution*
(Princeton, NJ: Princeton University Press, 2006), Chapter 2, especially
19, 24–28, 34–35; and Merrill Jensen, *The Founding of a Nation: A History
of the American Revolution, 1763–1776* (New York: Oxford University Press,
1968), 155–57.

17. For tax complaints in Great Britain, see Lewis Gipson, *The Coming of
the American Revolution* (New York: Harper Torchbooks, 1962), 57–58 and
170–72; Robert Chaffin, "The Townshend Acts Crisis, 1767–1770," in *A
Companion to the American Revolution,* Jack P. Greene and J. R. Pole, eds.
(West Sussex: Wiley-Blackwell, 2003), 134–50; and Thomas Purvis, "The

Seven Years' War and Its Political Legacy," in *Companion to the American Revolution*, 112–17, especially 115. For the Townshend Duties, see Benjamin Woods Labaree, *The Boston Tea Party* (New York: Oxford University Press, 1964), 15–37.

18. John Sainsbury, *John Wilkes: The Lives of a Libertine* (Aldershot: Ashgate, 2006), 64.

19. For an overview of the British politics, see Middlekauf, *A Glorious Cause*, 53–255, especially 111 for Greenville's dismissal; and Gipson, *The Coming of the American Revolution*. For more on the politics of this period, see Lewis Namier, *England in the Age of the American Revolution*, 2nd ed. (New York: St. Martin's Press, 1962), and Lewis Namier, *The Structure of Politics at the Accession of George III*, 2nd ed. (London: Macmillan, 1957).

20. Gregory Evans Dowd, *War under Heaven: Pontiac, the Indian Nations, and the British Empire* (Baltimore: Johns Hopkins University Press, 2004), 233–48.

21. George Croghan to Benjamin Franklin, December 12, 1765, *IHC*, 11:63.

22. Earl of Dartmouth to Sir William Johnson, February 3, 1773, *Documents Relative to the Colonial History of New York* (Albany, NY: Webb, Parsons, and Company, 1857), 8:348–49. Sosin, *Whitehall and the Wilderness*, 217.

23. The following is based on Benjamin Woods Labaree, *The Boston Tea Party* (New York: Oxford University Press, 1964), and my own reading of newspaper articles from the period. The estimated loss is on 141.

24. For the East India Company, see Phillip Stern, *The Company-State: Corporate Sovereignty and the Early Modern Foundation of the British Empire in India*, 58–79, and Benjamin Carp, *Defiance of Patriots: The Boston Tea Party and the Making of America* (New Haven, CT: Yale University Press, 2010), Chapter 1.

25. For more on the tea prices and smuggling, see Labaree, *The Boston Tea Party*, especially 3–14 and 58–79. For the poundage, see 67. See also David Ammerman, "The Tea Crisis and Its Consequences through 1775," in *Companion to the American Revolution*, 195–205, especially 195–196.

26. For the best summary of the Tea Act and the colonial response, see Labaree, *The Boston Tea Party*.

27. For more on the origins of the drawbacks, see Labaree, *The Boston Tea Party*, 66–68. For those opposed to the scheme, see 71–73. For colonists who supported the measure, see 107–108.

28. Ammerman, "The Tea Crisis," especially 196–107, and Labaree, *The Boston Tea Party*, 88–96.

29. "Lyons" quote is from John Shy, *People Numerous and Armed: Reflections on the Military Struggle for American Independence*, rev. ed. (Ann Arbor: University of Michigan Press, 1990), 102; Labaree, *The Boston Tea Party*, 170–216.

30. Fischer, *Paul Revere's Ride*, 299.

31. On Smith's service in the committee, see John Woolf Jordan, *A Century and a Half of Pittsburg and Her People* (New York: Lewis Publishing Company, 1908), 1:140–41. James Wilson, "Speech Delivered at the Provincial Convention, June 1775," James Wilson Papers, 2:3, HSP. This speech has also been republished as "In Vindication of the Colonies," which has a slightly different text. Instead of "his blessings," the text reads, "human blessings." See, for example, Marion Mills Miller, ed., *The Great Debates in American History* (New York: Current Literature Publishing Company, 1913), 1:150–58, quote 154.

32. "Westmoreland Resolves," May 16, 1775, *PA Archives*, 6th series (Harrisburg, PA: Harrisburg Publishing Company, 1906), 2:262–64.

CHAPTER 11: REVOLUTION

1. For a summary of this view, see Gordon Wood, *The Radicalism of the American Revolution* (New York: Alfred A. Knopf, 1992), 3–8. For those that emphasize the Revolution's failures, see also Barbara Clark Smith, *The Freedoms We Lost: Consent and Resistance in Revolutionary America* (New York: New Press, 2010), and Douglas Egerton, *Death or Liberty: African Americans and Revolutionary America* (New York: Oxford University Press, 2009).

2. For Johnson, see Fintan O'Toole, *White Savage: William Johnson and the Invention of America* (Albany: State University of New York Press, 2005). For New York, see Alan Taylor, *The Divided Ground: Indians, Settlers, and the Northern Borderland of the American Revolution* (New York: Alfred A. Knopf, 2006).

3. David Hackett Fischer, *Paul Revere's Ride* (New York: Oxford University Press, 1994), 30–44.

4. On speculation that Gage's wife was involved, see ibid., 96–97, 290.

5. For his death, see Nicholas Wainwright, *George Croghan, Wilderness Diplomat* (Chapel Hill: University of North Carolina Press, 1959), 300–310, and William Campbell, *Speculators in Empire: Iroquoia and the 1768 Treaty of Fort Stanwix* (Norman: University of Oklahoma Press, 2012), 206–7.

6. Ibid.

7. For a further discussion of this process, see Patrick Spero, *Frontier Country: The Politics of War in Early Pennsylvania* (Philadelphia: University of Pennsylvania Press, 2016), Chapter 10.

8. *Letters of the Delegates to Congress* (Washington, DC: Library of Congress, 1981), 7:625.

9. Ibid.

10. Ralph Izard to John Adams, October 8, 1778, *The Adams Papers Digital Edition*, ed. Sara Martin (Charlottesville: University of Virginia Press, Rotunda, 2008–2018).

11. The best account of the Penn family is Lorett Treese, *Storm Gathering: The Penn Family and the American Revolution* (University Park: Pennsylvania State University Press, 1992), 171–201.

12. For Smith's biography, see John Woolf Jordan, *A Century and a Half of Pittsburg and Her People* (New York: Lewis Publishing Company, 1908), 140–41, and James Smith, *An Account of the Remarkable Occurrences in the Life and Travels of Colonel Smith* (Lexington, KY: John Bradford, 1799), 73–74.

13. See especially David Freeman Hawke, *In the Midst of Revolution* (Philadelphia: University of Pennsylvania Press, 1961); Richard Ryerson, *The Revolution Is Now Begun: The Radical Committees of Philadelphia, 1765–1776* (Philadelphia: University of Pennsylvania Press, 2012); and Steven Rosswurm, *Arms, Country, and Class: The Philadelphia Militia and the Lower Sort in the American Revolution* (New Brunswick, NJ: Rutgers University Press, 1987).

14. The best work on Pennsylvania's divided loyalties is Anne Ousterhout, *A State Divided: Opposition in Pennsylvania to the American Revolution* (Westport, CT: Greenwood Press, 1987). For Adams's role see Patrick Spero, "Creating Pennsylvania: The Politics of the Frontier and the State, 1681–1800" (PhD diss., University of Pennsylvania, 2009), Chapter 7.

15. Hawke, *In the Midst of Revolution*, 186, fn 14. See Spero, *Frontier Country*, Chapter 10, for more on this shift.

16. "Learned fellows" is from Thomas Smith to Arthur St. Clair, August 22, 1776, Philadelphia, *The St. Clair Papers: The Life and Public Services of Arthur St. Clair*, William Henry Smith, ed. (Cincinnati, OH: Robert Clarke and Company, 1882).

17. *The Proceedings Relative to Calling the Conventions of 1776 and 1790* (Harrisburg, PA: John Wiestling, 1825), 48, 56.

18. Ibid., 55.

19. See Terry Bouton, *Taming Democracy* (New York: Oxford University Press,

2009) for more on this theme, especially his "rings of protection" in Chapter 7 for the effect of this change in the post-war period. For opposition to the new office holding, see Edward Shippen to Jasper Yeates, September 13, 1776, Yeates Collection, HSP.

20. Gregory Knouff, *The Soldiers' Revolution: Pennsylvanians in Arms and the Forging of Early American Identity* (University Park: Pennsylvania State University Press, 2004), 16; Hawke, *In the Midst of Revolution*, 192.

21. *PCM*, 10:726.

22. Smith, *An Account of the Remarkable Occurrences*, 73.

23. Ibid. For more on this skirmish, see "January 5, 1777" in *The Revolutionary War Memoirs of William Heath*, ed. Sean Heuvel (Jefferson, NC: McFarland, 2014), and John Cunningham Clyde, *Rosbrugh, a Tale of the Revolution* (Easton, PA: 1880), 67.

24. Smith, *An Account of the Remarkable Occurrences*, 73–75, and "From the Pennsylvania Council of Safety, February 10, 1777," in *The Papers of George Washington, Digital Edition*, http://rotunda.upress.virginia.edu/founders/GEWN-03-08-02-0323 (accessed December 15, 2014). For more evidence of Smith's activity, see Spero, "Creating Pennsylvania," Chapter 7.

25. Smith, *An Account of the Remarkable Occurrences*, 75; "From Timothy Pickering, May 19, 1778," in *The Papers of George Washington, Digital Edition*, https://founders.archives.gov/documents/Washington/03-15-02-0162#GEWN-03-15-02-0162-fn-0001-ptr (accessed April 17, 2018).

26. Smith, *An Account of the Remarkable Occurrences*, 75–76.

27. Hugh Henry Brackenridge, "Thoughts on the Present Indian War," in *Incidents of the Insurrection*, ed. Daniel Marder (New Haven, CT: College and University Press, 1972), 41.

28. Hugh Henry Brackenridge, February 2, 1792, *National Gazette*, and Smith, *An Account of the Remarkable Occurrences*.

EPILOGUE: LEGACIES

1. For a wonderful analysis of the clothing in the portrait, see Mike Burke, "Portrait of a Frontiersman: James Smith," *Wilderness & Warfare: The Fort Pitt Museum Blog*, Senator John Heinz History Center, November 17, 2015, http://www.heinzhistorycenter.org/blog/fort-pitt-museum/portrait-of-a-frontiersman-james-smith (accessed April 17, 2018).

2. For Smith's later life, see William G. Scroggins, *Leaves of a Stunted Shrub: A Genealogy of the Scroggin-Scroggins Family* (Cockeysville, MD: Nativa, 2009), 6:603–4.

3. Hugh Henry Brackenridge, *A Hugh Henry Brackenridge Reader, 1770–1815*, ed. Daniel Marder (Pittsburgh: University of Pittsburgh Press, 1970), 317.

Index

About the Author

Patrick Spero is the librarian and director of the American Philosophical Society Library in Philadelphia, an internationally renowned research institution. The library holds more than 250,000 books and 13 million pages of manuscripts, including the Papers of Benjamin Franklin, the Journals of Lewis and Clark, the largest collection of Charles Darwin's correspondence outside of Cambridge, ethnographic material relating to more than 400 Native American communities, and the papers of seven recent Nobel laureates.

A scholar of early American history, Spero has published more than a dozen essays and reviews on the American Revolution. He is also the author of *Frontier Country: The Politics of War in Early Pennsylvania* and *The American Revolution Reborn: New Perspectives for the Twenty-First Century*, an edited anthology.

Prior to his appointment at the American Philosophical Society, Spero served on the faculty of the History and Leadership Studies Departments at Williams College and held the post of historian at the David Library of the American Revolution. He received his PhD in 2009 from the University of Pennsylvania. He lives in Narberth, Pennsylvania, with his family.

www.patrickspero.com